The
EDWIN POPE
Collection

ALSO BY EDWIN POPE
Football's Greatest Coaches
Baseball's Greatest Managers
Ted Williams: The Golden Year 1957
On the Line *(with Norm Evans)*

Series Editor, Carlton Stowers

SPORTSWRITER'S
EYE

The
EDWIN
POPE
Collection

Introduction by
JAMES MICHENER

TAYLOR PUBLISHING COMPANY
Dallas, Texas

Published by Taylor Publishing Company
1550 West Mockingbird Lane
Dallas, Texas 75235

LIBRARY OF CONGRESS
Library of Congress Cataloging-in-Publication Data

Pope, Edwin.
    The Edwin Pope collection / introduction by James Michener.
      p.   cm. — (Contemporary American sportswriters)
    Includes index.
    ISBN 0-87833-609-5 : $14.95
    1. Sports.   2. Newspapers—Sections, columns, etc.—Sports.
I. Title.   II. Series.
GV707.P59   1988
070.4'49796'0924—dc19
[B]

ISBN: 0-87833-609-5

Printed in the United States of America

0   9   8   7   6   5   4   3   2   1

To my son David, who as
a small boy asked why I had
to leave home a week early
for a Kentucky Derby
that lasts two minutes.

And to my wife Eileen,
who understands why.

Introduction

Introduction

During my frequent stays in Florida in recent years, I acquired the habit common in this area of reading the *Miami Herald,* a very solid newspaper, and thus became acquainted with the writings of Edwin Pope, its learned sports columnist. I found him to be one of the best in the nation, a master of detail and infused with a desire for common sense in the conduct of sports, whether high school, college or professional.

In fact, I became addicted to his column and this was helpful, for I was then striving to clarify my own thinking about the position sports ought to occupy in American life. Consistently, Pope struck a sensible note. He loved sports but recognized their weaknesses; he defended athletes but appreciated the temptations they faced; and he well understood the importance of professional teams in the life of a great city. He served his community well and in doing so provided his readers with a constantly interesting mix of information, emotion and insight.

He was, I concluded in those days when I had only read him and not yet met him, in the great tradition of Grantland Rice, John Kieran, Red Smith, Jimmy Cannon and Shirley Povich. I realize that I am citing only those sportswriters with whom I would have been familiar on the east coast of the United States, and I'm sure there were other writers in the mid and far west sections just as good, but I had not been nurtured in their writings. Indeed, had I not moved to Florida at various times I would probably have missed Pope's fine writing.

He was, therefore, one of those experts like Furman Bisher of Georgia and Blackie Sherrod of Texas who spend their lives outside the New York-Chicago-Los Angeles axis and who dominate by their skill the areas they serve. Any fan who followed faithfully the writing of such men, and who understood what they were saying, would acquire a solid understanding of American sport.

I came to expect from Ed Pope a reasonable presentation of facts and a sensible interpretation of their significance. He was not an excessive home-towner, and I agreed with him in September 1987 when he lambasted big University of Florida at Gainesville for canceling future games with the University of Miami. A natural rivalry was thus extinguished, at least for a four-year period and for the most improper reasons. I forgave Pope for chortling when Miami in the last scheduled game of the series lambasted Florida 31–4 in a remarkable meeting in which the loser's two scores came when the Miami center, passing to his waiting punter, threw the football clear out of the playing field, giving Florida two safeties, perhaps the only time this has happened in major college or professional football. Pope had a right to gloat, and he did so within the limits of propriety, by which I mean that if he had gone overboard some Florida partisan might have bounced one off his noggin.

Like some other writers restricted to an outlying area, Pope's universality suffered because Miami had neither a professional baseball or basketball team, which meant that he could not write with that intimacy which comes from daily contact with the coloful men who operate in those sports. However, his general writings in these two fields had a statesmanlike quality, and anyone following his column would gain an understanding of what was happening in the professional leagues that centered in other parts of the nation.

As a visiting professor at the University of Miami I watched with great interest as Pope tackled two complex sporting developments. In the 1986 football season, my Miami team had several heart-stopping victories over major teams like Oklahoma, and a chain of wins over less-than-big-time schedule fillers. They wound up the season undefeated, and headed for a Fiesta Bowl showdown with Penn State. In Arizona, confident that they would crush Joe Paterno's Nittany Lions, they behaved so arrogantly and abrasively that the sporting press of the nation rebuked them, and properly so.

I watched eagerly to see how Ed Pope would handle this ugly situation in his backyard and was gratified to see that he reported it fairly, compassionately and with the proper degree of condemnation. In fact, he was instrumental in ensuring that Miami would not engage in such excess in the future, a proper role for an important newspaper.

I was less happy about Pope's declared vendetta against my

friend Joe Robbie, owner of the Miami Dolphins professional football team. I have known Robbie for many years and am aware that he can be abrasive, bullheaded and quick on the draw. I concede that he forms a justifiable target for local reporters. Furthermore, his stubborn determination to take his team out of the antiquated Orange Bowl in the heart of Miami in favor of a bright new stadium far removed in the outskirts was strongly opposed by local patriots. I understood why Pope rebuked Robbie for most of the moves the latter wanted to make, but in the end it seemed to me that the interests of Miami, the Dolphins and Pope's own paper were best served by what Robbie wanted to do. In the end Joe made American history by building a splendid new stadium with private rather than public funds, and in so doing may have established a revolutionary pattern for American sports.

I was therefore delighted to see that when the job was completed ahead of time and under budget, giving Miami one of the country's finest stadiums, Ed Pope was among the first to congratulate Robbie and the Dolphins. His articles about the opening were the finest published, and although I'm sure he reserves the right to take off after Joe if things go sour, he was gracious in applauding him when things went right.

A final good word about Pope as a professional sports editor. He has worked closely with *Miami Herald* executive sports editors Ed Storin and Paul Anger, and together they have enlarged the Herald's outlook, strengthened its coverage, encouraged hard-hitting comment and generally moved it into competition with the similar departments of the *Los Angeles Times* and the *New York Times,* two of the finest in the nation. Much of this improvement and maturity can be attributed to Ed Pope, who knows what sports are and how they should be integrated into a community. Unfair knocking by an area's leading newspaper can kill a franchise; uncritical adoration can make the paper or television look ridiculous; judicious support and intelligent criticism can make the area bloom as a home for sports.

I will watch how Miami in general responds to its new basketball franchise, and how it progresses in its efforts to obtain a major league baseball team. As a friend warned the other day: "They have to be careful about baseball. If they don't field a first-class nine, either Cuba or the Dominican Republic might come here and clobber them." If that happened, I would expect Ed Pope to report it accurately, fairly and with a sense of humor.

James A. Michener
Coral Gables, Florida

Contents

Pro Football / 61

College Football / 99

Baseball / 141

Horse Racing / 169

Fishing / 193

Boxing / 207

Golf / 219

Olympics / 229

And Other Trips / 243

Index / 261

Preface

I solemnly promise this preface will not pretend to be any kind of seminar on sports writing. Nothing is more embarrassing than telling someone how to do something and then falling on your face the next time you try to do it yourself.

I also solemnly swear to avoid any suggestion of solemnity in this pre-discussion of children's games, other than to chide myself for too often taking these adolescent exercises too seriously in the pages of the *Miami Herald* and other Knight-Ridder newspapers.

I do feel compelled to warn you of the degree of celebrity you now hold in your hand.

Quite recently, seeking God knows what trivia, I telephoned a retired press agent who had been famous for his media contacts among media.

"Ah, Eddie!" he said cheerfully. "How are things in Atlanta?"

Stunned is far too mild a word for my reaction. "I don't know how things are in Atlanta," I finally said, not at all effusively. "I left there 32 years ago."

"Oh," he said.

That is fame. And there is more where that came from. You are reading a combination of schlemiel and schlimazel. Know the difference between a schlemiel and a schlimazel? A schlemiel is one who goes into a restaurant and spills his coffee. A schlimazel is the one he spills it on. You can look it up in *Webster's Third New International Dictionary*.

If I have proved anything in 48 years of sports writing off and on, in some 8,000 columns including around 8 million words, it is that I can make a fool of myself in any language.

Covering my first women's golf tournament, I wrote that Babe Didrickson Zaharias, the greatest female athlete, was so skilled as to be "beyond conception." An editor saved me, the first of many miraculous catches on my behalf by journalism's unsung heroes.

Unfortunately, no editors were around to bail me out years

later in Paris. I approached a French airline staffer after an English Channel jump from Wimbledon. He said, "May I help you, sir?"

"Parlez vous Anglais?" I inquired.

The clerk stared at me as only Frenchmen can stare at Americans. He icily pointed out that he had just spoken to me in English.

Oh.

Gullible's Travels.

At the 1972 Summer Olympics in Munich, I found myself baffled by an unfamiliar attachment inside a shower. It was situated about three feet above the floor and seemed to be the only mechanism that would deliver water. No matter how I bent or twisted, I was unable to shower vertically.

I finally decided I had been assigned to a dormitory designed for pygmy journalists from New Guinea, and may as well make the best of it. I thus began showering in prone and supine positions. Granted, it felt a bit odd, but if athletes had to compete in 10 events to win the decathlon, who was I to complain about having to lie down to shower?

Emerging from my room one morning after the usual prostrate ablutions, I was perfunctorily asked, "How's it going?" by Stan Hochman of the *Philadelphia Daily News*.

"OK, except for the shower," I said, and blurted out the story.

"You are an idiot," Hochman said quietly. "That is a hose. You remove it from the wall and hold it and rinse yourself."

Oh.

Gullible's Travels again.

That was just before I mistook the "men" and "women" symbols on the restroom doors in the Munich press center.

I had installed myself inside a stall, as it were, when I heard snippets of conversation all too close. In German. By females.

Trapped! The consequences of discovery bulked like a thunderhead in my mind. Deportation? Imprisonment?

There was one thing to do. I did it for fully 15 minutes until the voices quieted and the voices' owners departed. I crouched atop the commode, mute in terror. Then fled.

These are the things I remember more than the touchdowns, home runs, field goals. These in retrospect are why my job has been such sheer fun. It has not hurt, either, that I have spent more than three decades working with only three superb executive sports editors—Bob Elliott, Ed Storin and Paul Anger—in the best newspaper company in the world.

Privately, sports columnists complain all the time. We "travel too much." Deadlines are "impossible." We curse the day *prime time* entered the language and sports events began brushing midnight. We bemoan having to interview young morons—college graduates, many—who cannot utter a sentence without including a dozen you-knows.

At bottom, though, it is more fun than any business I could imagine. How many sports columnists quit, especially after serving long apprenticeships to become columnists?

It seemed interminable in my case. Although I lucked into my first sports-writing job on the *Athens* (Georgia) *Banner-Herald* at age 12, I was 37 before I saw in person and wrote about a World Series. My columnar arrival at other events was relatively late as well—39 at the Masters, 40 at the Olympics, 47 at the Kentucky Derby.

Waiting didn't hurt me. It made me all the happier to get there, and please spare me from balderdash about how great it was in the old days, except for people who considered it great to starve and owe three loan companies at once.

Who has it better? We see and describe exploits we all first wanted to perform ourselves, before we turned out too short or too myopic or too slow, or all of them. Management seldom tries to restrict our opinions. What does management know about linguistic goofs in Paris or showerheads in Munich or press agents who don't know where we've been the last 32 years?

We are not expected to be infallible, or even sane, for that matter. If a business editor makes a mistake, it can bring down a whole company. Our goofs are taken in the context of the toy department in which we function. In fact, the more often we screw up, the better readers seem to like it.

I take small pride in confessing that the standard column which most pleases my readers is sarcastically called "Love Letters." No complimentary letters are printed, only those flagellating me for some error of fact or judgment. Readers therefore never run short of ammunition. The pseudo-psychologist in me considers "Love Letters" a classic outlet for the tensions of abused husbands, tapped-out bettors and other just ticked off in general. Better they should flail at me by mail than take an Uzi to someone else.

Granted, I make an easy target. When NFL owners debated on and on in Bal Harbour before hiring Pete Rozelle as commissioner a million or so years ago, I mentioned "their indecisiveness as the sun sank slowly in the Atlantic."

If Columbus had been as precisely oriented, we would still be wearing headdresses.

Regular readers need not be reminded of my remarkable clairvoyance. I predicted the Chicago Bears would "wipe out" the Miami Dolphins in 1985. The Dolphins played their best game in more than 11 years, since they won Super Bowl VIII. They destroyed the Bears, 38–24.

And it is still fun. Most games run together after awhile, but antic moments outside the games stick lovingly in the mind.

I was awakened in Jacksonville one football-season morning by a roommate/writer with an equally devastating hangover. "Did I pick up the check last night?" he asked blearily.

He was assured that he had not. "Good," he said, rolling back over. "Usually it costs me a lot of money to feel this terrible."

No matter how boring some of the games get (for a real adrenalin rush, try commenting on a decathlon or pole vault), someone or something always comes along to make us laugh.

It helps to have the right traveling companions, as poet W. H. Auden noted. "Among those whom I like or admire, I can find no common denominator," Auden said, "but among those whom I love, I can: all of them make me laugh."

Thus, Jim (*Los Angeles Times*) Murray lying in a Miami hospital bed after suffering a detached retina, detailing why he can't watch TV: "All the stagecoaches look like alligators jumping into trees."

Thus, Bob (*Chicago Tribune*) Verdi, frostily answering a Sarajevo Winter Olympics waiter's question as to how much cream he wanted in his coffee: "Two lumps, please."

Thus, the night at a U.S. Open when Blackie (*Dallas Morning News*) Sherrod and I were set upon by a certifiable loony. He— the loony, not Sherrod—began raving about everything from the effect of the juxtaposition of planets on the golfers to his personal theory that Arnold Palmer was the reincarnation of

Napoleon. He finally paused long enough to say, "You know, I'm on leave from an insane asylum."

Ever so softly, Sherrod said, "I never would have guessed *that.*"

Blackie has that way about him. I am only sorry I could not have been in his office the day he was visited for the first time by a publicist already terrified by Blackie's reputation for aloofness and/or withering humor. The poor guy was so scared just walking in he got his feet tangled and actually fell down. Sherrod gave him The Stare and asked dryly, "How long have you been with the ballet?"

Our lives are crazy, but never uninteresting. Most columnists utterly fail the requirement that Flaubert outlined for writers in a letter to his mistress: "Be regular and ordinary in your life, like a bourgeois, so that you may be violent and original in your work."

Even the inanities often become curios. Consider the question most often tellingly asked of us: "How long does it take you to write a column?"

Surgeons are asked about lobotomies. Lawyers speak of torts. Brokers discourse on price-earnings ratios and reverse stock splits. Even the most animalistic of professional defensive football players can deliver perorations on inside-outside moves. We are only asked, how long does it take?

The answer is, how long will you give me? I have written columns in 10 minutes. Others have taken months. Squirrel-like, we gather and sequester nuts, to be hauled out in the midnights of our days, when the editors scream, "I don't care whether the game is over or not! Write *something* and we'll plug in the score!"

Editors always speak in exclamation points. Their jobs are exclamation points. They, like columnists, spend their lives trying to convey to the reader, as Henry Luce did with *Time* and *Life* and their offshoots: "Hey out there! We're alive here at this end and we have something to tell you!"

What sports columnists say is not often important in the great, grand, cosmic scheme. People *do* care about sports, though, and that helps when one is recovering from yet another chapter of Gullible's Travels.

Besides, as that conversation with the press agent proves, it's so wonderful to be famous.

Personal Favorites

'WHO'S HE GOING TO SHOOT?'

DECEMBER 22, 1986

They ought to wedge in at least one rendition of *Auld Lang Syne* tonight. One time for the Dolphins' life and times in the Orange Bowl. And while they're playing it for all the big plays everybody finally saw one way or the other, how about an extra chorus for some extracurricular episodes only a few saw? The other side of the curtain. *People* stuff instead of X's and O's.

A staffer rushes up to Don Shula after a game. Shula has won, so he's all smiles. "Coach, meet Don Johnson of *Miami Vice*," the staffer bubbles.

Johnson sticks out his hand and says, "Great job, coach!"

Shula doesn't watch TV except for news and football, but he's a law-and-order man. "It's you guys who do the great job," Shula says, beaming.

"Hey, thanks!" Johnson says. "Why don't you come out and watch us shoot some time?"

Of course, Johnson means shooting *film*. But Shula doesn't know *Miami Vice* from *La Traviata*. Cheech and Chong came up to a Dolphin practice a couple of years ago and Shula said he didn't remember any comics since Fibber McGee and Molly.

Anyway, there in the Orange Bowl underbelly, Shula stares quizzically at Johnson. "Shoot?" Shula echoes. "Oh . . . yeah, right. That would be fine."

Johnson leaves. Shula turns to the staffer. "Who's he going to shoot?" Shula asks, motioning at the departing Johnson. "A bunch of crooks?"

Shula thinks Johnson is a real Miami vice cop. That's a different world down there. Understand, we're not talking about normal, individuals. What we are dealing with here are driven, isolated, insulated specialists who look at life through the narrowest of tunnels, men who wouldn't know if World War III started unless NFL Films shot it.

2

Here's Norm Evans, who *doesn't* run on a narrow-gauge track, driving his family home from the Orange Bowl to Hollywood the 1972 night Bob Griese gets his right ankle pulled apart. Suddenly, 30-year-old, 6-foot-5-inch, 246-pound Evans pulls his car to the side of I-95 and begins sobbing.

"It was my fault," Evans is saying, more to himself than his wife or daughter or son. "I'm the offensive right tackle—I'm to blame. Deacon Jones was my man and he was one of the guys who hit Griese."

It isn't Evans' fault. Griese is already a one-legged man by the time Deacon cleans up on the play. That's just the way offensive linemen think. And that's as memorable to me as any touchdown pass or twisting catch or historic interception.

Why is it the "little" things stick the longest? Why can't I thumb the mental Rolodex back to all the breakaway runs one Dolphin made, instead of the time he wants out of a game so badly he simply lies on the field and resists every attempt the Dolphin medical corps makes to pry open his eyes? He has them squinched so tightly shut a crowbar won't open them. He means to be through for the day, and he is.

Of course, looking back, it isn't all goofy. Some of it is good and sound and solid, stuff you *want* to cling to. You have the Dolphins everybody wants to talk to, win or lose, because they will always state the case—Doug Betters, Dave Kocourek, Ed Newman, Jim Langer, Roy Foster, Nick Buoniconti, Jimmy Cefalo, Billy Neighbors, Don Strock, Frank Jackson, Bruce Hardy, Jim Mandich, Jim Kiick, Glenn and Lyle Blackwood, Andra Franklin, Mike Current, Doug Moreau, Steve Towle, A.J. Duhe. Ah, so many.

You also have a Manny Fernandez, smoldering so in the rare defeats of his day that no one dares approach him. You also have a Jeris White, whose m.o. if things are tough in the secondary is to pretend the game never happens. "Touchdown pass?" he asks blankly. "What touchdown pass?"

Strange things happen upstairs, too. Executives of visiting clubs occasionally sit in the Orange Bowl press box. The box is supposed to be for working press only, but nobody cares about that if the visitor is Bucko Kilroy, the Patriot vice president who will be in there tonight, or, say, President Dan Rooney of the Steelers, or Vice President Gil Brandt of the Cowboys, because they will answer questions.

They also stay out of the flow of the game, unlike Al Davis, the Raider boss who tends to become a bigger show than what's happening on the field. Or, in this particular context, General Manager John Sanders of the Chargers.

Sanders perches with assistant GM Tank Younger on the second row of the press box for the Chargers' 41–38 overtime victory in '81. Sanders is a former Occidental College runner; Younger a former Rams' fullback. Between them they make a load. And Sanders is on the officials' case every play. "Knaves! Cutpurses!" he yells, or something, every time a call goes against the Chargers.

It happens that Rudy Martzke, now the sports TV columnist of *USA Today*, occupies the spot beside Sanders. Martzke knows who Sanders is. Martzke also knows the rule: No demonstrations in the press box. After Sanders' fourth or fifth outburst, Martzke says softly, "That's enough now. You be quiet."

Sanders pays no attention. "Trolls! Undesirables!" he shouts at the zebras, or something.

One more time Martzke remonstrates with Sanders. "I told you once," Martzke says. "This is the second time. We're trying to work up here. You'd better not yell again."

Sanders goes right on. "Blunderers! Dolts!" or something.

Martzke rises. "You!" he wags a finger under Sanders' nose. "Out! Now!"

Sanders looks up ominously. Small humanoids along press row wait for either Sanders or Younger or both to squash Martzke like a grape.

Instead, Sanders and Younger move meekly out of their seats. Vanish. Poof! Just like that.

You can see this is anything but the definitive overview of the Dolphins in the Orange Bowl. It's just a hobo stew of offbeat things I remember best.

I'm not sure whether I'm going to miss the Dolphins playing in the Orange Bowl. But something is going to be lost after tonight, if nothing more then just the familiarity of the backdrop for people who have been so much fun to watch, and especially to listen to.

A Greg Koch as well as a Bob Kuechenberg, the mightiest line warrior. A Jeff Dellenbach as well as a Larry Little, the most talented lineman the Dolphins have had. A John Offerdahl as well as a Doug Swift, that iconoclastic linebacker, the only doctor the Dolphins turned out. A William Judson as well as a Dick Anderson. A Tony Nathan as well as a Jim Kiick, two good guys. A Bob Brudzinski as well as a Mike Kolen.

There isn't any "as well as" when it comes to Jake Scott—unique, rattlesnake-mean, panther-quick, the ultimate loner. Nor is there any "as well as" with Larry Csonka.

When the smoke clears, no matter who has been burnt, you can always talk to Zonk. It isn't true of several others, especially as the salaries go up and up and some player's opinions of themselves do, too. Generalizations stink, but this one you can take to the bank: A player making $50,000 is four times easier to talk to than one making $200,000.

Shula *never* changes. You just have to take care with him for at least an hour after the game, because he is coiled so much tighter than most coaches.

Here, in the oddest unseen scene of the Dolphins' 21 years in the Orange Bowl, is Shula holding forth to his players at bitter length after a certain disaster. He is suddenly shocked to spot a stranger against the wall. This postgame segment is for Shula and players and coaches only, but now the boss Dolphin spots a man he doesn't even know in the room, and taking notes.

Taking notes! In Shula's most private meeting of the week!

"Who the *bleep* are you?" Shula roars.

A Dolphin front-office man hustles up and whispers the stranger's identity to Shula. It is an author—world famous, doing a book on sports. It isn't the author's fault. A member of management has stupidly brought him in. But the author's name flies right by Shula in the heat of defeat.

"An author!" Shula shouts. "What the *bleep* are you doing in here? Checking out the animals? Visiting the zoo? Get the *bleep* out of here!"

And James Michener, one of the world's most distinguished scholars and novelists, trudges humbly out of the locker room beneath the Orange Bowl.

TIMMY'S HEART TAKES OVER

NOVEMBER 14, 1978

Most kids talk sports with their fathers. Timmy limped in to his mother with this particular sports matter because his parents are divorced and he lives with her. "They're having a mini-marathon, six and two-tenths miles," Timmy said. "I'm going to enter."

Martha Brattain blanched. God had played it down the middle with her Timmy. Eleven years ago he was born with a 50,000-watt glow in his heart. And cerebral palsy.

"Timmy, you can barely run around the block," she said gently. "How can you expect to race more than six miles?"

Timmy grinned and said he didn't know but he was going to try.

She thought he would forget the Key Biscayne mini-marathon. Then, one Sunday last month, he shouted: "Mom, hurry! The race starts in a few minutes!"

They barely made it. Seven hundred runners were at the starting line on Key Biscayne. Timmy took one look at that mob. "I better get to the end of the line," he grinned, "or they might run over me."

Mrs. Brattain watched the runners start. Then she went back to their home a few blocks away. She was sure Timmy would stop the first time by the house. So were the rest of us who had seen him drag his unsynchronized right leg through soccer and baseball games, grinning, forever grinning, every heaving half-stride.

"I waited in the house," she said, "but he didn't come back in."

Mrs. Brattain bicycled across the island asking if anyone had seen Timmy. They had. "He's still going," they said.

Policemen had shut off traffic into Cape Florida, the state park at the tip of Key Biscayne, because the race route led into and around and back out of the park. Timmy entered Cape

Florida more than an hour behind the other runners. Policemen saw him and held up motorists. No car would go inside until Timmy came out.

They waited. And waited. Timmy emerged, gasping and flushed, nearly two hours behind the pack. His mother wanted to ride the rest of the way behind him on her bike. But Timmy sent a message: "Tell Mom to stay 'way behind me."

Out of the park and down the finishing stretch came Timmy. He was half-running, half-hopping, all on his better left leg.

An old man on a lawn hailed Mrs. Brattain. "Was that your kid that just went by?" he asked.

She nodded.

"That . . . is . . . the . . . damndest . . . thing . . . I . . . ever . . . saw . . ." the old man said. The moisture on his cheeks was not sweat.

Jerome White won the mini-marathon in 32 minutes and 23 seconds. Timmy crossed the line in two hours and six minutes.

His mother tried to be casual. "Are you all right?" she asked.

Timmy grinned. He said he was "a little tired, that's all."

I told his mother I couldn't believe what he had done.

"You have to understand," she said, "Timmy is a very special boy."

VINNY'S HEISMAN IS MORE THAN ACADEMIC

DECEMBER 7, 1986

Those new voices insisting scholarship should be a factor in the Heisman Trophy had best take it up with New York's Downtown Athletic Club. The rule is that the Heisman goes to the "outstanding" player. It is hereby submitted that Vinny Testaverde meets the standard as well as or better than anyone who ever won it.

It is further submitted that Testaverde stands as more than the best college player. He is just as good a man as he is a quarterback.

Reflexes alone did not induce Vinny to look out at his father Al in the Heisman presentation audience and say, "We dreamed it together, we lived it together, and now I could probably say we won it together."

That play came from the soul, not the sideline. And his mom was not talking about Vinny's feet and arm when she said, "Every mother should have a boy like him." She was talking about what is inside that "boy"—what makes him a model of citizenship despite some cavilling over what one critic calls his "disdain for academics."

Times make one leery of idealizing any celebrity. They can blow up in a blink of a snow-burst. But if Vinny has any character flaws deeper than a merely human aversion to bookishness, they have not yet emerged.

Goodness will out. Even in that stilted and anticlimactic setting in New York, he came across as the kid from down the street. Vinny placed a hand protectively around a shoulder of his teary-eyed father and closed his acceptance remarks with, "Thank you and God bless you."

Real heroes on any level don't worry about how archaic anything sounds as long as it expresses gratitude and humility. It isn't necessary to be either a stand-up comic or a blowhard to be responsible and dedicated.

Which do you find more attractive? Testaverde's plain earnestness? Or the megalomaniacal ravings of a Brian Bosworth who happens to make high classroom grades?

Is it hopelessly old-fashioned to believe that some obligation to society is involved here?

A few years ago, bothered by the decreasing numbers of true sports heroes, I mentioned the anything-goes approach that Joe Namath made so chic. It was a philosophy that said, *I can do anything I feel like doing as long as it doesn't hurt anyone else,* and no credo has ripped the fabric of sports as savagely as that.

At the time, for whatever it was worth, I added: "I have never known a real hero who opposed that philosophy any more vigorously than Oklahoma's Billy Vessels, the '52 Heisman winner . . ."

A handful of other Heisman honorees fall into that same exceptional category as humans. TCU's Davey O'Brien in 1938. Georgia's Frankie Sinkwich in '42. Princeton's Dick Kazmaier in '51. Army's Pete Dawkins in '58. Navy's Roger Staubach in '63. Florida's Steve Spurrier in '66. Penn State's John Cappelletti in '73. Georgia's Herschel Walker in '82. Plus, surely, some we never knew.

Let us now be grateful for Testaverde in '86. For you run short of Heisman winners to emulate in the recent flood of scandal. You have to go back a long way to recall a Staubach detailing the depth of his feeling toward the Heisman, and what it represented to his family.

"My dad wasn't very well at the time," Staubach said, "and they asked him to give a speech, and he said, 'I only had one child, and God gave me a good one.' "

Staubach added, "I couldn't possibly tell you what that meant to me."

All right, so keeping the Boy Scout oath isn't as important in Heisman voting as deeds of magic on a football field. But it is at least stimulating to find a later-day winner as trustworthy, loyal, helpful, friendly, courteous, kind, obedient, cheerful, thrifty, brave, clean and reverent as Testaverde.

Inarguably, a playground instructor may exert every bit as significant an impact as any high-ranker. The whole point is productiveness, and Testaverde's anti-drug activism scores for him off the field.

On the field, no question.

Ask Gil Brandt, the Dallas Cowboys' talent expert who first held up Testaverde as a national exemplar. "If you would design a linebacker for the pros, it would be Bosworth," Brandt says. "If you would design a quarterback, it would be Testaverde."

Boz, by the way, was dead wrong when he opened his big yap—yes, again—to vent his personal dislike for Boston College's Doug Flutie. Bosworth said Flutie won the '84 Heisman "because of one pass he threw, but he was not the best player in the country."

Wrong. Flutie had the Heisman won before he launched the legendary rocket that snuffed Miami, 47–45. If he wasn't the best player in college football that year, I'd hate to play against a better one. And Flutie still can't play in Testaverde's league on sheer talent.

For comparison's sake, it would have been helpful to see Testaverde start more than 22 games. Nonetheless, the opinion here is that he ranks as a college quarterback with Spurrier, Staubach and Heisman non-winners Bob Griese, Dan Marino and John Elway.

As a human, too.

We would all so love all God's children bringing home straight A's, but every parent can testify that other matters become just as important in the end. If you saw the Heisman ceremony, you know what the other matters are.

SNOWFLAKES IN MIAMI

JANUARY 20, 1977

I feel betrayed. Twenty-one years ago I came to Miami for the weather. Did you ever once hear me kick when it got down to 60? No, you never did, because I never did.

But in the gray weirdness of post-dawn, radio voices drifted into our chickee. They told of snowflakes violating Miami.

Snowflakes! Say Jack Dempsey has taken back the heavyweight championship. But snow on Miami?

Snowflakes! Show me headlines that Billy Martin has entered a monastery, and Sparky Anderson has opened a go-go joint. But snow on Miami?

Snowflakes! Tell me Richard Daley wasn't a politician. But snow on Miami?

Snowflakes! Prove Dick Butkus is a sissy, and Ted Williams couldn't hit to right. But snow on Miami?

Snowflakes! Produce a picture of Ted Hendricks joining The Singer Midgets. But snow on Miami?

Snowflakes! Tell me the Unser brothers can't drive in traffic. But snow on Miami?

Snowflakes! Say Barry Goldwater is a Communist, and Mao Tse-tung was a Republican. But snow on Miami?

Snowflakes! Tell me Ernest Hemingway couldn't put two sentences together. But snow on Miami?

Snowflakes! Give me a speech that Eddie Arcaro never learned to sit on a horse. But snow on Miami?

Snowflakes! Lay it out for me how Sammy Baugh or Johnny Unitas or Joe Namath or Ken Stabler never threw a spiral. But snow on Miami?

Snowflakes! Make me believe Bob Jones putted with a sledgehammer and Jack Nicklaus slices every drive. But snow on Miami?

Snowflakes! Go ahead, be my guest, bring out affidavits that

11

Jim Langer can't block a lick, that Muhammad Ali is the worst fighter ever to draw on a glove, that Bobby Hull doesn't know a hockey puck from a dropkick, that Vince Lombardi and Don Shula and Tom Landry will be remembered as losers. But snow on Miami?

Snowflakes! They never promised me a rose garden. But snow on Miami? They never mentioned snow at all. I feel betrayed.

THE FACES OF A NATIONAL CHAMPIONSHIP

JANUARY 8, 1984

How should we remember The Night? As The Two-Day War? The Monday-Tuesday Classic?

Miami's Hurricanes lead Nebraska's Cornhuskers, 17-0, on *Monday*. They finally win, 31-30, on *Tuesday*. The Orange Bowl Classic usually is played January 1, but this one starts January 2 and ends January 3.

Doesn't matter. I'll probably forget the score. And the date. But not the faces. The faces stay with you. *No. 1* faces. National championship faces.

Bernie Kosar's is an unwhiskered cross between Joe Namath and Dan Marino, eyes searching, always listening. Except when he carries in a bulging breakfast tray the day before the Notre Dame game. Then his mouth opens and downs huge containers of pop, chocolate milk, tea, orange juice.

Orange juice. A symbol, perhaps, more than three months before the Orange Bowl Classic?

"Naw," Kosar says, grinning. "I've just got permanent cotton-mouth."

The cottonmouth bites 11 teams—in a row.

Try Rocky Pomerance's face, a weightlifter's face, muscles *on* muscles. Pomerance is UM right down to his squashed soles. The former chief of Miami Beach police worked so hard at being nice to friends in the stands, he still is so sore he's going up and down stairs sideways. His shoulders are the size of Atlas Van Lines. To keep from blocking the view of people sitting behind him in the Orange Bowl, Rock hunkered down in front of his seat. His legs feel like giant boils.

I thought about the faces a lot of the rest of the morning the

13

national championship game ended. Got home about 2 o'clock and started *schlepping* around the house, too tired to do anything, still too far off the ground to sleep.

My wife woke up. Her loveliest of Irish-Canadian faces still twitched from the game. "Better sleep, you have to go in early," she said.

No. I had waited 28 years for this. I had worn lines in my own dumpy puss, waiting. I wasn't going to let go of the faces just like that.

All those faces. All those years.

Jay Brophy's. Not lovely. Scary. The last you would want to see in even a lighted alley. A melon standing on its end, with hair. The face of a soldier.

Tad Foote's. The UM prez. Patrician. Dancing eyes sunk in an angular bank of reserve.

I reached into the pantry and dug out a bottle of Soave Folonari a friend gave me a year ago. Poured a spritzer. Sat. Thought about all the sad faces it took to make these new ones light up.

Talked to myself. "You can't appreciate this," I told the imagined faces in the 3 a.m. room, "unless you've been through all those psyched-out coaches and beaten-down players who came before. All that despair. Good faces. Bad times."

Nick Spinelli, dark, handsome. George Mira, Latin light shining out. Ted Hendricks, that oversized sprite. Pete Banaszak, with the look of a dock brawler set adrift on grass. Charlie Tate's little muffin nose.

Fran Curci. Nobody could talk to those mamas of prospects like Curci, the Valentino of coaches.

Pete Elliott, All-American, blond right to his pearlies. Super guy. Maybe the right coach. Definitely in the wrong place.

Twenty-eight years of covering UM football; more than a quarter century that would have passed like a finger snap other places, richer places, with five generations of alumni dangling gold watch chains.

Nobody ever loved a job more than I love mine. But I can't lie about most of those 28 years around UM. They were awful. The face of Cleopatra couldn't have made writing about those old Hurricane teams fun. The sun's face usually turned black when UM took the field. Even the moon over Miami frowned.

Look at the next face you see looking at a firing squad. That's how it was. Twenty-eight years of running around like a blind dog in a frankfurter factory.

It had been longer than that for UM between Orange Bowls, 33 years. But I didn't check in until '56. That's far enough back.

It wasn't actually that brutal in the beginning. It was OK for a little bit there because of Andy Gustafson. Gus was an old Pitt and West Point man who immediately evoked images of columnist Westbrook Pegler's decades-earlier description of Knute Rockne, which Rockne despised: "He has the appearance of the preliminary fighter who becomes a doortender in a bar. His nose is a bit smashed. And when he talks, it is like an old battered oil can giving champagne."

Gus could coach up a storm even when he was talking about a morning (before he joined AA) when he wanted a drink and figured the one place nobody would recognize him would be a little bar out on Bird Road by old Tropical Park.

Gus pulled a newsboy cap down over his forehead and put on shades and stooped his shoulders and named his poison.

The bartender shouted, "Coming right up, *Coach!*"

Gus put his head on the bar and said, "God! You're not safe anywhere."

Coaching at UM could do that to a man for a long time before Howard Schnellenberger stiffly walked in and gradually opened up until the most natural place in the world for him was in front of a microphone.

He was a one-man gang at the Omni the other morning. In the last week he had talked about how hungry the Hurricanes were.

"When you're hungry," he said, "a piece of Wonder Bread tastes like angel-food cake. If you're not hungry, it tastes like Wonder Bread."

UM was hungry, all right. So was Schnellenberger. "This is our angel-food cake," he said.

So it was, and so he stood Tuesday morning, eight hours after gorging himself on Nebraska, still having his cake. It was the crowdedest post-Orange Bowl classic press conference I ever saw, and many of the faces in that crowd peered at Schnellenberger as though scanning deity.

He was ready, quick, upbeat, glib. "Double dog trio," he described the defense the Hurricanes used to stop the Cornhuskers' passing attempt for two points when Nebraska still

15

could have won by 32–31. "You put pressure on the passer [Turner Gill] so he can't roll out, and cover the receivers."

Especially you cover Jeff Smith, who had just run 24 yards on the option play to pull Nebraska back in there. And when Kenny Calhoun tipped the ball away from Smith, it was all over.

So many times, so many years, fourth quarters slashed the smiles off University of Miami faces. That was before Snels and his defensive coaches, poker-faced Tom Olivadotti and bright, happy Mike Archer and the grave but amiable Harold Allen and impish Bill Trout, put this all together.

That was before Schnellenberger walked the Hurricanes to the middle of Greentree Practice Field and said, "Men, we lost to Notre Dame and Maryland in the fourth quarter last year. We aren't going to lose any fourth quarters this year."

At a certain point late in practice, he would blow his whistle and bellow, "Fourth quarter!" and they practiced just as though it were.

They won the last three games in the fourth quarter. East Carolina went down, 12–7, when Kosar threw 52 yards to Eddie Brown. Florida State fell, 17–16, when Jeff Davis, the tiny mannequin every matron wants to take home and set on her mantelpiece, kicked a 19-yard field goal.

And Nebraska.

All those games were something like Schnellenberger's first genuinely huge victory in the Orange Bowl. That was 10–9 over Florida State in 1980, when Jim Burt deflected a Rick Stockstill pass to abort FSU's two-point attempt with 39 seconds left.

A crowd of 50,008, big for UM then, had watched it. "How much did that crowd mean?" a man asked the coach.

Schnellenberger's mustache twitched. "One point," he said.

And his innermost emotions when Burt tipped away Stockstill's pass?

"Like a man playing Russian Roulette, when the hammer goes *click!*"

This droll face came as a sunny shock after Miami's stretch of despair all the way back to the 1960s.

I remember the nadir, hard as I tried to forget it. No use saying his name, but he was one of the bosses between the time Gus quit after '63 and Schnellenberger came in in '79. A day before the Hurricanes were flying up to play in Gainesville, I asked this particular coach how were tricks.

"I've got a cold," he said.

I thought, *A cold? Hey, get a cold the Fourth of July. Get a cold Labor Day. Get a cold Christmas. But don't tell me two days before you play Florida you've got a cold.*

He was gone pretty soon after that. He is still a man I think about when I ponder the utter, abject hopelessness of UM's program just a relatively short time ago.

The difference between now and then is that UM finally got enough gifted bodies to put under all those good-old-boy faces, all at once. Enough so that one injury wouldn't wreck a season. Or one game.

A bunch of people in Miami's traveling party turned their faces away from me, livid, when I said the Hurricanes didn't have a chance in the opener at Gainesville. But they didn't.

It's the only time I ever felt more confidence in a team after it lost by as much as 28-3. "The thing to remember," I wrote that night at Florida Field, "is that a 19-year-old freshman who never threw a varsity ball before moving into this madhouse outpitched [Wayne] Peace, 223 yards to 146."

I never thought the Hurricanes would go on as they did. Not in a trillion years. Schnellenberger thought they would. While Tony Fitzpatrick's ruddy and usually smile-split mug was dragging the floor after the Florida game, and Albert Bentley stared expressionlessly into his locker, Schnellenberger explained why he hadn't put in Kyle Vanderwende or Vinny Testaverde.

"It was good practice for Bernie," Schnellenberger said.

Your eyes swept the rest of the dressing room, looking for tears or maybe even somebody cracking a shrill joke. But there were only clenched teeth. Tight faces. Pursed lips.

Sharp, articulate John Smatana. Hollywood-handsome Speedy Neal. Quiet, contemplative Ken Sisk. Each stared at one wall as though he were determined to run through it.

They did. I may forget the scores. I won't forget those faces. The faces, though no one dreamed it then, of a national championship.

MICKEY MEETS THE BABE

MAY 17, 1984

BALTIMORE—Mickey Mantle, meet Babe Ruth.

He finally did, in a way.

"Boy, I'd loved to have played on a team with him," Mantle said, standing in front of an automated figure of the Bambino in the Babe Ruth Birthplace Foundation here. "Billy Martin and I used to sit in the Yankee clubhouse with Pete Sheehy, the equipment manager who was there when Babe was, listening to stories about him. We would have listened all night if the beer hadn't run out."

Mantle grinned, a slow and easy crackling of that country-boy face still rugged and handsome at 52.

"I guess me and Babe had something in common," he said. "No, no, not the home runs. I wasn't even in his league as a ballplayer. I mean, like staying out all night."

The second greatest Yankee slugger came to the shrine of the greatest almost by accident. An acquaintance ran into Mantle here and said, "You must have seen the Babe Ruth place."

"Never did," Mantle said. "Could we go?"

Mantle was there on the dot when the building opened at 10 a.m. It took awhile to convince staffers that it really was M. Charles Mantle in person, which embarrassed our hero no little bit, for he is basically a humble man.

It would be easy for Mantle to be different after three American League Most Valuable Player seasons (1956, '57, '62) and a niche in history as the only player to win baseball's Triple Crown in the 1950s. In '56, he led the league in homers with 42, runs batted in with 130 and batting average with .363.

"It's the closest I'll ever come to meeting the Babe," Mantle said. "Geez, what a fabulous record! He was always one of my idols, but I was just 17, the year before I started in pro ball, when he died in 1948."

Mantle hit 536 home runs but refuses to bracket himself with the man who held the record with 714 before Henry Aaron pumped it up to 755.

"Babe was a world apart to me," Mantle said. "I'll tell you this, though. This old place is a mansion compared to what I grew up in back in Commerce, Oklahoma. We had holes in the floor so big that when the wind really blew, you had to jump over pieces of linoleum flapping up.

"It's sort of crazy, but Billy Martin had this idea to turn my old house into a museum. We went down to see it a few years ago. Actually drove a bus the owner of the Tulsa ball club loaned us. And Billy got obsessed with the museum idea. But the next time we went back, it had been torn down."

Mantle walked over and peered into another glass-enclosed case labeled *The 500-Homer Club*. He looked back at his own likeness beside those of Aaron, Ruth, Willie Mays (660), Frank Robinson (586), Harmon Killebrew (573), Jimmy Foxx (534), Ted Williams and Willie McCovey (521), Ernie Banks and Eddie Mathews (512) and Mel Ott (511). He kept staring at Williams' picture.

"Ted Williams," Mantle said softly. "My *number one* idol."

A female visitor standing nearby heard him. "Ted Williams," she said. "Wasn't he a singer?"

Mantle was flabbergasted. "A singer? Ted Williams? My God, lady, you must be thinking of Hank Williams."

"Oh," the woman said.

Mickey rolled his eyes and took another long look at a replica of one of the huge flannel uniforms Ruth wore.

"We used those when I started out in pro ball in Independence, Missouri," Mantle said. "We were a Yankee farm, so we got all their hand-me-downs. Just think of going out and playing a double-header in the worst heat of summer in Yankee Stadium in one of those suits, with a hangover. It was hard enough in the uniforms we wore when I was on the Yankees, but they weren't this hot."

Mantle checked out a plaque bearing Ruth's stats with the Boston Red Sox, 1914–19; Yankees, 1920–34, and Boston's National Leaguers, 1935.

"All the guys with the big numbers played a long time," he said. "Look here. Ruth went 22 seasons and quit when he was 40. Me, I should have played longer than 17½ seasons, '51 through '68. But I was stupid. Helling around."

His friend said, "Mickey, the helling around didn't have anything to do with the knee that finally stopped you."

"Yes, it did," Mantle said. "When I first hurt it, trying to pull up beside Joe DiMaggio in the outfield in '51, the knee popped right through the leg. I mean, right out of it. They didn't have arthroscopic surgery then. I was in a cast for a long time, and the muscles deteriorated. And then I was supposed to do a special set of exercises to rehabilitate the knee. But I never did. Just stupidity. If I'd done them, the knee would have been all right, and I could have gone a few more years."

Mantle looked around and said he was awfully glad he came to Ruth's place.

"I guess this sounds corny, but anything that has to do with the Yankees moves me, and there never was a Yankee like the Babe. I often wonder what his biggest thrill was. I get asked that a lot of times.

"Well, I played 2,401 games, the most of any Yankee, and that's a hard question to answer. But when I think about it, it has to be when they had a Mickey Mantle Day in '69. They had only retired three numbers up until then, Ruth's No. 3, Lou Gehrig's No. 4 and Joe DiMaggio's No. 5. And that day they retired my No. 7. That was it for me."

Mantle turned at the door and looked back.

"So long, Babe," he said. "Sleep tight."

THANK YOU, JIM BURT

JANUARY 13, 1987

Cup this moment and hold it close: nose tackle Jim Burt piling into that gone-crazy crowd in Giants Stadium and making himself one with it.

The scene is too precious to belong merely to Burt or his team's interminably tortured followers. It belongs to sports, for it is what sports should be but so searingly seldom is—the property of the fans who pay the freight, and wait, and wait.

Thank you, Jim Burt.

Remember Jim Craig draping himself in the American flag and skating across the Lake Placid ice in desperate search of his father after the U.S. Olympic hockey squad rode down Russia in the winter of 1980?

For history, that was bigger.

For what is in the heart, though, it was no bigger than this.

Jim Burt, 27, the kid Lou Saban gave a chance at the University of Miami, the reject the pros wouldn't even draft, paid off Sunday.

He ran over just to wave at his wife in the stands after the Giants gored the Redskins, 17–0. Then, caught up in the Super Bowl dream he helped make possible, he clambered over the wall and into the stands.

Most had turned their televisions off or away from the rout by then. Those that didn't saw the rarest of pictures. High-fiving, hugging, a professional athlete gave himself back to the fans, and for golden minutes sports was good and glorious and innocent again.

Bellowing, beaming, he drove away the bogeymen of commercialism, arrogance, drugs, churlishness and contracts.

Thank you, Jim Burt.

As Burt bobbed in the swell of humanity, a few from down Miami way thought back six years and 11 days ago. Miami's Hurricanes had beaten Virginia Tech, 20–10, in the Peach Bowl in Atlanta. There was no swelling crowd that day. Atlanta didn't care who won. UM buses were loading up to leave, but Burt sat in half-frozen rapture on his locker-room stool.

"The bus is leaving, Jim!" assistant coach Kim Helton yelled.

"I'm staying," Burt yelled back. "I'm staying right here. I love it, I love it."

"Come on, Jim," Helton repeated. "We can't leave you here."

Burt slowly smiled. "All right," he said. "I'll leave the locker room. But I don't feel like ever leaving this football team."

The pros were in no sweat to pry Burt loose. Burt finally got his free-agent shot from George Young, the Giant general manager, the same way he had gotten it in Miami from Saban—barely, at the last minute. He gave it all back and more when he went up there and joined Sunday's party.

Steve Carlton talks maybe once every 10 years. Vince Coleman tells World Series reporters he will "evaluate the questions" before deciding whether to answer them. Jim McMahon informs waves of Super Bowl media—and, by extension, fans—of their "stupidity." Dwight Gooden can't make the victory parade. But Jim Burt goes into the stands with the "common" folk.

He has always been different. He got married in the middle of Miami's 1980 season, by special dispensation of Howard Schnellenberger. Jim and Colleen Kempf tied the knot in the Nativity Catholic Church in Orchard Park on an open-date Saturday before Miami lost to Mississippi State, 34–31.

There wasn't any point in Burt going up into the Orange Bowl stands that day. He couldn't have found a crowd with a telescope. Only 17,806 were there.

There were 76,633 in Giants Stadium. Finally, crawling back over the barrier and down onto the field, Burt danced up and down the Astroturf like a deranged teddy bear.

Sheer celebration. No litigation, negotiation, renegotiation, arbitration. Just celebration, from one grateful heart to thousands of them, a metaphorical beacon in the sordid fog of sports.

"I only wanted to thank them a fraction of what they deserve," Burt said.

Thank *you*, Jim Burt.

A TIME FOR FLAGS IN LAKE PLACID

FEBRUARY 23, 1980

LAKE PLACID, NEW YORK—All this frenzied night, until red timing lights atop the Olympic Field House showed 10 minutes remaining and suddenly the green numbers blinked *US 4, USSR 3,* a sense of doom sat like spiritual bankruptcy over Americans.

I was glad it wasn't World War III.

I was glad, among other reasons, we weren't dodging missiles the way American goalie Jim Craig was smothering, slapping and gloving away pucks shot at him by Russian athletes racing toward what seemed sure to be their fifth straight Olympic ice hockey gold medal.

Then a Massachusetts player named Mike Eruzione put the accumulated sinew and skill and patriotism of his 25 years behind a shot past goalie Vladimir Myshkin.

Lights flashed. Skyrockets went off in American hearts. The United States had beaten "invincible" Russia, 4–3.

Plenty is wrong with Olympics, both the Winter and Summer Games. But this was what is right about them.

This was *spectacle.* I never saw anything like it for ferocity, for courage, for naked emotion.

A Yank named Henry James Miller went directly from the field house to American Legion Post 326 just down the street. He passed out red, white and blue flags.

"Go on the street and start waving them," Miller said. "Tonight is a night we are all proud to be Americans. I got down on my knees this morning and said, 'Dear God, lead our nation to regain its way of life that was established long ago when people gave up their lives for something they believed in.'"

Miller said, "I cried then and I am crying here again tonight because our young team did something out there tonight that no team on earth could have done. They brought to life the conscience of our nation."

Is that maudlin?

Think about it.

Two countries just a red telephone away from destroying each other were warring on skates with sticks and a tiny round piece of hard black rubber.

Take less than one-tenth of the people at football's last Super Bowl.

Multiply the intensity of that crowd by 10.

This was America rocking Russia in Olympic ice hockey.

Our team still has to beat Finland for the gold. That will take awhile. So did this.

Dave Brooks, the brother of U.S. coach Herb Brooks, refused to celebrate ahead of time.

"Watch the Russians put the pressure on now," he said when Eruzione fired in the go-ahead 4–3 goal. "Our kids are getting tired."

And every time the red-clad Soviets with CCCP emblazoned across their uniform fronts flashed down-ice, handling sticks with the apparent delicacy of an ophthalmologist wielding his tiniest instrument, Dave Brooks would moan, "Oh, murder! Is this murder!"

It was murder, all right. Murder for Mother Russia when the final horn cut through the smoke and hysteria, and American players tumbled deliriously together on the ice like overcoated St. Bernards, hugging, kissing, screaming.

Orange phosphorescent stripes glittering from their sticks, the Americans refused to quit at every point.

They were down 1–0, 2–1, and 3–2 before history kicked in.

Americans had been beating on 19-year-old left wing Vladimir Krutov most of the belly-churning evening.

Finally, midway through the third and final 20-minute period, Krutov retaliated by high-sticking an American, slamming his blade across the nearest neck he could find.

Into the penalty box for two minutes went Krutov. Now it was six Americans against five Russians, and just eight seconds before Krutov came out, Mark Johnson took a pass from Dave Silk and rocketed at goal past Myshkin, who for some reason was playing the second and third periods in place of the leg-ended Russian goalie Vladislav Tretiak.

That tied the socre, and Eruzione's goal made the unbeliev-able believable.

The score was hardly up before coach Brooks received a call from President Carter.

"The President told me we had made the American people very proud, that we reflected America's basic ideals, and then he invited us to come to the White House Monday for a couple of cases of Cokes," Brooks said.

The first man in the Coke line should be Craig, the 22-year-old goaltender from North Easton, Massachusetts, who fended off all but three of the Russians' 39 shots on goal. Americans hit an incredible 25 percent of their 16 shots on goal.

In the end, though, it was Eruzione, with an assist from tiny (5-7, 160-pound), baby-faced Mark Pavelich of Eveleth, Minne-sota, who handed the Russians only their fourth loss against 40 victories and two draws in Olympic competition since 1956.

"It's amazing," Eruzione said. "We're thrown together in September and now we're incredibly close."

The very last and most poignant words of the night came from Tony Lorente, a Cuban expatriate now living in nearby Saranac Lake.

He threw his Russian hockey pin onto the ice. He said, "This might have meant something to some people, but it meant everything to me. The Russians drove me out of Cuba. I love America."

ZONK AND LANGER HIT IT BIG

JANUARY 28, 1987

Larry Csonka drew a long breath and let it out in the literal burst of a lifetime. A new life. It started Tuesday when he and Jim Langer joined Paul Warfield as the only Dolphins in the Pro Football Hall of Fame.

"When you're playing," Zonk said, "it's all *is*. Every goal is that season, that game, even that play. All of a sudden, that's over, and it's *was*.

"You sit around at fan meetings and reunions and beer promotions and talk about what used to be. None of what you talk about *is*, it's all *was*."

Then the Hall of Fame says come in and a radiance of fresh glory beams in, and neither Csonka's nor Langer's lives will be the same, for they are Hall of Famers.

I believe all four Dolphin nominees—Csonka, Langer, Bob Griese and Larry Little—belong in the Hall. But there is no realistic way to think that, in a field of superstars, even one is a cinch to make it. Landing a pair is a stunning tribute to how football sees Zonk and Langer and others on the only team to make three straight Super Bowls.

Csonka said he was "real sorry" neither Griese nor Little made it. Well, they will get more chances, and probably make it yet.

The point is, Zonk and Langer are where they deserve to be. Zonk was the heart of the Super Dolphins—17–0 in 1972 was the greatest, but 32–2 for two seasons was even greater—and Langer was its war-club.

Bob Kuechenberg won't be eligible for the Hall until 1990, five years after the close of his career. He can look at both his old brothers in blood more vividly than anyone.

"I roomed with Jim for 10 years after both of us had been

rejected by other clubs," Kooch said. "I never saw a more inspirational leader than Zonk, and I never saw a center as good as Jim until Dwight Stephenson came along."

Langer's election came as a surprise. Most offensive linemen nominated for the Hall sweat bullets for decades. Langer held one special ace among the four Dolphins. It was impossible to say that Csonka was the best running back of history, or Griese the best quarterback, or Little the best guard. But Langer from 1973 through '79 was regarded as the best center who ever played, all through that time.

"I don't think most realized one unusual thing about Langer," Kuechenberg said. "He was left-handed. So was I, but the nuns made me change as a kid, so I do a lot of things right-handed. Langer never changed. It gave him a tremendous weapon. He could snap the ball with his right hand, but the left hand is the one centers do their damage with, and Langer used his like a war-club—an ax.

"Jim was like Popeye. His legs were huge. He was the biggest person I ever saw from elbows to fingertips, and knees to toe tips. He'd snap the ball right-handed, and put all that tremendous power into that hammer of a left arm. Just devastating."

Langer was faster, too, than most thought. Csonka was starting long before Langer arrived in '70. The fullback wasn't altogether sold on the center until one of their first games together.

"We were playing the Colts," Zonk remembered, "and that was hairy back then because you just couldn't get outside when Mike Curtis was in there, because he was the fastest middle linebacker there was. You'd see the action start and then Curtis was gone and no center could catch him, but there was Langer doing it. I don't mean Langer would knock him down. No center was ever *that* fast. But Jim would knock Curtis off stride, and that gave us the edge."

Csonka and Langer were as different personally as two men could get; Csonka gregarious, Langer private. They still had something besides leadership in common. They refused to wrap themselves in that arrogance characteristic of so many sports mercenaries who obviously believe their God-given talent sets them apart from "ordinary" people.

To act ordinary in pro sports is to be extraordinary. Csonka and Langer did it. They shared themselves, even if it was sometimes difficult for Langer in his reserved way.

27

On field, by Kuechenberg's lights, it was total antisociability with Zonk and Langer.

"Out there, they were both to the right of Attila the Hun," Kooch deposed. "Sheer savages. I'd have to say Paul Warfield, who's already in the Hall, is the most talented teammate I ever had. Zonk was the most inspirational—best I ever saw at turning two yards into four yards, or four into six. What a factor!

"But the image I carry of Zonk is him staggering back to the huddle, bleeding like a stuck pig, and still growling. You'd be in the line bleeding, and to see a skill player doing the same thing just made you play like hell. Langer and I had a standing bet which side of Zonk's face his nose would be on at the end of the game."

But Csonka's body paid, and so did Langer's, and both will be paying the rest of their lives in aches from toes to skulls.

"Let me put it this way," Csonka said. "I have a little cabin on my farm in Stow, Ohio. We drill gas wells out there in the winter, and it's cold in that cabin.

"The first thing I do when I get out of bed and feel the jolt in my knees is think of Roy Winston. On the second step, my calcified Adam's apple starts bobbing and I think of Carl Eller. A few more steps in the dark and it's Willie Lanier. By the time I get to the bathroom, I'm flashing back to Dick Butkus and Ray Nitschke. And when the light finally comes on, I just hope that somewhere in the darkness they're thinking of me, too."

THAT SAND WAS REAL FOR CHARLES ATLAS

MARCH 1, 1973

I'll always remember how lonely he seemed. We had been four hours in his luxurious Palm Beach condominium. Finally it was time to leave. Charles Atlas stood there, a 77-year-old millionaire with a body that looked as though it had been freshly quarried, and you could see in his face the ache for company. I think he would have climbed into our car and gone on with us, just for someone to talk to, if he'd been asked.

Now I wished we'd asked. That was three years ago, and Hubert Mizell of the Associated Press and I had spent most of the day with him on our way to Lakeland to see Denny McLain. A couple of months ago, Charles Atlas died. I couldn't believe it. He was the symbol of indestructibility. He had been an idol of mine and other generations who saw that body and his published promises to give everyone one just like it.

In the 1930s and 1940s we grew up on Charles Atlas. For $30 you could take his "dynamic tension" course. Now it's simply isometrics.

Charles Atlas was the hero of all the spindly nearsighted weak underweight kicked-around kids in America. They didn't kick sand in HIS face. Not more than once anyway.

His advertisements showed a bully striding along a beach and kicking a shower of grit over an emaciated youth trying to court a beautiful girl. A few panels later, after taking the Charles Atlas body-building course, the kid was all muscles and punching out the bully.

Charles Atlas launched one of the unforgettable advertising campaigns. But it wasn't all Madison Ave. It really was Charles Atlas. He was no phony.

He was too good to be true: reverent, sincere, polite, the

29

total gentleman. But he was true. It was a shame he had to live his last year pathetically reaching out for someone else like himself.

Women all over America, rich women, actresses, bored play-women, propositioned him by the hundreds. He would have none of that. He wanted someone real, like his adored wife—"more than a wife, a sweetheart for 50 years"—until she died in 1965.

His ads told how he transformed himself "from a 97-pound weakling into the world's most prefectly developed man." They did not lie.

"I lived in Brooklyn," he said, "and I took this pretty young lady out to the beach. Two big fellows came walking by and looked at me. They were wondering what a scrawny little guy like me was doing with such a beauty. Finally one of them drew back a foot and kicked sand in my face.

"I didn't do anything. The girl wanted to know why I didn't fight back. I told her, 'In the first place, he is too damn big. In the second place, I am blind from the sand in my eyes.'"

Charles Atlas even had a sense of humor.

His original name was Angelo Siciliano. He had come from Italy with his father in 1904. Through "dynamic tension"—straining one muscle against another—he developed the celebrated body that could tear New York City telephone directories in half and pull a Pennsylvania Railroad car 112 feet down a track.

Even at 77, every morning he did 50 knee-bends, 100 sit-ups, 300 push-ups. When weather kept him in his apartment, so he couldn't run or walk on the beach, he would do the equivalent of 20 to 30 miles on a stationary bicycle.

He had borrowed the name "Atlas" from a statue he saw as a boy. He threw in the "Charles" for American effect. Eventually his customers numbered more than seven million. Few asked for their money back. They could get it if they wanted. Atlas wasn't greedy.

"What would I do with more money, anyway?" he asked. "Just give it away."

What he really wanted was someone, not something. I'm just sorry he didn't have anyone there at the end.

BACKSIDE AT THE DERBY

APRIL 30, 1982

LOUISVILLE—The groom called himself Buddy Brown. He was thin enough to work as an advance man for a famine, and the beard over his black face would bring a rabbi's envy. But he wore the beard only as protection against wind that cut to the bone even when the sun first hit Churchill Downs' green-roofed barns at 6:49 Thursday.

He shivered when a friend pointed to Barn 43 and Nelson Bunker Hunt.

"Nelson Bunker Hunt, international silver king," Brown's friend twanged, "and his horse Rockwall. Imagine. The guy's got 600 horses and half the silver in the world, and this is the first time he even brung a horse to the Derby."

Brown grunted. "Ain't that too bad?" he said. "And I got caught with a hotplate in the dorm, and they said one more time and it's goodby backside for old Buddy boy."

Brown picked up a hose and shot a stream at a raggedy roan's forelegs. "And you know something?" he said. "I wouldn't trade this for all of Nelson Bunker Hunt's silver and horses and everything else."

Welcome to the Kentucky Derby backside. Officially, backstretch. But always The Backside to the homeless nomads who nest in on short money and long hopes, chasing horses and rainbows.

You know about the front side. TV brings it up close in glorious color. Cameras zoom in on clothes that would cost a $150-a-week backsider two months' wages. Cathy Lee Crosby and Andy Warhol and Patrick Duffy and Averill Harriman will weep when the band plays *My Old Kentucky Home*. But that's only the wrapping. It is the veneer of the backside world of hot-walkers, exercise boys and girls, grooms, trainers and jockeys—the most fascinating world within a world in all sports.

"Nothing anywhere can grip you like The Backside," said Charlsie Cantey, a TV commentator whose husband, Joe, trains horses.

"You have to be a part of that camaraderie to understand it. When we won the 1980 Belmont with Temperence Hill, the gathering afterward by the barns was one of the most touching things of my life, for simple love and sharing."

The front is packed with phonies, pickpockets, dukes and kooks. The Backside is *people*. "All kinds," Charlsie said, "from grooms who have to sign their W-4 forms with an 'X' to others who have doctorates from the finest universities."

One of Joe Cantey's employees is a former stockbroker and management consultant whose wife had written three books. "They just got tired of bucking the system," Charlsie said. "They went to the track and they've been on it ever since. It's a kick, a high. It's the only place I ever worked where I didn't feel like I was working. What would *you* rather look at? Horses and sunshine, or typewriters and stacks of paper? The Backside is total freedom."

The Backside is deliberate, self-sought, magnificent insulation. Backsiders joke on the square that they probably would never hear of World War III unless *The Daily Racing Form* twinned off a headline: SPRINTERS VIE AT CHURCHILL; SIX GO IN WORLD WAR III TODAY.

"The Backside is dreams," in the words of trainer Wayne Lukas.

Frontsiders pay up to $500 a day for rooms at the Seelbach Hotel. Backsiders live in free dormitory rooms that would make a cell look sumptuous. Frontsiders worry about scratching their Mercedes. The Backside is the only place where it's worse to run over a horse than a human.

If The Backside is heaven on earth, Churchill Downs is as surely that earthly heaven's capital city this week. Churchill Downs looks as though it was tacked together by cross-eyed carpenters using Jack Daniel bottles for hammers. But not a pin or a bridle is out of place among the hoses and pails of The Backside.

Buddy Brown happens not to be the real name of the thin man who said he would not trade places with Nelson Bunker Hunt. That, too, is part of The Backside.

"Buddy Brown is just a name I use," he said. He is on the lam from alimony payments. "If my ex-old lady ever found out I was back here," he said, "she'd break one-fifty-nine-and-two getting here."

That is Backsidese for one minute, 59 and 2/5 seconds—the way Secretariat ran the fastest Derby ever, in 1973.

"I got to hide out somewhere," Brown said. "What's better than this? If you ain't got nothing and ain't never going to have nothing, where would you rather do it than here? I get fresh air and sunshine and one regular meal a day."

Lukas stood out by Barn 42 just before Thursday's post-position draw, thinking about The Backside *and* the Derby.

"Look around," Lukas said, "and tell me truthfully if this isn't the greatest place in the world to be this week."

Lukas glanced over at a girl in jeans grazing a horse. "Annie, how long have you had him there? Thirty minutes? OK. Take him in."

The horse nibbled at Kentucky bluegrass. *Poa pratensis.* The grass here is only called bluegrass; it is as green as any anywhere. It is the best for growing horses strong enough to last but light enough to exert minimum energy, because bluegrass springs from earth left by billions of shells when central Kentucky was an ocean bed.

Lukas plucked a burr off chaps covering designer jeans. "Just once," he said, "I'd like to ask every trainer when they load the Derby horses into the gate, 'Would you give up the purse if you knew you could win this Derby?' And every one would holler, 'Yeah!'"

Until that time comes, the 1,000 citizens of The Backside will dream. Few will see the finish. They will either join the infield, where some people have stood for 30 years without seeing anything but six-foot humans, or on the roofs of the barns off the backstretch, or the top of the track kitchen, Thompson's Restaurant. Steve Cauthen saw his first Derby up there the day he turned 16, two years to the day before he won the '78 derby with Affirmed.

"They bring their own stepladders and climb up there," said Gladys Farmer. She and her husband, Charles, run the track kitchen. Nobody knows The Backside better than Gladys and Charles.

Gladys calls it "a wonderful world of wonderful people." But the wonderful world stops at requests for kitchen credit. The kitchen operates 15 hours a day, 4:30 a.m. to 7:30 p.m., and hears more hard-luck stories than anybody except the track chaplain. It serves the best food at the best prices of any place in Louisville. Two eggs with hash-browns and toast go for $1.30. Eighty-cent biscuits and gravy are the *piece de resistance*.

But no credit. Especially not at night when betting has tapped out most backsiders.

"We had one man come in and signal with his hands that he couldn't speak," Gladys said. "He wrote a note that he had money coming in three days. We fed him three meals a day for three days. And then he wouldn't pay."

The Farmers cut him off. "Then he opened his mouth," Gladys said, "and gave me the worst cussing I ever got."

If a backsider is stone busted, the chaplain will take him to the kitchen and charge his meal to the Horsemen's Benevolent Protective Association. This is Rev. Jesse Hood, 47, a Southern Baptist who chaplains the state's backstretches.

"The only time these people leave The Backside is to die," Rev. Hood said. "They have the same problems everybody has. Alcoholism. Gambling. But you'll never find anybody that shares like backsiders do. They have more togetherness than a lot of churches."

One night, the rev held a little Bible service in a recreation room that also is unofficially and illegally used for card games. "When our service was over," Rev. Hood said, "a couple of guys walked up to me. Each one pressed a dollar bill into my hand. It was their only way of expressing themselves, of thanking me. These are not highly educated, articulate people."

Joe Hirsch is. Hirsch has spent 34 of his 54 years as top columnist for *The Daily Racing Form,* the world's most expensive daily publication at $1.75. He knows every groom, every dog, every trainer, every jockey. When Hirsch walks into a backside mob and quietly asks, "How did the horse work?" every trainer snaps to attention, not because of Hirsch's job but because he has done more favors for backsiders than anybody.

Hirsch introduced a friend this week to Winston Neil, 64, who has been a trainer for 42 years and typifies The Backside because he has never gotten a horse to the Derby.

"Any friend of Joe is a friend of mine," Neil said. "You want to know about The Backside. Well, I'll tell you straight, there's not much profit back here. If there were, there'd be unions, and there aren't any unions."

Neil's chuckle jounced his ample belly. "Overtime? Are you kidding. A horse don't know it's Sunday."

Still, horses are Neil's first love. "Noble animals," he said. "You remember Gen. Nathan Bedford Forrest, the one who said you have to get there fustest with the mostest? By the way, the general was a distant relative of Henry Forrest, who won the '66 Derby with Kauai King.

"Anyway, Gen. Forrest's favorite horse was named Chadwick. Chadwick was wounded at the front, and the general sent him back of the lines with his son. But the horse loved the general so much he found his way back to the front lines all by himself. And was killed. That's a horse for you."

Neil wished his visitor good luck. Then he said wistfully, "I wouldn't mind having a horse run in a Derby before I die. I got plenty of them that could go a mile and a quarter. Trouble is, it might take them until sun-up Sunday to do it."

Neil is a literary man. Another such, named William Faulkner, came to The Backside 27 years ago and said his own piece:

"And now in the gray early light we can see them, in couples and groups at canter or hand-gallop under the exercise boys. Then one alone, at once furious and solitary, going full out, breezed, the rider hunched forward . . . not of the horse but simply (for the instant) with it, in the conventional posture of speed—and who knows, perhaps the two of them, man and horse both: The animal dreaming, hoping that moment at least it looked like Whirlaway or Citation, the boy for that moment at least that he was indistinguishable from Arcaro or Earl Sande, perhaps feeling already across his knees the scented sweep of the glorious garland . . ."

Every backsider says it differenly. Leonard Imperio, who trains Star Gallant, dreamed as a child of becoming an Australian rancher. For him, The Backside is the next best thing to Australia's outback.

"I don't bet," Imperio said. "If I don't have a horse racing, I don't even go to the track in the afternoon. But I love the tranquility of The Backside so much that I'll go back to Star Gallant's barn at 1 a.m. or 2 a.m., just to be there."

Imperio pencilled some figures. "It costs our owners, Buckram Farm, about $2,000 a week, not including insurance, to keep Star Gallant going," he said. "We pay $200 a week just for water for him. Imported mineral water."

Buddy Brown earns $50 a week less than Star Gallant's water bill.

"I guess," said Imperio, "that's why they call it the sport of kings. And The Backside makes you feel like a king."

BACK FROM OBLIVION IN TALLAHASSEE

OCTOBER 3, 1987

TALLAHASSEE—With 17 minutes and 45 seconds remaining in the zaniest game in Miami's football history and the Hurricanes lying bleeding and apparently dead, down 16 points, Florida State cornerback Deion Sanders felt it necessary to inform Michael Irvin that UM's day was done.

"He told me the game was over when they had us 19–3," said UM wide receiver Irvin. "Deion said, 'Michael, you might as well quit running so hard and blocking so hard, 'cause it's all over for today.' "

Irvin responded, All-American Man fashion: "Oh no. A Hurricane never quits."

Irvin claims no gift of prophecy, but this was industrial-strength clairvoyance in Miami's utterly grotesque 26–25 victory.

Talking courage is one thing. Turning word to action is another, as the nation witnessed on CBS-TV in what must have been a fit of bafflement.

Irvin completed touchdown hookups of 26 and 73 yards with quarterback Steve Walsh. They came after halfback Melvin Bratton went 49 yards with another Walsh pass for UM's first touchdown just before the end of the third quarter.

Irvin initiated a conversation of his own when Miami's defense was trying to stop FSU's last chance pass attempt for a two-point conversion in one of the wackiest college games I have seen in going-on 50 years.

"You guys stop this," Irvin shouted, "and I'll spend all day in church tomorrow."

They did. He will.

Beating a brilliantly talented FSU team that was leading 19–3 with barely more than a quarter to play is surely worth a day of thanks. While Irvin and his Hurricane buddies are at it, they can also thank the Seminoles.

Actually, I'm a little surprised UM didn't just turn its plane toward Las Vegas instead of Miami late Saturday.

They could have shot everything they had on one roll and left with Vegas in their pockets. That's how their luck was running.

"Never played in a game that was so much fun," said senior guard Scott Provin. "So it was crazy. Hey, that's why we're the most-watched team in America."

True, luck notwithstanding. Their triumph was as much a tribute to courage and patience as to Florida State's seeming death wish.

There simply was no way UM was going to win—unable to run, unable to stop Sammie Smith (the best runner they have faced since anyone can remember), unable to throw consistently until Walsh started pulling rabbits out of his helmet.

The Seminoles formulated the brightest of game plans before blowing it. They felt that demon UM pass rusher Danny Stubbs took such a wide path that they could run inside him, and they did. They thought faking reverses would turn Miami's pursuit in the wrong direction, and it did.

And then they just loused it all up. They lost seven points on two missed field goals and an extra point by Derek Schmidt, who specializes in winning games, not kicking them into the loss column. The Seminoles also set up Miami's first quarter field goal on a terrible oversnap when Schmidt lined up to try his first field goal.

If victory seemed an outright gift, the Hurricanes still had to pick up the package and haul it.

"Sometimes they're ugly and still go in the right column," said UM defensive line coach Butch Davis. "That's what makes college football so great."

Don't try to sell that to the Seminoles.

Danny McManus' fourth-quarter pass that was intercepted by Stubbs never should have been thrown. Why put up the ball with an eight-point lead and wildman Smith running for 189 yards on the day?

Then, on the fatally failing two-point passing try, why would FSU line up without Smith even in the lineup?

Almost everyone figured that FSU Coach Bobby Bowden would run Smith for the game-deciding two-pointer. He was averaging 6.3 yards a pop, and had only three yards to go.

"We called timeout after they broke the huddle so we could see who they were lining up with," Davis said. "That's when we saw no Smith."

That was a dead tip-off that FSU was going to pass rather than run, and gave Bubba McDowell the mental jump to bat away McManus' pass intended to Pat Carter.

The hard truth is, FSU kicked the stuffing out of Miami everywhere but the scoreboard for 45 minutes.

An even harder truth for FSU: The scoreboard is the only place it counts.

GRIESE'S LEGACY AS A MAN

JULY 16, 1981

All too little can be accurately described as difficult in sports writing, which is the kindergarten of literature. The only hard part for any practitioner with an IQ of more than 40 is taking it seriously. What could possibly be less important to civilization than the scores of children's games?

For myself, the single professional agony of the last 14 years has come in the rare instances when I have felt it necessary to criticize Bob Griese's quarterbacking as his eyes and arm and then his shoulders deteriorated to the extent that he officially retired Thursday.

Even this in any reasonable sense is hyperbole. Griese is an adult who has been handsomely paid for his work. As such, he is no less immune to criticism than any other professional entertainer.

Yet, even the few times I denigrated Griese's quarterbacking, I could not avoid a sense of guilt as deep as though I had spit on the grave of Thomas Jefferson or kicked the Lincoln Memorial.

This sounds puerile and may be. It was just that, well, he had *done* so much for Miami and the Dolphins, and *was* and *is* so much in so many other ways.

That was part of what Griese had to sacrifice to eventually earn $400,000 a year, which by contractual agreement he will—and should—receive even while not playing this season.

It was not the larger part by any means. Much the larger part was the time he had to spend away from wife Judi and sons Scott, 12, Jeff, 10, and Brian, 6.

For years, as Griese progressed from the second-time Super Bowl championship quarterback of 28 on into his labored 30s, we arranged an annual appointment for a sort of Griese a Year Older piece. He never enjoyed them, or any other interviews that I ever heard of. As a private man, he despised public attention, though not the public.

There came one year when he absolutely refused the birthday bit, and I must go back some summers to explain.

For all his outward cool, Griese carries a pranksterish streak that manifests itself at grotesque times. The Dolphins make clear a policy that no players sit with newsmen during meals in training camp at Biscayne College. Sometimes, I would be the only media type around for the evening meal at Biscayne College. Griese would breeze right past Don Shula's summit table, and audibly repeat a comment I might have made about Shula—especially if my comment had been even fractionally negative. Then Griese would proceed directly to the table where I sat alone, and plop down his tray.

Nobody ever called Griese on that. Kings pick their own dining spots. And heaven forbid that anyone should think Griese was seeking publicity, the absolute last thing he ever wanted.

At those times, Griese presented a single though unenunciated taboo.

No football talk.

He delighted then as now in discussing children. Once, I mentioned a birds-and-bees book I had found helpful with my own son, a classmate of Griese's oldest. Griese did not mention it again unitil I called him for the annual State of Griese's Arteries interview about a week before the February 3, 1977, he turned 32.

"No," he said. "No more of those. Nobody is interested."

"You're wrong," I said. "Everybody is interested."

"No," he said again.

I was about to drop it when he said suddenly, "Do you still have that book you mentioned at training camp? The one for kids?"

"Yes."

"OK," Griese said. "If you'll let me borrow the book, then we'll talk."

He would do nothing to enhance his own image, which mostly was that of a cold and cryptic man. But he would, and will, do anything for his children. Or anyone else's.

This alone will not put a quarterback in the Hall of Fame. Nor should it. But if you couple this sense of responsibility with the magnificent quarterback he became despite an arm less powerful than hundreds of others' before and since, it makes a rather nice combination to decorate the Hall.

I would suggest a bit more than the mere bust honoring Griese when he inevitably is voted in.

A monument to him should be erected outside the Orange Bowl, or whatever new stadium hopefully follows, just as Stan Musial's statue enhances St. Louis' stadium.

This monument need not show Griese in football clothes. His decency transcends all he did on the field.

If some insist his statistics be chiseled in stone, all right. But a single quote from H.L. Mencken would say more about Robert Allen Griese than all the arithmetical rigamarole.

"Honor," it would say, "is simply the morality of superior men."

WHAT DO CHILDREN KNOW ANYWAY?

MAY 7, 1982

One kid hung his head for maybe 30 seconds. "It's embarrassing," he said softly, "to walk in six runs with your dad watching."

One coach insisted for maybe 15 seconds that his batter should not be declared out on a tipped strike. "It was the third strike," a teenage umpire said simply. "The catcher caught it. Batter's out."

The coach said, "Oh," and sat down.

It was a kids' baseball game. It had to be a kids' game. Could you imagine sensible adults conducting a game so illogically?

No owner fired a manager or coach, or threatened to move his team unless the area provided a new stadium. A church provides the field, and isn't about to shift *its* franchise.

Not a single player held out for a trade or a bigger contract. Nobody recruited anybody or induced them to play with new cars. Not even a tricycle.

In two hours, I never saw an obscene gesture. Nobody spilled beer on anybody. Not one fan bloodied another. Nobody demanded anything except another turn at bat, or an extra cup of Gatorade.

When a mother brought out the thermos, the wild pitcher forgot how embarrassed he was for his dad to see him walk in those runs. Besides, dad didn't care. "I just enjoy seeing him play," said the father. You see right there how unwise the man is in the ways of sports.

One pitcher broke out into a smile wide as a slice of watermelon every time he threw a strike. He forgot himself once and pegged the ball as hard as he could, some 20 miles per hour.

"Don't throw it so fast," the batter pleaded.

"OK," the pitcher said, and both smiled.

No native-born American kids complained because some others were Cuban-born. Poor little pinheads, so untaught to hate.

I listened as hard as I could, and still could not catch a single voice raised in anger. The simple-minded people who run this league restrict verbal expressions to rooting for one's own batter. When one kid got carried away and joyously shrieked at the opposing pitcher, "Throw the ball wild!" the pitcher stopped cold.

"They can't do that," he told the umpire, who gently advised the bench jockey to desist.

The most unworldly of all sights presented itself in a small group of parents. They applauded every play by either team, oblivious to such insidious assault on the fabric of our society.

One kid got a special hand. He came to the game with a hurt finger after taking a blood test for admission to a summer camp. The lab technician, who invariably keeps a cigarette lit in a nearby ashtray, hit the kid's thumb a brutal shot with a needle. The kid screwed back his tears. Still holding his thumb at the game, he finally firmed up his thoughts.

"I'm glad that guy smokes," he told a buddy.

It was the only bitter line I heard all day.

They're only kids. How are they supposed to know what sports is all about?

BASEBALL SPRING:
It's the Promising, Not the Keeping

MARCH 7, 1987

My heart knows why it loves spring baseball training.

My head thrums up great stacks of reasons for the game's loveliness in lush springtime: the symmetry and sunshine in which rich and famous men perform with such indolent grace.

My heart knows better.

My heart loves spring training because the world turns virginal again then, and our lives start over.

So, of course, our lives don't start over in every way. Baseball isn't *that* strong. So, of course, no surety is involved. So what? What guarantee can truly stir the soul?

It is the newness of it all that stirs; the newness with which we see baseball now, the same as when we first saw it and want our children to see it. It is the kind of newness that fell about us in a great dazzling light the first day we would fish the baseball out of the closet's winter mess and dash out into the first slush of spring, rolling and reveling in mud and crud.

As a personal quirk, I am anti-new in terms of possessions. You could call me downright cranky in my dislike for new cars, new clothes (just take a look), new houses—just about anything new that will wear out.

Not to get all big-domed about it, the only investments in newness I truly relish involve human experiences—a new scene, a new friend, a new situation.

Baseball in springtime is exactly that to me. Its enchantment is its freshness. It is true that spring baseball makes millions more promises than it keeps. But baseball is unlike love. In baseball, making promises means vastly more than keeping them. Baseball promises, like records, are made to be broken. The promise is all that counts. We look anew, and we are stimulated, as first-time pictures on a blackboard arouse a kindergartner.

What if the pictures are only fantasy? What is more fantastic than fantasy? Especially if we are holding a father's or grandfather's or child's hand on the historic day that a Ted Williams or Henry Aaron or Dwight Gooden or Stan Musial or Mickey Mantle breaks in. Or—and this really is the point—even if it is only the *promise* of a Williams, Aaron, Gooden, Musial, Mantle.

My own spring training "father" left when Paul Richards left. He and Gene Mauch were the smartest, toughest managers who never won a pennant. The last night I spent with Richards, in a little hotel where the Texas Rangers quartered at Pompano Beach, we had laughed at his remembrances of the Joe DiMaggios and Mike Schmidts and Sandy Koufaxes and Reggie Jacksons and Steve Carltons and Robinsons (all of them, Jackie, Brooks, Frank) and Roy Campanellas and Warren Spahns flying through spring training. Mike Cuellar. Boog Powell. Duke Snider. Luis Aparicio. Herb Score. Ron Guidry. Mike Flanagan. Men Richards managed or managed against, or just admired, clinically, professionally.

"I'll be gone pretty soon," Richards said that night, cheerfully enough. "Baseball won't miss me. It starts over every spring with or without you. Maybe that's the trick of it. Makes no difference what happens, it's going up to bat fresh every year. The thing is, if you're there, you feel that way, too—fresh."

That was April 1986. A month later, at 77, Richards died on the golf course at Waxahachie, Texas. He once owned the newspaper there. "The *Waxahachie Daily Light*," Richards would lovingly reel off its name. "We had the greatest slogan of any newspaper ever. Right over the masthead, it said, 'We are for an early spring and against the boll weevil.' "

The slogan made a perfect metaphor for the simplicity of spring baseball. Simplicity makes much of baseball's beauty; much of the reason children so revel in their rhapsodic original look at the game as played by the best; much of the reason we go back and back and back to it in such open-hearted expectation.

"It's just throwing and catching and hitting and running," Richards said. "What's simpler than that?"

Yet every throw and catch and hit and run is new. And baseball, at least in the spring, before winning's frenzy and losing's despair set in, relaxes enough to give us time to share it.

My son was 6 and wondering where to throw the peanut shells the first time I took him to Miami Stadium to see the Orioles open the spring against the Yankees.

On the floor, I said.

"The floor!" he said in a paroxysm of wonder spilling over into delight. For him, baseball will always be that wondrous place where you can throw the peanut shells on the floor, and I hope he remembers I was the one who told him.

See, spring baseball gives us time to share. Football so sweeps us up in its rat-a-tat violence, it is impossible to communicate even during exhibitions. Basketballs whir into rims too fast to allow any but the tiniest snippets of conversation. Tennis frowns upon conversation in the grandstand, and golf—ha! Heaven forbid we should raise a voice, even to continue to share a golden shot more than two minutes after it is struck.

Baseball was made to share, and spring baseball to share the most. The sharing is as freshening as the promising.

In the off-and-on decades that I tracked Paul Richards from my boyhood, I would see him haggard in late summer from hard playing, managing, general managing, even consulting. But by the beginning of the next spring he was new again.

Every spring training meant new life, until the end. For Richards, as for so many, the thrill of baseball's annual renewal was as basic as perhaps the most basic baseball poem ever written. The poem is as odd as it is bewitching. It is called *Benediction*. John Perlman wrote it, and Kevin Kevane and Richard Grossinger included it in their unforgettable volume, *Baseball, I Gave You All the Best Years of My Life*.

One day I showed Richards the poem:

A ball batted foul

askew

out over the wall—
which I stab
one-handed
passing by:

All
> *Right!*

says a boy
chasing after

as I make my catch

All
> *Right!*

Richards looked it over. "That's poetry?" he asked.

"Hey, you've been around a long time," I said. "Think back to when you were a kid. Think back to when you were seeing baseball for the first time, when maybe you reached out and just *speared* one out of nowhere."

Richards thought back. He rubbed his leathery old chin. He said, "Yeah. That's how it was. I guess that is poetry."

An unsentimental sort, Richards looked a little embarrassed. He turned his head slightly away. "There's a lot of poetry in baseball," he said. "Especially in the spring. When it's all brand new, and looks so good, whether it comes true or not."

In the wonder of it, he was almost whispering. "Damn, son," he said, "it's so good right then."

GETTING CREATIVE ON OKEECHOBEE

MARCH 19, 1986

OKEECHOBEE—My 16-year-old boy and I hadn't been here 10 minutes before they marked us as city folk. I must have stood too close to the razor this morning.

"What's the first thing a Miamian hears when he gets a three-piece suit?"

"Go ahead, tell us, Roy Lee."

" 'Will the defendant please rise?' "

By supper time the second night, my whiskers were out far enough to blend into the crowd at Lightsey's, where entrees include cooter—Lake Okeechobee turtle.

And one yarn-spinner's voice floated over all the rest.

"Tried all day and couldn't get a bite to save my soul," said the voice. "So I'm putting the boat back on the trailer when I look down and see this snake with a frog in its mouth. I take the frog. I'm grateful to the snake, so I give him a little sip of whiskey."

The whole gang in the restaurant was listening by then.

"A little later, I feel this tapping on my foot," the voice went on. "It's that same snake with another frog in his mouth. I didn't catch any specks, and the bottle's empty, but boy I came home with a mess of frog-legs."

The place roared. It was tale-telling time on Lake Okeechobee, where some fishermen will swear their fathers built the Natural Bridge of Virginia. That's not to mention the Texan who measures his fish only between the eyes. Or the Clewiston farmer talking about a day so flat-calm they had to take down a barbed-wire fence to let in enough breeze to turn the windmill. And the Iowan who caught a bass so big right in his pond that the water went down so far it made the mill run backward so fast it unground 50 bushels of corn right back onto the cob.

Stranger yet, fishing hereabouts is serious business. You ask a question when an Okeechobeean is watching a bobber, your answer is bound to come out of the side of a mouth.

None of those drugstore cowboys from down U.S. 27. Not around here, no siree. None of those salt-water party people throwing out a line, parking the boat and rushing the beer cooler.

Real Okeechobee fishermen hit the bulrushes before dawn with fire in their eyes. They come back at sundown, either jubilant with their baskets overflowing with speckled perch or bluegill or shellcracker or bass, or empty and inconsolable.

Okeechobee fishing isn't play. It's life.

"Child, does your mother know you're out fishing on a Sunday morning?"

"Why don't you ask her? She's right over there—the lady using the Rockefeller XZ806T spinning jig."

Around here you learn to touch up the truth just a speck now and then, or get downright embarrassed. God wouldn't punish a man for a lie as long as it was about fishing.

From the top of a lock, a sunburned matron who looked right out of Westchester Country, New York, gave us a magisterial stare and demanded, "Oh, where are all the fish?"

We ignored her. She tried nice-nice. "Catch any?" she trilled.

"Oh yeah, a bunch," I lied. In tandem, David and I rolled our eyes at a cooler that actually was holding a lot more pop than perch.

She bought the act. We figured we had done right by her. Deep down, tourists want to hear only good news.

You just don't want to have to dissemble real often. We didn't have to. Things picked up. David is a fishing fool. He started picking off shellcrackers on spinners.

It took longer than we thought it would; story of my life. We had read where a fisheries biologist said specks were "thicker than fleas on a hound dog" at Okeechobee. After two days of more squalls than fish, my son concluded, "That hound dog must have been dipped and clipped."

He stays at it, though. Sometimes you need a block and tackle to get him up for school, but his mattress has rockets in it over here. Five a.m., *whoom.* He wants to be out amongst the reeds before sun shows.

And never mind the mosquitoes down in the locks when rain has really hit and the bugs start pumping iron. After one downpour, a farmer near the levee missed a horse. He looked down by a nearby lock. Two mosquitoes had eaten the horse and were pitching horseshoes for the saddle.

My son loves Okeechobeeans' pleasant guile. He recognizes this territory for what it has become since the lusty days painted in Patrick Smith's novel, *A Land Remembered*. What it has become is a unique cluster of a seeming million mobile homes whose tourist owners grew so entranced with this part of crackerland they just pulled over and stayed, like tents expanding out into a village, from one kind of tribe to another.

The first tribesmen used canoes. These use high-tech craft that get faster and fancier as the stock market goes up. But the nature of the Okeechobee fisherman doesn't change. He is grim and then some.

It's pride more than hunger. That has cost some manners. Few fishermen bother any more to slow down while passing those at anchor. If one spot doesn't work, speed on. Keeping moving is the name of the game. Reputations are at stake out there. That isn't why I fish. It eats right into the grain of the fun. Here, though, a man's catch is his cachet.

His catch, and his story.

I told my boy about All-Pro tackle Big Daddy Lipscomb going out in Chesapeake Bay with his Baltimore Colt teammate, Long Gone Dupre, in the 1950s. The halfback fell asleep. Big Daddy fastened a bucket onto Long Gone's line and then woke up his buddy by shouting, "Fish on! Fish on!"

When Long Gone finally dragged the bucked to the surface, Big Daddy bellowed, "Man, look at the *mouth* on that sucker!"

That's an Okeechobee kind of story.

Listen here, bubba, some of that land over around Pahokee is so rich, you flip a seed in the muck and jump out of the way.

"And that wind off the lake the other day . . ." said a man wearing a snuff cap and a week's beard. "It was just like back in Kansas. I had this 500-pound hog fenced up, and a wind came up so hard it blew that hog through the knothole and made a mile-and-a-half of sausage in five minutes."

ON THE ROAD WITH CASSIUS CLAY:

SHOULD A KING TOTE HIS OWN WATER?

APRIL 1, 1965

EN ROUTE TO CHICOPEE FALLS, MASSACHUSETTS—
Cassius Clay stretched himself on a chaise lounge in front
of his northwest Miami home and declined a road map.

"Don't need no map," he said. "Just going to point that old
bus north and be in Boston in nothing flat."

Thus began the most improbable cross-country trip by
a heavyweight champion since John L. Sullivan boozed and
wenched his way across America three quarters of a century
ago.

Clay does not booze, nor does he wench. He does not do a
whole lot of advance planning, either. The closest he came to
any logistics for this 1,400-mile journey was to ask his wife Sonji
to fry a batch of chicken.

The chicken was late, and more like enough for seven people
than 17.

"Won't be quite on time leaving," Clay explained to sparring
partners, reporters, bottle-washers and fellow Black Muslims.
They had gathered to accompany him to his Chicopee Falls,
Massachusetts, training camp for his May 25 bout with the
Sonny Liston he TKO'd 14 months ago in Miami Beach.

"Got to wait for the chicken," Clay said. "Leastwise we'll have
enough food to get us out of this part of the country."

Famous last words.

Clay looked proudly at the red and white bus parked at curb-
side. "Just put in a new $7,000 diesel engine," he said. "This is
going to be a trip you can tell your grandchildren about."

Nobody knew then how right he was.

Finally, the chicken was ready. Clay began supervising loading. His wife interrupted. "Ali," she called, using the last part of his Muslim name, although almost everyone else calls him Cassius or champ, "you see about my dry cleaning?"

"All sent," said the champion.

"How about my shoes at the shop?"

"Done," he said.

"Then take out the garbage," she said.

Clay put one finger to his mouth. "Shh," he said, "champs don't take out garbage."

He took out the garbage anyway and then started hauling bottles of distilled water to the bus.

"Don't seem right," he said. "Here I'm the king and still got to tote my own water. Some of these people would rather run through hell in a gasoline coat than do any work. I mean they'd rather jump off the Empire State Building and hope the ground wouldn't be hard, if you asked them to do anything."

Loading done, Clay stood on the steps of the bus and enjoined passengers from flirting during stops on the trip.

"Don't worry about us," I said, for the journalistic contingent. "We'll all be writing." The only journalists, and only whites, were George Plimpton, Mort Sharnik of *Sports Illustrated*, Bud Collins of the *Boston Globe* and myself.

"All aboard!" Clay shouted. He climbed inside, took the wheel and spun toward the Sunshine State Turnpike.

"By the way," he said, "anybody got any money?"

Everybody looked the other way. I was closest. "Give me $100," Clay said. "Remind me to give it back to you in Boston."

"Don't worry about that," I said. "There's no use both of us worrying."

Clay levelled me with a look. "Just think," he said. "The whole world would love to be on this bus with me, but they ain't, and you are. We're going to breathe fresh air and look at pretty trees and eat that chicken and you can interview me while I'm driving my beautiful bus along at the cruising speed of 85."

Some days a fellow is just lucky.

ON THE ROAD WITH CASSIUS CLAY:

UGLINESS IN YULEE

APRIL 2, 1965

FAYETTEVILLE, NORTH CAROLINA—The champ's traveling circus stalled in a frantic amalgam of thirst, hunger, back-biting, mechanical failure and racial trauma.

The last stood bitterly first in the minds of Cassius Clay's bedraggled entourage as it sat stranded a few miles north of Fayetteville, North Carolina, after 24 hours on the road from Miami.

The bus blew out here. This troupe's whole little world blew up in a hole in the road called Yulee, Florida.

The 17 passengers, all black except for four white reporters, had expected trouble along the way to Clay's Chicopee Falls, Massachusetts, training base for his return match with Sonny Liston. Just not so quickly.

It came when the bus pulled into a service station outside Yulee for refuelling late the first night.

Trainer Bundini Brown went into the station's lunchroom. Clay, now a Black Muslim, refused to enter because "I might not be welcome, and, besides, I don't believe in forcing integration."

He taunted Brown, "You go ahead, though, Jackie Robinson."

The station's proprietor told Brown that Negroes had to go around to the side for service.

"You mean the champion of the world can't get served like other people if he wants to come in here?" Brown asked.

"That's right," said the proprietor.

Brown began arguing. Clay raced inside and hauled the trainer outside. "You fool!" Clay shouted, manhandling Brown onto the bus. "Didn't I tell you what would happen in a place like this? Why you want to go into a place where they don't want you?"

Bud Collins of the *Boston Globe* asked the proprietor, "Isn't this discrimination against the law?"

"Not in this (Nassau) county," the proprietor said.

"Isn't this county in the United States?" Collins persisted.

"Not yet," the proprietor said.

The group finally was served in a restaurant in Brunswick, Georgia. But nobody had forgotten what happened in Yulee. Least of all Brown.

"One of these days," Brown told Clay, "we're going to find out which one of us is crazy. I think it's you."

That blow-up came as traumatic interruption of a ride that until then had been mostly laughs. Clay drove the first leg out of Miami, waving at motorists as he passed. As a driver, the champion is a cross between A.J. Foyt and Sarah Bernhardt. He goes 75 to 85 with elbows and knees only, using his hands to punctuate endless perorations, often turning his head away from the road to address querulous captive passengers.

Clay gave up the wheel after a bit, but reminded all that he was still in charge. "Anybody don't like anything on this bus better see me," he announced. "I am the navigator, the instructor and the provider."

The navigator, instructor and provider then went to sleep.

He was awake and talking non-stop again early Saturday when the cry of "fire!" came just outside Fayettteville.

A flaming tire was doused, but the bus would not start.

"Poor old bus," Clay said. "I guess we been pushing her too hard. She don't have no rest at all."

She was resting now, all right.

ON THE ROAD WITH CASSIUS CLAY:

'GOODBYE, LITTLE RED BUS'

APRIL 3, 1965

FAYETTEVILLE, NORTH CAROLINA—Cassius Clay stands beside his private bus on a deserted highway. One end of the bus is jacked up. A charred axle lies on the cockle-burred ground. A repairman summoned from town surveys the remains of the axle.

Clay: What's the story, baby?

Repairman: When were the bearings last packed on that wheel?

Clay: Don't know for sure. Maybe 30,000 miles ago. But I got a brand-new $7,000 engine in there.

Repairman: Wonderful. The bearings ought to be packed every 10,000 miles. It really helps to have a new engine when the grease dries out of the wheel bearings.

Clay: Well, I got to get to Boston, can you fix it or not?

Repairman: I'd have to drive 16 miles back to Fayetteville to see if we got parts.

Clay: I'll go with you. Then we'll roll.

Seven hours later, Clay's party is scattered beside the forlorn highway in various stages of lassitude. No one has slept in a bed in 31 hours. No one has eaten for what seems like forever.

Jimmy Ellis, sparring partner: Champ's been gone seven hours now. That's bad.

Bundini Brown, trainer: He's left us here to die.

Rahaman Ali, also known as Rudy Clay, the champion's brother: My brother wouldn't do that.

Otis Shabazz, bus-driver: Then why don't he come? I've starving and thirsty. We don't even have any paper cups.

Ellis: Lie down, Otis, and I'll pour water into your mouth from the jug. (He does.)

Shabazz: Oh, that's delicious. I never knew water had a taste before.

Ellis: Look, everybody. Bundini is so hungry his eyes are rolling back in his head.

Clay's brother: Give him a soda cracker. It will taste like cake.

Ellis: No, mix the cracker in some water. Cracker stew might save him. (Then, bitterly, to Brown): It is all your fault, Bundini. This is a judgment on us because you tried to integrate that lunchroom in Yulee last night.

Bundini (weakly): I wasn't trying to integrate it. I just wanted something to eat.

Suddenly, a sleek Trailways cruiser approaches. The party salaams and chants, "Ali has come . . . "

Clay: Relax, brothers. It is I, the king.

All in unison: Are they going to fix our wheel, or what?

Clay: They say it will cost $1,100. (All groan.) And I don't hardly got even $11 left. (All groan again.)

Bundini: I knew we should have caught a plane.

Clay: No, brothers, we shall ride into Boston on an air-cooled Trailways bus.

All cheer, except the Miami reporter who already has been nailed for a $100 loan.

Miamian (suspicious): How much is it going to cost to rent that new bus?

Clay: $650.

Miamian: What do you want me to do? Wire my paper for the $650? I didn't know when I signed up I was financing this whole trip.

Clay (soothingly): No problem. My people will pay for the new bus when we get to Boston.

All cheer as luggage is transferred to new bus. *Exeunt* new bus toward Boston, C.O.D. Clay's old bus remains by roadside.

Clay (waving): Goodbye, little red bus. I am too good for a bus like you, anyway.

ON THE ROAD WITH CASSIUS CLAY:

SO HARD TO BE RIGHTEOUS

APRIL 4, 1965

CHICOPEE FALLS, MASSACHUSETTS—Pulling out of Fayetteville, North Carolina, in a Trailways, Cassius Clay looked mournfully back at his abandoned private bus.

"My poor little red bus," Clay said softly. "You was the most famousest bus ever in the history of the world. Leastwise you the onliest one ever to come on a trip like this."

His melancholia soon gave way. "One thing about it," Clay said. "I'm glad we wasn't on no plane. A bus catches on fire, you don't fall no 30,000 feet."

The cruiser was heading into Rocky Mount, North Carolina. "You think," Clay asked no one in particular, "we far enough up the road for a nigger to eat?"

He told the driver to stop. He had just been seated in a roadside restaurant when an old man hobbled over.

"You really the champ?" the old man asked.

"Sure am," Clay said. "The Greatest. You'll see when I whup Sonny Liston again."

The old man picked his teeth contemplatively. "Greater than Joe Louis?"

"Sure am," Clay said.

"Greater than Sugar Ray Robinson?"

"Sure am."

"Greater than Cassius Clay?" the old man asked.

"Listen, mister," Clay snapped, torn between hurt and amusement, "I *am* Cassius Clay."

There was no problem with the vittles, as there had been in Yulee, Florida. The iced tea wasn't the greatest, but it is a sad fact for the champion as well as everyone else that the farther north you get, the worse the iced tea. Everyone's senses were dulled by then, anyway. We had been on the move for 40 hours without a shave or a change of socks.

At Fredericksburg, Virginia, I asked Clay if he would stop the bus so I could call my office. He nodded. By the time I returned to the bus, six pretty young things were at the champion's side. One wanted a souvenir. "I'd give you my shirt," Clay said, "but I can't get at a fresh one."

"That's all right!" photographer Howard Bingham hollered out of a bus window. "Take mine, sweet thing!"

"Hush, Bingham," Clay warned. "These little foxes want to talk to the champ."

Instead, he shooed away the girls. "Ooh," he moaned, re-boarding, "sometimes it's so hard to be righteous."

After 50 hours on the road, the bus pulled into the Chicopee Falls motel where Clay was supposed to train for Liston. This was Mecca, and the Great Prophet Muhammad Ali Formerly Cassius Clay had delivered us at last. All we needed were scissors to cut ourselves out of our clothes, and lye soap.

The room clerk must have thought we were advance men for a convention of chimney sweeps.

"I'm Cassius Clay," the champion told the clerk. "Give me the $60-a-day suite."

"But somebody is in there right now," the clerk said.

"Well, get him out," Clay said. "The Greatest is here."

Rooms were duly secured. One of the bus drivers went into the dining room and wolfed down an enormous meal without ever removing his cap. It seemed a terribly uncouth ending to such a couth trip.

Pro Football

SHULA THE CONSTANT

SEPTEMBER 4, 1980

This was just another day in another airport until football's most recognizable face appeared in the Newark terminal. Don Shula was heading back to Miami from a charity dinner. Instantly, humanity closed in on him like fans at an old-time movie premiere.

Shula offered each a separate and somehow different salutation. Only politicians *learn* to talk that way. It had to be born in Donald Francis Shula, who is the furthest thing from a politician.

A youth in his late teens rushed up and blurted, "You're the greatest coach ever!" Either the youth had been seriously fasting or in training for ballet. His waist, 24 inches tops, would make a middle-ager weep.

The last boarding call came. Shula said a gracious goodby to No-Belly. Then, casually, the kid said, "By the way, coach, you're taking on a little weight."

Shula's smile vanished. Face darkened. I thought he would spring. "*Me?*" he bellowed. "It's *you* that's taking on weight!"

The words were barely out when Shula discerned their absurdity. Hilarity burst, quicksilver, the mark of a man who has learned one of mankind's dearest lessons: how to laugh at yourself.

"Wasn't that a stupid answer?" Shula said, striding the passageway to his jet. "Did you see the *waist* on that kid?"

If Shula's answer typified his impetuousness, his self-chastisement also told how he has changed. Ten years ago, when he arrived from seven winning seasons in Baltimore, he might have boiled all the way to his seat.

He remains a transfixing mix—brilliant, stubborn, devout, profane, demanding, compassionate, sensitive, proud, bullying, humble, self-deriding.

"But now," says All-Pro safety Tim Foley, who has spent the decade with him, "he sees the gray between the black and white."

At 50, when so many men swamp emotions for symptoms, Shula's only obvious physical concessions are the white chest-hair showing beneath his neck and the half-glasses he uses to read small type.

His legs and head and shoulders seem pure gristle. He still resembles a stone sphere. In bestowing so many other talents, The Almighty also built a low center of gravity into Shula's 210 pounds. But neither the years nor the growing gift of laughter have diminished his drive. He continues to convey the impression of a person who never will feel he has completely caught up with what must be done.

To Foley, the most remarkable aspect of Shula is that of a certified giant of his trade altering his methods to cope with changing society.

"The nature of the pro athlete has changed tremendously in the last 10 years," Foley says. He confirms pro sports as a classic example of a cynical law of experimental psychology that says that any well-trained mammal, in a controlled environment, will do as he damn pleases. "That means, in Shula's case, a *genius* having to switch the approach that made him that in the first place."

Foley cites summer '71, when he was still struggling as a second-year cornerback.

"My wife was out of town during training camp and I had to look after our puppy, Kelly. I'd keep Kelly in my dorm room at night. Then, when we were in meetings or practice, I'd put him in a big pen behind the coaching offices.

"One day Kelly escaped and came yapping right between the two lines. Shula berserked. 'What the *bleep* is this?' I was terrified. I looked up at the sky as though I didn't even know Kelly. Then Shula roared, 'Whose *bleeping* dog *is* that?' And Kelly ran right to my feet and looked up at me, with his tongue out. I thought Shula would go out of his mind."

Shula still berates Foley for bringing Kelly to camp. "But now he laughs afterward," Foley says.

Shula can afford to laugh from his aerie.

Who but one of his charisma could be voted NFL Coach of the Decade, even considering his three early Super Bowls and the unique Perfect Season of 1972, while Pittsburgh's Chuck Noll has wiped out four Super Bowls since Shula last won a postseason game in the '73 season?

The explanation is grade-school basic. Noll lives inside himself. He appears to wish that no one know he coaches the Steelers, and he has partly succeeded in that. Before the Dolphins keelhauled the Steelers, 34–14, in last year's playoffs, a long-time Steeler-watcher wrote, "It will be football's best team against football's best coach."

Nobody had to fill in names.

All of Shula goes so directly outward that he is more eagerly coveted as a coach and sought by commercial sponsors than any coach since Knute Rockne, who died in an airplane crash a half-century ago. Shula's face is more familiar than Rockne's because of TV. Several commercials do not even trouble to identify him by name.

Shula's Dolphin decade has convinced all but a grudging few that Shula and sunshine present this strand's two consistently most positive images to the world. If Shula declared tomorrow as Christmas, most South Floridians would have their stockings up by sunlight.

Barry Halpern, a Miami lawyer of standing, addresses himself to this: "Dade County has had little to be proud of the last few years. We have had rioting, racial imbalance, an influx of Cubans, Haitians and other minorities that brought dissatisfaction in this community. When one thinks of Miami now, one does not always think of it with pride. But always above everything, we take pride in the Dolphins and especially in Shula, the greatest ever to coach."

It would be idiotic to say that no other person could successfully coach the Dolphins. No one is indispensable, right? But when you employ a genius, it would be, at the very least, difficult to find a suitable replacement.

"From hero to zero is about the average hero's fate," Miami's Eddie Rickenbacker said before he died in '73, barely six months after Shula had brainstormed the Perfect Season. Shula has not descended to anything close to average, although equivalently he has bailed more lifeboats than Rickenbacker.

He remains unshakably positive through the most negative times. This, too, bears upon his anointment as Coach of the Decade.

One picture stands starkly against the celebratory scenes dotting Shula's office walls. It shows snow beating upon him in Cleveland during the '76 game the Dolphins lost, 17–13, when Bob Griese, that most cerebral of quarterbacks, forgot what down it was.

"You're such a positive man," a visitor says. "That picture seems so negative."

"It's not," Shula says. "It reminds me not to get in another situation where the same could happen.

He remembers. Oh, how he remembers. His memory is all but photographic. "Do you always wear the same shirt two straight days?" he needles a newsman on the edge of the practice field.

Time has taken the sharp edge off his vanity but failed to erase it. "What the hell do you mean my hair isn't combed? What do you think *you* are? A portrait?"

He has earned some egocentricities. Shula, Noll, Dallas' Tom Landry and Minnesota's Bud Grant remain the only continuous NFL head-coaching forces in what a not-so-long-ago Chrysler Corporation president, Eugene Cafiero, called "a very radical world of discontinuities."

Meanwhile, Shula chastens players less and pokes more fun at himself. Though he unabashedly adores his parents, who came here from Hungary, he enjoys painting himself as a "dumb hunky." It is not unique for him to answer a bewildered look after one of his technical explanations with, "That's the best I can do for a Hungarian."

The prototype kidding-on-the-square Shula surfaced in a confrontation with a bricklayer after losing a mid-'70s game to the Jets in Shea Stadium. The noise of the laborer's hammer obliterated Shula's attempt to hold a press conference. Shula looked over with eyebrows arched. The message was clear: be quiet.

"Don't look at me," the man said, "I ain't stopping. I'm working!"

"It's all right," Shula said. He politely moved some 50 yards down the corridor. "With a little different luck," he said, "I could be doing that myself right now."

Only when directly asked does he mention that he majored in sociology, got a teaching minor in mathematics, and a Masters degree in physical education at John Carroll University.

He prefers recounting pratfalls. One was kite-skiing at Acapulco "when I got up there and all of a sudden asked myself if I was out of my mind." In college, he challenged a boxer who had fought Michigan State's Chuck Davey, later a pro star, "and by the end of the second round, I couldn't even get my hands up."

This is the funny side of Shula. The professional, passionate side is Ted Hendricks, his old Colt linebacker now with the Raiders, calling him "the most honest man in the U.S."

I have known pro coaches who would steal a hot stove. Never, even in our least cordial days, have I found reason to so much as suspect Shula of any deliberate breach of ethics, let alone rules.

Of course, there are no perfect coaches, including Shula. I think, sometimes, he has been overly inflexible in leaving regulars in games already secure, as when Griese was injured with some six minutes remaining with a 20–3 lead over the Patriots in '78. Largely because Griese was hurt in that freak accident, the Dolphins lost their playoff game to the Oilers, 17–9.

"I suppose I should have known Griese was going to fumble and get a freak injury in a pileup," Shula said sarcastically.

No, but Griese couldn't have been injured if he hadn't still been in the game.

Shula just may be pro history's most effective communicator, despite dismissed tight end Loaird McCreary's plaint in '79: "As a communicator on a scale of 1 to 10, I would rate Shula below zero." The dear hearts remaining in camp greeted Shula the next morning with a sign depicting a scale from 1 to 10. Far below the bottom line was scrawled "Shula."

You may ask, then, why, if Shula is such a hot ticket, have the Dolphins found all their mountains turn to glass near the top for the last seven years?

Part of the answer is in overall managerial structure, inordinately inferior to those of at least the Steelers and Cowboys. Shula has achieved greatness with many players who never were great. He usually finishes so high that the Dolphins are reduced to run-of-the-mill draft picks, and he has made mistakes in talent evaluation. He has been *good* with many barely better-than-average players.

At his worst, Shula qualifies as excellent. At best, unsurpassable.

A George Bernard Shaw character in the play *Misalliance* said something that applies here: "The strength of a chain is no greater than its weakest link; but the greatness of a poet is the greatness of his greatest moment. Shakespeare used to get drunk. Frederick the Great ran away from a battle. But it was what they could rise to, not what they could sink to, that made them great."

FLIP SIDE FOR ZONK

FEBRUARY 22, 1987

I don't know whether this is too personal to be public, or too public to be personal. I wouldn't even bring it up if Larry Csonka hadn't first. I bring it up now only to show that there is another side to the outcry, justified though it usually is, over the sums some sports superstars earn both while and after they are playing.

Not that there's any great moral to this story. There isn't. It's just a chunk of sadness that might make some people wonder about how much money really means.

Csonka left the Dolphins for money; no two ways about that. He also left the World Football League with close to $1 million cash. He picked up some more back in the NFL, and literally caught financial lightning in a bottle when he joined the light-beer TV celebrity force.

That's the money side. The other side belongs to Pam, Larry's wife of 21 years. Pam probably will be in the audience when Zonk and old teammate Jim Langer go into the Pro Football Hall of Fame in Canton, Ohio, this summer. But she probably won't be Mrs. Larry Csonka by then.

"I hate it being this way," Zonk said. "The only thing is, it's better than trying to be something you're not. We're getting a divorce. We're getting it because I'm what Pam always called a rolling-stone guy, and she's a cottage girl. She needs a 9-to-5 guy who'll be at home, and I'm gone all the time."

When Zonk said it, he had been on the road 21 of 29 days. He makes no excuses. He earns a great deal of money at it, but it isn't something he has to do to survive economically. He likes it out there.

"Being at these conventions and all is the closest thing I've had to team unity since I quit playing after 1979," he said.

"That's my kind of world. I can't expect it to be Pam's, too, much as I hate what's happening."

"I want to be everywhere with everybody. That makes it pretty tough being Mrs. Larry Csonka, and Pam's been that, or close to it, since she was 14 or 15 years old. When the kids were growing up, I'd rush home, more or less. Now, though, they're up and out, and I'm not there, either."

Nobody except the people inside a marriage ever knows exactly what it is. But Zonk knows what he's not, and that's a guy who can stay home.

Although it had nothing to do with him making the Hall, part of the reason he's in so much demand for commercials and appearances is that he talks as well as he ran. Uncustomary as it is to requote people in this space, something he said the day he was named to the Hall still sounds so soulful it bears repeating:

"I have a little cabin on my farm in Stow, Ohio. We drill gas wells out there in the winter, and it's cold in that cabin. The first thing I do when I get out of bed and feel the jolt in my knees is think of Roy Winston. On the second step, my calcified Adam's apple starts bobbing and I think of Carl Eller. A few more steps in the dark and it's Willie Lanier. By the time I get to the bathroom, I'm flashing back to Dick Butkus and Ray Nitschke. And when the light finally comes on, I just hope that somewhere in the darkness they're thinking of me, too."

Doubly unfortunately, the wife also has to live with the pain. One way or another, Pam absorbed every shot Larry ever took.

"She's the best," Zonk said. "We lived in 17 different places in 21 years. Pam sacrificed so much. We finally just decided there's no point in trying to be Mr. and Mrs. when I'd be gone for 28 days in a row. She's the best person I've ever known, and that's no life for her."

After that, there isn't much for Zonk to say, except that he hopes Pam will be there when he goes into the Hall. I hope so, too. I always thought she did more than anybody to help put him there.

SUPER SCROOGE I

JANUARY 24, 1967

SUPER CITY—formerly Los Angeles—Even the officials are grooving on the first Super Bowl. They'll come on in saucily radical outfits, presumably styled by Super-designer Don Loper. I guess they'll call them Superficials.

It's getting to be a sort of parlor game. Even before the Super Bowl, two networks have been Superloudly proclaiming "Super Sunday" in their quest for Super ratings.

Seems apt enough in this Super-tawdry territory of Super folksinger Bob Dylan, Super pop artist Andy Warhol, Super beatniks and Super smog. Not to mention Super hoopla. No less than nine press agents are scurrying around representing both the National and American leagues. They are not Superfluous. As of Friday there were 719 writers, photographers and radio-TV men here.

Then there is Super Vince, Super-surname Lombardi. He is the Super boss of the Packers. Super Vince is nothing loath to compare himself with Super attackers of the past. Asked if he might follow his frequent pattern of directing his attack against the opponent's strong point, he retorted: "Well, if I do, it won't be original with me. Napoleon did it, and so did General MacArthur."

As an afterthought, he tossed in Red Blaik, his old head coach at Army. I was a little surprised he didn't mention Nietzsche, who started the Superman theory in Germany more than a hundred seasons ago.

This much is Super-sure. The Chiefs had better not expect Super mercy from Super Vince. It requires no Super memory to recall last summer when the College All-Stars were preparing to meet the Packers in Chicago. Johnny Sauer, Lombardi's old coaching mate at Army, was handling the All-Stars. Strictly as a humane gesture, Sauer made it clear he would not damage any of the collegians' pro chances by keeping them around if they were hurt.

Eventually Gail Gillingham, the Super guard from Minnesota, got himself racked up. Sauer accordingly dispatched him on the Packer camp and forgot about him.

Super Vince didn't forget. He used Gillingham as part of the turbine that chewed up the All-Stars.

Super Vince? How about Super Scrooge?

This Super thing is catching. Fred Williamson, Kansas City's caveman cornerback, keeps insisting he is going to drop the "Superhammer"—the kind of jet-propelled elbow that turned Dolphin Howard Twilley's cheekbone into pulp—on some Packer receivers. To that, Packer end Carroll Dale said, "It just might give us some extra incentive for downfield blocking on Williamson."

Appraised of Dale's solemn comment, Williamson chuckled. "Well, now," he said, "That's just Super. Already I've got them worried about the Superhammer."

They're even planning a Superhalftime show in the Coliseum, with Super hornblower Al Hirt as Super attraction.

Lamar Hunt, the Chiefs' owner, blushingly confesses to coming up with the first reference to this world championship game as the Super Bowl. Not coincidentally, Hunt is the Super-rich gentleman of the executive set of this whole wild scene. Lamar has holes in his shoes but none in a bank account estimated at a modest $150 million. If he wins, he may buy Los Angeles. If he loses, he may sell Texas. And he isn't making any advance plans. Hunt is Superstitious.

Hunt never could have imagined that his brainchild could make such lousy poets out of such great writers out here. One anonymous wit, however, is drawing laughs out of Packer halfback Elijah Pitts' exotic academic origin, which is little Philander Smith College in Arkansas. This unSuper rhyme was posted on the pressroom bulletin board:

"There's one idea that gives me fits,
"It bothers me a lot.
"Philander Smith, Elijah Pitts,
"Which one went to what?"

THE LONGEST GAME, AND SILENCE

DECEMBER 26, 1971

KANSAS CITY—Suddenly it was silent.

Thunk! went the sound of 5-foot-6-inch Garo Yepremian's left foot meeting football.

Swish! went the ball, bobbing 37 yards through the Christmas night America was beginning to think would never end.

Holiday feasts congealed. Wives, mothers, grandmothers and chefs everywhere wrung their hands. Dolphin fans back home all but crawled into their TV sets.

Then, in a transfixing grain of a second, the placekick tumbled through the uprights and silence came over the crowd of 45,822.

Yepremian had knocked them speechless. The Longest Game was over. The Dolphins had beaten the Chiefs, 27–24, in double overtime—82 minutes and 40 seconds that truly became Christmas for the fledgling 6-year-old franchise.

Not very sudden death for Kansas City. At the end it was not a matter of who could run the fastest or block the hardest or tackle more tellingly. It was who could still breathe.

The shortest man in pro football turned out the biggest hero. Toulouse-Lautrec would have been proud. So was Yepremian, the lovable pixie who had been lower than ever the last two days after being snubbed for the Pro Bowl in favor of Kansas City's Jan Stenerud.

Yepremian nicked that field goal through like a 9-iron, and now the Dolphins move on into the second round of the playoffs with a chance to become the youngest expansion team to make a Super Bowl.

The "nick" became an explosion, a shattering blast ending in that zombie-like pall in the stands.

It was almost as though someone had been murdered. Some Christmas for K. C. Worse yet, the Chiefs could have won it without even going into overtime if Jan Stenerud had hit a "gimme" 31-yard attempt just seconds before the end of regulation.

Yepremian didn't miss.

"I knew I'd make it," the bubbly multilinguist from Cyprus said precisely. "The 14-yarder that tied the score in the second quarter was no problem. And I felt I barely missed the 52-yard try in the fifth period."

He nodded and looked up at the mob of interviewers. Garo looks up at toadstools.

"After coming so close then," he said, "I was positive I could not fail on anything less than 50 yards. Then Bob Griese positioned the ball in the middle of the field for me. Mike Kolen made a perfect snap. Karl Noonan held the ball just right. I'd been dying for the chance to get everything over with. I never had a doubt."

Stenerud kicked only one of four. "I know how he feels," Yepremian said. "I missed three in our 10–10 tie with Denver. But I can't say I'm sorry Jan missed so many."

Then, contriving an air of solemnity, Yepremian added, "I only hope I can make the Pro Bowl next year when I have improved in my profession."

A laugher.

We do not hesitate to convey our opinions on forgettable games, so we should be specific on this one. Until the Dolphins win a Super Bowl, this will be their finest moment.

It was joy unconfined in the Dolphin dressing quarters, as ecstatic in the stadium's belly as it was gloomy upstairs among the thousands filing out glassy-eyed.

For the Dolphins, though, a laugher.

"That's what I did," said Griese. "I busted out laughing. I looked over and saw Karl Noonan jumping up and down and waving his arms in the air after he had held the ball for Garo, and I busted out laughing. I couldn't help it. I'm still laughing."

It was a Griese decision that sprang Larry Csonka on a 29-yard run and set up Yepremian's kick.

"I was trying to think of plays we liked but hadn't used yet,"

Griese said. "This one involved Csonka coming back against the flow. He got some great blocking."

Griese laughed again. Understand, he isn't that much of a laugher. But now he couldn't hold it in. He was laughing uproariously, tension rolling out uncontrollably.

"All you have to do is turn Zonk loose," Griese said, "and he'll get what you need."

And then set up the ball for Yepremian, and turn out the lights. And the voices. Sometimes it just takes an awfully long time.

UNSUPER BOWL VI

JANUARY 17, 1972

NEW ORLEANS—Don Shula looked as though he had been hit with a sharp ax. But his head was up when he said, "What's so sad is for a bunch of ballplayers to come this far . . . so many sacrifices, so much sweat, so many great games, and then . . ." Shula's voice faded almost imperceptibly, ". . . to have it end like this . . . "

For the second time in four years, Shula had lost a Super Bowl. First with Baltimore to the New York Jets, 16–7, in 1969. Then Sunday with the Dolphins, by a skull-shattering 24–3, to Dallas.

"That other Super Bowl doesn't have anything to do with this one," Shula said. "In '69 we were favored and had opportunities to score and didn't. Today we never even challenged them."

How terribly, dismally accurate.

The Dolphins' effort was nothing to be ashamed of. They did the best they could against faster, smarter, stronger talent.

On the other hand, it was nothing to write home about. Miami didn't even give Dallas a game.

The slash that let the last ounce of blood out of the Dolphins was Chuck Howley's interception of a Bob Griese pass early in the fourth quarter. The Cowboys finalized the score four plays later.

"But that wasn't the turning point," Shula said. "The series that hurt the most was right after half. We went out behind only 10–3. We thought we could come back and establish the offense that hadn't worked the first two quarters. We talked about keeping our men in the pursuit lanes defensively instead of getting them cut off on the Cowboys' cutback plays. But when they took the kickoff and went 71 yards, that did it."

All along Shula had been more afraid of Dallas' running than its passing. He was right, to his regret.

Dallas' offensive line overpowered the Dolphin defense in creating gaping holes for Duane Thomas, Walt Garrison and Calvin Hill. I am not sure I would not have given the Most Valuable Player award to either Thomas or Garrison rather than Roger Staubach, because they kept the Dolphins in a fine bafflement for Staubach's touchdown shots.

The Cowboy defensive line shut down Jim Kiick and Larry Csonka, who picked the world's worst time for his first fumble of the season, and Mercury Morris sat sullenly on the bench. The Dolphins live by the running game, and Sunday it was dead.

The Cowboys finally played the way Coach Tom Landry's computer says they should always play—and so seldom have when the dice were rolling for the bundle.

Either a lot of us overrated the Dolphins or underrated the Cowboys. Or both. One thing to remember in any case is that these losers were born as a franchise only six years ago. Nobody reached an NFL championship game that fast since the earliest days of the league.

"We can't just drop our heads and cry," Shula said. "The Cowboys were just about perfect. We have to walk away feeling as though we've gained something."

That something was hard to define after this trampling.

Griese's quarterbacking was uninspired, and made to look worse by a first-quarter 29-yard loss on the kind of scramble he often has turned into a game-buster. Bob Lilly, Dallas' all-planet tackle, flung Griese backward like a sack of salt.

"But how can a quarterback get going when he doesn't get the ball any more than we did in the first half (eight minutes to the Cowboys' 22)?" Shula asked.

A latecomer interrupted Shula's lachrymose interview. "What did you think of Lilly?" the man chirped cheerfully.

Shula just stared at him.

'THAT FUNNY LITTLE TEAM'

JANUARY 21, 1973

Mr. Jim Murray
Los Angeles Times
Big City, U.S.A.

Dear Jim:

Just a few lines on the back of corn-shuck to let you know the rubes got back OK from the society ball. You'll be glad to hear they didn't go busted in the big town, you were so worried about 'em. Their dancing partners in Super Ball VII in L.A. treated 'em real nice. Gave 'em $15,000 apiece, they liked 'em so much.

Now, Jim, we're pals, and that's why I'm writing from back here on the farm. To fill you in on what you called that "funny little team from the funny little conference . . . the rube who comes out of the audience to wrestle the bear . . ."

'Course not all the rubes are home yet. Some of 'em had to jump off the hay-wagon in Dallas to play in the Pro Bowl today. The pro coaches thought the Dolphins were so funny they invited more Dolphins than any other team's players to compete in the Pro Bowl. Nine of 'em. You know. Just for laughs.

What did you say was the name of those unbeatable monsters from the nation's capital? Redskins? No wonder Indians all over the country are complaining that those sports nicknames are degrading.

You wondered what a Kiick is. I was still curious about that after the 14–7 score that should have been 31–0.

I asked Big Chief George Allen and he mumbled something like, "I still don't know what a Kiick is . . . It went over the goal so fast I couldn't identify the species."

Another Redskin told me a Kiick must be a doll: You wind it up and it scores four touchdowns in three playoffs.

77

"What's a Csonka? A hammer?" Gee, Jim, you ask good questions.

Check with Diron Talbert or Jack Pardee or some of those other slickers in the checkered vests. They will agree Csonka is a hammer—a jack-hammer, not a tack-hammer.

By the way, we heard here that Allen got tired of waiting for President Nixon to call him, so Allen called the President instead. Collect. That funny little team from the funny little conference barely left Allen a change of clothes, let alone change for the phone.

Some of the Dolphin defensive men were curious about your asking, "What do those front four do during the week—make pizza in a window?"

The only pizza 75 million folks watching on television saw was slices of Bill Kilmer and Larry Brown being chewed up by Manny Fernandez, Bill Stanfill, Bob Heinz and Vern Den Herder.

And you had to ask: "You're going to give them Jake Scott, Larry Seiple and that funny little guy from Cyprus?"

Yeah, they gave 'em Scott, and Kilmer was so grateful he gave Scott back two passes. (Look, Jim, just because Kilmer played at UCLA in the big city doesn't give him automatic dibs on that rube from Indiana, Bob Griese.)

They gave 'em Seiple, too, and Seiple gave 'em back seven punts averaging 43 yards.

As for the funny little guy from Cyprus, what are you complaining about? That play of Garo Yepremian's will be remembered longer than any in Super Bowl history. He even set a record: Right-handed passes by left-footed Armenians from Cyprus—one.

The rubes from Miami sort of enjoyed it, distractions, interviews, game and all. Ask 'em back to the next ball, will you Jim? I think they're beginning to get the rhythm. Next time just find 'em an opponent who can keep up with the music.

Sincerely,
Your little pal from that little conference,

Eddie

GRANT'S TOMB? SHULA'S SHRINE?

JANUARY 14, 1974

HOUSTON—Call it Grant's Tomb. Re-title it Shula's Shrine. Or Csonka's Causeway.

Or let 'em keep the name Rice Stadium. No matter. Henceforth this fog-bound battleground will be known as the one where the Dolphins settled themselves by any reasonable measure as football's all-time kings.

Forget Super Bowl VIII's final score of Miami 24, Minnesota 7. It was no more a reflection of Dolphin superiority than that 14–7 victory over Washington in Super Bowl VII indicated the one-sidedness there.

Do remember that both Washington then and Minnesota now were and are excellent football clubs. And that the Dolphins did much more than win by 17 this soggy Sunday.

This was murder. It made the St. Valentine's Day Massacre look like a draw. The world finally learned why Don Shula had been grinning all week. He knew what he had. Now everybody knows what he's got, which is something nobody had before, the Kohinoor Diamond of football teams. A 32–2 record over two seasons, back-to-back Super Bowl champs.

The Dolphins buried once and for all the myth that other teams have better material. That Miami wins on unity rather than speed or muscle.

Jim Langer and Bob Kuechenberg and Larry Little and Wayne Moore and Norm Evans picked up Bud Grant's fabled Front Four from the Northland and shook them like a gang of King Kongs dangling a cluster of Fay Wrays from the Empire State Building.

Scorning audible check-offs at the line of scrimmage and

79

throwing a Super Bowl-low seven passes, Bob Griese aimed Larry Csonka through the debris and Csonka flung it aside like confetti in his Super Bowl record (145 yards) running show.

Between Shula winning his second Super Bowl in four starts and Csonka truck-trailering up and down the Astroturf, the Hungarian press missed a great bet. Newsmen were here from such distant spots as Egypt and Hong Kong and Norway and Romania and even the Ivory Coast. Too bad: the Hungarian forebears of Shula and Csonka will have to read of The Great Goring in English.

You also have to hang some jewels on the defense when it's 24–7 on the scoreboard and even more so in the punching pits.

The Dolphins' speciously named No-Name defense pounded Viking runners into such terror that they did not get a first down rushing for a stultifying 44 minutes and 17 seconds.

Bill Stanfill and Vern Den Herder came up hard on the inside. Manny Fernandez blocked the middle. Where else could a Viking runner go, except nowhere or crazy?

The defense forced Fran Tarkenton to waste time throwing short because he couldn't throw long when it meant anything. They just blanketed him with impossibility. Tarkenton was down 24–0, where he could not hope to win by running, and with no chance to do anything but make it worse by throwing deep into the Dolphins' spider web.

Alas! Poor Grant. He is a gracious coach who is not without wit. He had the perfect answer when asked what he would do differently if he had to do it all over again. "Not show up," he said.

He could not possibly have known he would find himself slapped down so ignominiously by textbook football.

Shula wrote it. The Dolphins played it. Between them, they posted the highest mark in National Football League history.

STABLER'S SHOT PUT

DECEMBER 22, 1974

OAKLAND—It wasn't so much the score as the way it got scored. This was the first pro football playoff decided by a shot put. That's how Raider Ken Stabler delivered the touchdown ball to Clarence Davis that dynamited the Dolphins from dynasty.

Camelot disappeared on the clumsiest, and cruelest, of clutch plays.

The team with the mightiest succession of achievements in pro football history—three straight Super Bowls and the last two winners—went down, 28–26.

"Two *bleeping* minutes and 68 yards to go," Benny Malone said, slumped abjectly at his locker. He and everyone else thought Miami was home-free after Malone's 23-yard run put the Dolphins ahead, 26–21.

Then came Stabler, timing himself and his passes as precisely as if arm and mind were wired to a chronometer, pick-pick-picking downfield.

Thirty seconds left on the clock in the gloaming of Oakland Coliseum and Vern Den Herder had Stabler by the ankles near the 10-yard line. Stabler was falling to the ground. Reflexively, almost convulsively, he pushed—really shot-putted—the ball toward Davis in the end zone.

"It looked like a wounded duck going through the air," Den Herder said.

Mike Kolen, Larry Ball and Charlie Babb all were around Davis. No receiver was ever better-covered. "Some of us tipped it," Kolen said. "But somehow Davis just took the ball."

Some Dolphins still would not believe that they were out of one of the most remarkable of all games. Manny Fernandez, savage pride surfacing, said: "I never thought we were dead until Phil Villapiano intercepted Bob Griese with 13 seconds left."

Don Shula knew. When incredible passes mingle with circus catches, it begins to come home to you that this is not your day. Shula was as close to tears as he ever will be as a coach when he said it just wasn't meant to be.

Shula's voice quivered although his chin never dropped.

"Stabler did it when he had to," Shula said. "That 72-yard TD play, Stabler to Cliff Branch, was a fluke, with Branch on the ground and getting up and running, but Stabler's last drive was really something."

The plane ride home would seem six continents long. "The best two teams in football were on that field," Larry Little said. "The game showed it." He shook his great head. "I'm having an awful time convincing myself that I won't be going back to practice Monday."

Tim Foley sat completely squeezed inside his wide locker. Only his back was visible, his head between his knees. If he was crying, he wanted to avoid an exhibition, and no one saw it.

Malone, after his brief burst of anguish, went into his shell. He is a child of heartbreak, a onetime child migrant worker who lived in a tin shack. But now he could not even remember such pain of spirit.

"Losing has never hurt like this before," Malone said haltingly. "Ah, please, don't ask me to talk about it. Talking only makes it . . . "

His voice trailed off. The shot put lingered on. Adios, Camelot.

OVERCHARGED IN OVERTIME

JANUARY 3, 1982

Like Lazarus rising and then slipping on a banana peel, the Dolphins ashenly watched their Super Bowl dream die on a simple end-over-end kick in the most spectacular of pro football games.

Irony of ironies.

A man who lay at the point of death two years ago beat the Dolphins, 41–38, in playoff overtime for the San Diego Chargers.

His finishing 29-yard field goal came 73 minutes and 51 seconds and 1,030 offensive yards into a dizzying, dazzling kaleidoscope of Don Strock's (397 yards passing) and Dan Fouts' (433 yards) virtuosity, and everybody else's sheer courage.

The goal by Rolf Benirschke, who almost died of an intestinal disease two years ago, seemed too grotesquely simple to make sense.

But neither did anything else after the Dolphins fell 24 points behind after they had run only six plays for minus six yards.

The Dolphins came into this critical match in almost perfect condition. Down 0–24, they must have felt like old light-heavyweight champion Willie Pastrano after taking a vicious punch to the groin.

"Ain't no way you can train for that," said Pastrano.

Then, in an unceasing roll of points covering four hours and five minutes, the Dolphins turned the all-time National Football League topper into the doggedest show of determination as well.

"They're going to talk about this one for a long time," Dolphin receiver Jimmy Cefalo murmured through numbed lips. "Sometimes it seemed we were destined to win, and other times it seemed we were destined to lose."

He paused, and dropped the final, heaviest thought. "I guess we were destined to lose."

Destiny took its dramatic time deciding.

Strock sprang off the bench in the second quarter to relieve starter David Woodley and strong-arm his team back to a 24–17 halftime deficit on a 40-yard flea-flicker play involving Duriel Harris and Tony Nathan. He molded a 24–24 tie on a 15-yard bullet to Joe Rose, and finally took seeming command at 38–31 before the Chargers closed to 38–38 in regulation.

And then Uwe von Schamann's 43-yard field goal attempt, which would have won it with four seconds left in regulation, was blocked.

"My head's high," said stunned guard Ed Newman. "I'm proud of this club."

He should be.

The Orange Bowl's shrieking crowd was, too. That assemblage was counted at 73,735. In years to come, it will approach millions, for no one will admit he was not there for the only game to eclipse, for sheer watchability, the Dolphins' double-overtime, 82-minute-40-second, 27–24 playoff triumph in Kansas City on 1971 Christmas Day.

Nine Dolphin records fell in Saturday's merciless air onslaught. As amazingly, the Dolphins rushed for only 78 yards, nearly five times less than their overhead total.

Maybe that lost it.

Maybe von Schamann's second blocked kick—tipped by Leroy Jones from 34 yards out with 11:27 gone in overtime—helped lose it.

Maybe not.

The final answer may go back to the final few words of the pregame invocation. The Dolphins trotted out a big gun, Archbishop Edward A. McCarthy, for that.

"May the best team win," the archbishop closed, "and you know which one that is."

Nobody thought he meant the Chargers.

RIGGINOMICS

FEBRUARY 2, 1983

LOS ANGELES—No use keeping on carrying on out here in Hog Heaven that the Dolphins are really better than the Redskins.

They weren't on the day they had to be.

Why they weren't is what's on the minds of Miamians, as well as the violently pro-Redskin crowd that rooted for the offensive-line Hogs who rooted the Dolphins into the nickel seats on some plays.

First, too many people underrated the Redskins. They're the best. Not the best ever, or any such Hogwash. Just the best on the 17th Super Bowl Sunday, 27–17, which is nine more points that it takes.

The Redskins get the Vince Lombardi Trophy, and the Dolphins get motion-sick before even starting the long ride home. Quarterback Joe Theismann and his running backs and receivers jumped around so much, the Dolphin defense didn't know whether it was on foot or halfback most of the second half.

And then, as Miami's bitterest single memory, there is John Riggins.

"I'm not strong on Reaganomics," Rep. Claude Pepper's voice popped onto TV sets out here in Monday's wee hours, "but those Rigginomics really work."

More than anything, Washington's befuddlingly simultaneous array of motion helped Riggins bust the 43-yard touchdown run for a 20–17 lead in the fourth quarter and pile up a record 166 yards rushing.

Riggins was a refrigerator rolling downhill Sunday because of what Coach Joe Gibbs had slicked up for the Dolphins. And Dolphin fullback Andra Franklin couldn't hack it, because the Redskins were ganging up at the line like the Chinese Communist army. The Dolphins tried to spread them out with long passes, some on first down. Quarterback David Woodley stood bravely against frightful pressure but couldn't hack it.

Just a few days earlier, Shula had tried his level best to point up the difficulty of Woodley's job. "When you think of how many times a guy like Dan Fouts of San Diego has taken the ball and dropped back," Shula said, "and compare it with Woodley in his third year, you see what David is up against."

Not to mention Theismann, who was drafted by the Dolphins when Woodley was 12 years old. Failing to complete a single pass in Sunday's second half, poor Woodley still looked about 12.

It wouldn't hurt, either, in future assessments of Woodley, to recall that his hot streak at the end of regular season and beginning of playoffs came against two notoriously weak defenses, Baltimore's and San Diego's, and another team, New England, that isn't bad defensively but certainly can't come close to a Washington.

There is nothing to be gained by piling vindictiveness on top of all Woodley's other troubles today, but the numbers speak for themselves.

WANTED:
One Dolphin Thug

JANUARY 23, 1985

SAN FRANCISCO—Save on postage, friends and neighbors. Here's the answer before you ask. Yes, Don Shula *can* win the big ones.

He had to win 52 big ones while losing only eight (and tying one) to get to the four Super Bowls he has lost. And that doesn't even address his going 30–2 to reach the two Super Bowls he won.

So maybe Bill Walsh outcoached him out here in the 49ers' 38–16 Super Bowl XIX runaway. Nobody's perfect. People have brought up maybe six times they figured Shula was outcoached in the 15 years he has blessed Miami by working there, and I've never agreed with them. This time I might.

Either the Dolphins didn't make the adjustments they should have, or they didn't have the players who could, which supports one theory that Shula takes some teams to Super Bowls that no one else could.

In either case, coaching or picking personnel, the buck stops with Shula, and it's the best place for one to stop, because he was winning Super Bowls seven seasons before Walsh even became a head coach in the pros, and Shula will be winning them years after Walsh has burned out and packed it in.

No one needs to tell Shula what he most needs to do just that.

First, he could use some of the types that 49er nose tackle Manu Tuiasosopo was talking about when he said, "I saw Gary Johnson put his helmet in Dan Marino's chest, and Michael Carter threw a right jab in Marino's face."

This is not to suggest that Shula depart from his fetishism over playing by the rules. He never will, as he should not.

It *is* to suggest that pro defense is getting to be less and less a place for perfect gentlemen. A learned friend put it to me bluntly the night of the Super Mugging. "What the Dolphins need on the D is some thugs," he said.

Since the 1970s incidents with Don Reese and Randy Crowder and some others that might never come into full view, the Dolphins may have placed *too* much emphasis on acquiring players who won't rock the boat. So much, anyway, that the club could be overlooking plain competitiveness.

I consider it advisable to repeat, before yet another mauling by mail, this is in no way a plea for Shula to draft or otherwise acquire a congeries of potential felons. Still, there are times when he overlooks players of massive gifts out of a reluctance to bring aboard anyone who could cause problems in discipline or morale or simply fall into some self-destructive habits.

Mark Clayton threatens now and then to fit into the last category. His mouthiness on the field begs for trouble. He isn't always the most mannerly of men off it, either. But if all the Dolphins had stuck their heads in there against the 49ers the way Clayton did, no one would even be hinting at the question as to whether Shula can win the big ones.

The cry for speed and orneriness in combat is nowhere more audible than in the pass rush and linebacking.

Now is the time to reconsider the incredible toll on some of the finest Dolphin players in the last four years alone. The deaths of Rusty Chambers and Larry Gordon and multiple injuries to A.J. Duhe and Earnie Rhone either took away altogether or reduced to unplayability an entire cadre of good linebackers *and* humans.

Too, the death of David Overstreet tragically removed the fastest back the Dolphins have had in years. They genuinely require a burner as a runner despite the consistent contributions of Tony Nathan and Woody Bennett.

Hardly anyone mentions these grievous losses when bringing up that claptrap about Shula "not winning the big ones."

He would not mention it, either. He shouldn't even have to hear the question. But he will. At least until he brings a thug or three to the defense.

KOOCH

Too many warriors walk away from their wars as only snapshots. Bob Kuechenberg leaves his at 37 as a full-sized portrait, powerful and vigorous and, more than merely adult, genuinely mature.

This is not a man to sit and pore over all the other snapshots of 14 years of Sunday thunder. Kuechenberg has new pictures to develop, in his old business of art dealership, his new business of travel agency and heaven knows what else.

His Dolphin days are over. He just made it official. You would worry about some people moving on after the career he had, with 190 regular-season games and six Pro Bowls and four Super Bowls. You don't worry about Kooch, even with the double vision that forced his retirement.

"Interestingly enough," he said, "I see double when I look out the top of my eyes, which is the way I looked out from a three-point stance."

His double vision should clear up. Things usually do for Kuechenberg. He clears them up, radiating energy out of the flinty face that could have been carved from a Rocky Mountain side, eyebrows jutting like boulders overlooking blue streams.

He came in here as one of football's hopeless itinerants. He had been cast off as flotsam by the Eagles and Falcons, two teams nearly hopeless themselves. He stayed to become, in the words of Fran Tarkenton, "not just the best guard in football, but the best who ever played the game."

He played through Super Bowl VIII with a broken forearm inserted with a steel rod so long that some TV stations were mistaking him for a transmitter.

Tellingly, though, the apotheosis of Robert John Kuechenberg arrived not as a guard but out where he supposedly was too short and too light to play, at tackle.

"It was about the most unselfish thing I've ever seen," Shula said. "I asked him to go to tackle after he made the Pro Bowl six times as a guard. His answer was, 'Coach, if that's what you need . . .'"

So the last link with The Perfect Season disappears. There aren't any more from 17–0.

Kooch played just long enough to get a glorious picture of Danny Marino: "Enough to make me feel disappointed I hadn't played five more years with Marino and five fewer with Zonk.

"We'd stagger down the field with Larry Csonka and Jim Kiick and Bob Griese and come out at the other end bleeding from every hole in our body. With Marino, it's just zap! touchdown! Boy, I envy those guys."

Maybe, too, Kuechenberg was disappointed he wasn't more popular with teammates near the end. He wasn't because he was the one Dolphin not to strike in '82. Some of his old friends resented that, as they resented his mansion on Star Island, and his fondness for French cuffs.

So what? "Just because you're a football player doesn't mean you have to dress like a bum," Kooch said.

He didn't mind telling off fans, either: "They don't see much of the offensive linemen. All they think about are long touchdowns. Cheerleaders. Show and tell. Pomp and ceremony. They don't realize it may be Tuesday before we can walk again. To them, football ends every Sunday evening."

Maybe, finally, he was disappointed that football may never really know how truly great Kuechenberg was because Larry Little at the other guard and Jim Langer at center were staking out Hall of Fame claims that Kooch very well may deserve even more.

"But I played inside the best," he said with satisfaction. "Langer and Dwight Stephenson on my right, maybe the two greatest centers in football history. And two good 79s on my left, Wayne Moore and Jon Giesler."

Kooch gets on with things. Now he is putting away the snapshots. Now the living portrait is moving further on out into the real world.

He will do fine. Just fine.

MIAMARINO
BURNS DALLAS

DECEMBER 18, 1984

The Cowboys swung from the floor and Miamarino hit them right on the button.

Worst of all, with two punches called "Texas 70."

Is anybody left out there with the slightest doubt that Danny Marino's 48-touchdown-pass season is anything less than the best any quarterback ever had?

Argue with the Cowboys. Or 74,139 bug-eyed live watchers in the Orange Bowl. Or millions more who will be telling the TV tale down at the shop today, in phrases once reserved for the Sid Luckmans and John Unitases and Dan Foutses that nobody ever thought anybody would top.

They won't remember the score—28–21 Dolphins.

They can't *forget* Marino, who stepped up into the middle of what looked like a thousand Cowboys and shot two touchdown passes 38 and 63 yards to Mark Clayton within a minute and 40 seconds, with only 51 seconds left in the game.

In Texas, they will see this in nightmares.

Danny White shaking off hysterical hostility reverberating from the stands and delivering a Don McNeal-tipped pass to Tony Hill for 66 yards and a 21–21 tie.

Then, *Miamarino!*

"Both the same play—Texas 70," Marino said, cool as John Wayne after busting more records like kindling—first passer to throw for more than 5,000 yards (5,084), an NFL completion high (362), helping Clayton outrun the old receiving high with 18 touchdowns.

Marino made it sound so simple.

"Both of 'em were square-ins," he said calmly. "The first one [for the 21–14 lead], three guys were coming and Mark and I both read it and he went deep and threw it high."

Marino never got to the second one. That's all right. Everybody saw it. With Marino, you must see to believe.

The Cowboys knew he was good. That's why they paid him the biggest compliment they know. They wrenched around their whole ironclad defensive scheme to try to stop him. And found out he couldn't be stopped. Not this season. Not this Monday night. The Cowboys went with a do-or-die blitz. Marino whipped it black and blue.

He has been devouring blitzes so gluttonously for two seasons now, most teams have grown leery of coming at him full-bore. Again, his passing has been so lethal, it comes down to a question of whether he gets you in a hurry or maybe takes a little longer against deeply deployed coverage.

The Cowboys felt that blitzing was their only chance and that if they were going to die in the Orange Bowl, they would go down swinging.

The blitz takes its name from the original *blitzkrieg*, a tactic that the German army made infamous in its first sweeps through the lowlands in what would become World War II. In German, *blitz* means lightning and *krieg* means *war*. The only thing that will stop it is firepower, and Marino brought that to bear as soon as the Cowboys started sending linebackers and safeties through the cracks.

At the end, all the cracks were Dallas', ruthlessly exposed by the best quarterback any pro season ever saw.

CONVERSATION WITH CLAYTON

MARCH 23, 1985

Mark Clayton was sitting alone, determinedly reading a newspaper, off to the side of a cocktail party preceding the Miami Touchdown Club's annual awards dinner. He was there to accept a trophy and TV set and cash award. He consented to talk beforehand, but he kept right on reading that paper when the two of us sat down at a nearby table.

What's he been doing since the Super Bowl XIX downer at the end of his record 18-touchdown season?

"Nothing."

What's been the reaction to his superb 73-catch season? Fan mail pouring in?

"Yeah, some."

Had he been working out?

"Nope."

Mark Clayton, 24, the Dolphins' newest superstar, was still reading the paper.

Have you ever tried to interview someone who is reading at the same time? I was starting to feel like a kid groveling in front of the campus queen while she puts on her makeup. If anyone else had seen or heard this episode in the middle of a huge hall in Coconut Grove, I would have been embarrassed. If my own son, 15, had heard me virtually begging for the remotest crumb of an answer, I would have been humiliated.

Long before going one-on-one with Clayton for the first time, I had decided that I was not going to plead for interviews with any more athletes whose primary contribution to society has been that they can run a little faster or jump a little higher or throw or catch a ball a little better than the next. And here I was, right back on the brink.

"Mark," I finally said, "do you want to read the paper or do you want to talk?"

"I can do both," he said.

"No you can't," I said.

"OK," Clayton said. He put down the paper. But then his answers grew even shorter, and the pauses before them longer. When Clayton smolders—for whatever reason, and that seems to be a lot of the time—the words come out like hot coals.

Was he trying to renegotiate his contract?

"Yeah."

Did he actually sign a new contract just last year?

"Nope."

This was threatening to become one of history's great dialogues. "Look, Mark," I said, "if talking is as painful for you as it seems, we don't have to go on with it."

He said, "No, it's all right."

Still, the petulance—was it petulance? How do you describe basic unhappiness when you can see only the tip, and not inside it?—would not leave.

Nope, Clayton said, he didn't really hate the University of Louisville, although he never got the recognition there that he deserved.

Yeah, he would help Coach Howard Schnellenberger spread the UL gospel if Schnellenberger asked him. But he wouldn't have done it for the previous coaching regime because they never gave him enough credit, which is one reason he isn't making superstar money now, only around $80,000 a year going up to $96,000 this fall unless he gets a new contract. That's what comes of people not paying enough attention to you, of not being drafted until the eighth round. But now people *are* paying attention and Clayton is still seething.

He said he resented a fan writing to the newspaper saying he wouldn't be doing anything if it were not for Dan Marino.

He also resented stories that he and Marino had had some words during a game.

"Then what did happen down there in the Eagle game?" he was asked.

"I was getting on an official and when I got to the sideline Dan told me not to do it any more," Clayton said. "I told him I would do whatever I wanted to do. Then he used some curse words. I told him if he couldn't talk to me without cursing, just don't talk to me at all."

Clayton went on to say that some movie people had flown

him to California recently. He said he was thinking about doing some acting. "Football isn't my whole life," he said. He added that one of the people he talked to in California was a former vice-president of Paramount Pictures. "I think I could be an actor, yeah I do."

Clayton already has given some extra performances on the field. I mentioned that people were beginning to perceive him as a hothead. He bristled.

"They've never thrown a flag on me," he said. "And I don't start most of that stuff. You don't think I go up to those defensive backs after a play and say, 'Hey, I beat your butt,' do you? I'm not stupid."

Clayton does come across as alert. Even at only five feet nine inches tall, he is about as quick as football sees. He functions on reflex and courage in crowds, on catches that few others could make.

Yet, with all this, he radiates anger. I talked with him 20 minutes and hardly ever felt a single vibration of anything but contentiousness from a young man who could easily become a millionaire from football long before he is 30.

Not one word of thanks for the doors to dollars that the sport is opening for him.

Not one word of anything except annoyance at even being asked about football.

Not one word of thankfulness for his $46,000 Super Bowl slice, even as a loser.

DANNYBALL OVER ELWAY

SEPTEMBER 30, 1985

DENVER—A man in a postman's uniform rushed up to John Elway in the bitter dusk of Mile High stadium after Danny Marino and the Dolphins had shot down the Broncos, 30–26.

"Take your picture with my little boy and girl, John?" the man pleaded.

Elway set down a small black duffle-bag in the bleak under-hang of the stands. He nodded wearily and posed with an arm around each child's shoulder. Elway even smiled, showing the teeth that a Denver newspaper cartoonist had caricatured in a "comparison chart" of the celebrated Elway-Marino quarter-backing shootout—biggest teeth, ability to leap tall buildings in a single bound, and best-looking shoe being endorsed by the principals.

Then Elway picked up his bag and started walking slowly away.

He stopped after two steps. He said one word, very softly.

"Marino."

Elway looked up at the dark sky. No one had to wonder whether he thought the word was a curse or a blessing.

"I'll tell you this," Elway said finally to one last visitor who wanted to shake his hand. "Marino is everything they said he was."

Dannyball is back. Marino won the shootout hands down, 390 yards and three touchdowns to Elway's 250 yards and no TDs.

Marino stood calmly in a towel wrapped around his middle and dismissed the Elway comparisons.

"John's a great QB," he said, "but this was the Dolphins play-ing the Broncos, not Marino playing Elway."

Yes, he said, he did miss Marks—the injured Duper and Clayton.

"But we've got so many guys who can catch, all I have to do is get it there."

That's nice, but not quite true. Dolphins dropped a half-dozen or so catchable balls. "Boy, Danny loves that challenge, doesn't he?" Shula said. "I've never seen a guy enjoy competition as much as he does."

Elway relishes it, too. I think he is fractionally less accurate than Marino, but he's close enough to stand right on the golden edge of greatness, and he moves on ballbearings, and he *is* going to be a great quarterback.

I don't know if you could call this a game for the ages. But it was the most significantly positive thing that has happened to the Dolphins since they wiped out Pittsburgh last season for the questionable privilege of meeting San Francisco in the Super Bowl.

And Dannyball did it.

People tend to forget that the Super Bowling Dolphins actually won only one more game than the Broncos did in the last regular season. In this show, with all but the faintest touch of rust rubbed off Marino from his 37-day training-camp walk-out, it was even easier to forget.

Especially for Elway, who ran and danced and ducked and dodged himself heroically into nothing more at the end than a bummer against unbeatable Dannyball.

College
Football

'RUN RIGHT THE BLEEP AT 'EM!'

December 5, 1984

"Let's play football!" Bernie Kosar rasps in the wind and the rain and the hysteria.

This is one of those happenings you see and hear so intensely you can't believe it will ever be funny.

Kosar's outthrust chin almost impales a Miami Hurricane assistant coach on the Orange Bowl sideline. And then the word crashes in for millions listening and watching on CBS-TV.

"Run right the *bleep* at 'em!" Kosar snaps.

It will be explained in due time, after this electrifying evening of Friday, November 23, 1984, that some UM coaches want to run a tight-end around against Boston College with 33 seconds left. Head Coach Jimmy Johnson argues against it "because the grass is so slippery, I'm afraid Willie Smith might slip down back at the five or six and we'd have a lot farther to go than the yard we already have."

Kosar obviously does not wish to run any gimmick play. That's when he blurts, "Let's play football! Run right the *bleep* at them!"

Except he doesn't say *bleep*, and a major part of the TV-connected nation hears what he does say.

"When you think about it," Johnson says now, "it was pretty hilarious. There's Bernie throwing for 447 yards and he says he wants to run at 'em. But he was right."

Kosar runs Melvin Bratton right the *bleep* over the Eagles. Miami leads, 45–41. Doug Flutie nods quietly on the sideline. He has 28 seconds to make his own special magic.

Mark MacDonald, a BC offensive tackle, says to himself: "How long is 28 seconds? I can't walk from the kitchen in my house to my bedroom in 28 seconds."

Four plays later, with :06 blinking out of the clock, Flutie walks to the line of scrimmage, Miami's 48. He looks over at Coach Jack Bicknell on the sideline. Flutie silently raises his left finger into the air toward the western end zone.

Flutie furiously backpedals. Back, back, back, past his 45. MacDonald grunts and heaves in a one-on-one match with Hurricane rusher Jerome Brown chasing Flutie. Brown slips and falls in the muck. Flutie sets his left foot at his 37 and his right arm flails through the drizzle.

Two weeks later, even Florida State Coach Bobby Bowden will sigh: "When Flutie goes back that far, I just turn away from the TV. There's no way he can throw the ball that far."

Oh yeah?

Astride the goal line, Gerard Phelan clutches the flying football to his groin. Eagles tumble onto each other in a human sandpile of blind glee.

BC wins, 47–45. Maybe the most entrancing football game ever televised is over.

Not the greatest—most entertaining. A game needs a little of everything to be great. This one is devoid of defense. But it is so enchanting that people still babble about Hail Flutie!

Oh, we've had others. San Diego's 41–38 overtime victory over the Dolphins in the 1981 playoffs. UM's 31–30 squeaker past Nebraska in the 1984 Orange Bowl, for the national championship of polls.

BC-Miami will be remembered as long as any. Turnstiles registered 30,235 customers, but a million people will claim they were there, same as Dolphins-Chargers and Hurricanes-Cornhuskers. If you are lucky enough to own a videotape of it, hang on. It's right up there with Indiana Jones.

So much that slipped through some cracks in the pandemonium can be seen on a replay.

Brent Musburger's commentary was trophy stuff.

Kosar looks almost all arm as a passer on TV closeups, more than he ever does to fans in the distant seats. You realize what Flutie meant when he said, "Kosar does all the things I've been taught not to do." Flutie throws on balance, Kosar off balance. Flutie plants his left foot and fires from his ear. Kosar lunges and often throws almost from his hip, baseball's old Ewell Blackwell back to life in shoulder pads.

As good as Flutie is, Kosar is better. Much better.

"In my day, if you met one or two top passers in a season, it was a lot," says Ara Parseghian, the CBS commentator from Notre Dame. "But these guys . . ."

Think about it. The Heisman Trophy and first-team Associated Press All-American quarterback against the AP's second-team QB, who is throwing to first-team AP All-American wide receiver Eddie Brown and second-team tight end Willie Smith.

Miami's Bratton scores four touchdowns. One goes 52 yards; he breaks four tackles along the way. Bratton is "filling in" for injured Alonzo Highsmith.

The game swings from 14–0 Eagles to 24–21 Hurricanes to 34–31 Eagles. Four touchdowns go across in the last nine minutes and 46 seconds. And Flutie's pass goes 63 yards in the air not only against the wind but in the rain.

Some second-guess Miami for calling time just before Bratton jumped over for 45–41. But with barely 30 seconds left, it's more logical to get the whole offense on the same page than to worry about BC scoring in that impossible sliver of time. It's like folks knocking Benny Malone for running in 23 yards and putting the Dolphins ahead of the '74 Raiders, 26–21, with 2:08 left.

What's a guy supposed to do? Run backwards and skip the touchdown just so the clock will keep ticking?

Letters also came in from people beefing about Kosar going off the field with his head down.

What should he have done? Cheer?

VESSELS' HYPELESS HEISMAN

DECEMBER 4, 1986

Billy Vessels asked one question of the first man who told him he won the 1952 Heisman Trophy.

"What's the Heisman Trophy?"

Harold Keith, Oklahoma's sports information director, gave his hammering halfback the news. And got a blank stare before the question.

"People think I'm making this up," Vessels says now. "But I had no dreaming idea of what it was when Harold told me."

He wasn't the only one. Later that day 34 years ago, Vessels informed his sweetheart Susie that he would have to go to New York to accept the Heisman.

"Congratulations," said Susie, who has been Mrs. Vessels the past 33 years, "but I've never heard of it."

Possibly you have heard of this year's Heisman and Vinny Testaverde, who will be working out a significant pro contract shortly.

Well, Vessels went directly from the Heisman to a season as most valuable player in the Canadian pros—for $10,000.

He did not even negotiate that year with the Baltimore Colts, the team that had drafted him No. 1. Vessels spent '54 and '55 in military service, wrecked a knee, and didn't do business with the Colts until '56. Then Colt owner Carroll Rosenbloom invited Billy and Susie to spend a week in New York and talk contract.

"I guess Carroll knew how a week in the big city would go over with a kid who had spent most of his life on an Osage Indian reservation," Vessels says. "I signed for a $12,000 salary and $2,000 bonus. I figured it was a lot more than I'd made in Canada."

Vessels isn't Osage. He just sort of grew up with the tribe across the river from his hometown of Cleveland, Oklahoma. Anyway, he spent a longer time with the Indians than the Colts. One NFL season was enough with that knee.

At 55, he is retired from real estate and the presidency of the National Association of State Racing Commissioners. It is safe to say that no Heisman Trophy winner has had more friends, including U.S. presidents, than Vessels. It also is fitting that he never traded on his Heisman history, for his was one of the softest-sell Heisman campaigns.

"We hardly even mentioned the Heisman," says Keith, now 83. "We didn't do any of the business that came along later—posters, T-shirts, that stuff. Not even with Vessels, as great as he was."

Even then, it was TV that put the Heisman winner over the top.

November 8, 1952, America's living rooms vibrated to the image of Vessels flying 44 and 62 yards for touchdowns and catching a 27-yard pass for another against Notre Dame. Oklahoma lost, 27–21, in South Bend, but Irish Coach Frank Leahy saluted Vessels as "one of the finest runners I've ever seen."

They had known it all the time back home. Vessels came off the Osage reservation with motors in his hips and heart and head. In one high school game, he carried the ball only five times—and peeled off touchdown runs of 97, 93, 90, 76 and three yards. With his right wrist in a cast.

He ran for 208 yards against Nebraska as a sophomore, beat a serious knee injury as a junior, scored 18 touchdowns as a senior. He rushed for more than 2,000 yards in his 24-game regular-season career and recently was voted the best Oklahoma player of all time. That's almost bigger than the Heisman.

"The thing I remember best," says Vessels, "is some of my Indian friends wanted to throw a stomp-dance for me right after I got home from the Heisman presentation. For the longest time, they couldn't find a place for the stomp-dance, but they finally got a town hall, and we had a time."

In a storage room in Vessels' home today still hangs the Indian headdress the tribesmen gave him. Nobody had to tell Vessels what that was.

SO LONG, SABAN

JANUARY 5, 1977

NEW YORK—The last time I talked with Lou Saban, I was convinced anew that he still had much to give and would give it to the University of Miami's football Hurricanes.

He gave it to them. Right between the eyes.

And then ducked, by not even having the common decency to tell them promptly and directly.

"I'm just having a glass of wine with my good wife here in the Keys," Saban said by telephone exactly a week ago today. "We're going fishing tomorrow, and then I'm going to get back to business."

The University of Miami got the business.

The U.S. Military Academy got Saban.

Today, at a big feed in Manhattan, Saban will be officially introduced as Army's new head coach.

Good luck, Army. You'll need it.

You're hiring the Louis Henry Saban so many of us defended, two years ago when he took the UM job, against charges of being a "quitter" twice with the Buffalo Bills, in between with the University of Maryland and, in his last stop before coming to Miami, after just 19 days as University of Cincinnati athletic director.

God forgive us our gullibility. What *The Racing Form* calls Past Performance charts should have been evidence enough of the dishonor replacing the precious intangible of decency in so much of sports today.

You want a deserter, Army? You've got one. Saban is a quitter.

If he wants to quit on himself, as now appears to be a proven pattern, that can be excused.

But quitting after two years on a school that believed in him enough to hand him a six-year contract at age 55 is something else.

Quitting on the two classes he helped recruit, reneging on

the promise he gave those athletes and their parents that he would coach them through their college careers, may be his largest forfeiture of obligation.

"What you're talking about," Saban said after Miami beat Auburn, 17–15, there this year, "is character."

What are we talking about now, Lou Saban?

And, while we're at it, whatever became of the honor of the Long Gray Line at West Point?

The U.S. Military Academy knew Saban had four years to go on his UM contract. Yet Army did not even observe the most basic amenity of asking Miami's permission to talk with Saban.

If Cadets had been as careless in honoring their personal four-year service contracts beyond graduation as Saban is in this instance, we might be Japanese and German territory now.

I've tried every way I know, within myself, to explain his splitting.

The closest thing I can find to a connection is the UM's failure to draw fans—only 83,912 for four home games against Florida State, Utah State, San Diego State and Syracuse. Once, at a more or less private meeting this season, he exploded: "We've got to get some people out there!"

But the Florida State game was televised in South Florida, and Saban should know Utah State and San Diego State and Syracuse aren't exactly big draws.

He knew, in fact, everything there was to know when he took the job.

That's why the University of Miami opened its purse-strings as it had for no other coach, including Fran Curci, who also pulled up stakes in 1972 after only two years on a self-perpetuating five-year contract. The UM guaranteed Saban in excess of $50,000 a year when, frankly, he was not in considerable demand elsewhere.

I know everybody wants to advise the Army. My two cents' worth is this: Don't count on building any long-range programs around Lou Saban.

He's a quitter.

FAMILY AFFAIR FOR BOWDEN

DECEMBER 8, 1979

TALLAHASSEE—It has been a very long time since Bobby Bowden, if indeed he ever did, read Leo Tolstoy's beginning of *Anna Karenina:* "Happy families are all alike; every unhappy family is unhappy in its own way."

Bowden would be the last to know, anyway.

He rules not just one but two happy families.

By all accounts, Bowden, a muffin-faced 50-year-old father of six, is among the most ecstatically married man in college football, where, curiously, considering its pressures, most head coaches remain firmly married.

Bowden also is father figure to a Florida State University team at a peak of state history. The Seminoles have given the peninsula its first unbeaten major-college team. They also will be Florida's first representatives in the Orange Bowl since Ray Graves' Gators beat Georgia Tech, 27–12, in 1967.

It took a real big daddy to bring order out of the FSU chaos that professionally buried one coach, Larry Jones, and would have left another, Darrell Mudra, for dead had Mudra's puckish will not taken him on to success at Eastern Illinois.

"We must be living right around here to have Bowden," said Bryant Underwood, a restaurant cashier on Monroe Street. "We actually passed over him when we hired Jones and Mudra."

Bowden has restored fashion to the plural pronoun "we" in connection with FSU football. It was "they" for quite a spell before he took charge in 1976.

"We've got the best coach in football," says Bill Schuessler, who runs Bill's Book Store just off the campus and hasn't missed a home game in more than three decades. "Not a doubt in the world. Bobby Bowden is *it.*"

One recent afternoon, two children pondered the innards of

a trophy case in FSU's Tully Gym near Doak S. Campbell Stadium, where Bowden's tomahawk falls.

"What's that old wore-out football there?" asked a boy who later identified himself as Tommy Dunlap, age nine.

He and his friend, T.R. Roberts, 10, read aloud the lettering on the ball: *FSU 10, Tennessee 0, 1950.*

"My daddy was just being born then," young Dunlap said. "Besides, nothing around here wasn't nothing until Bobby Bowden."

Yet, for all his gregariousness and as close as his Seminole following feels to him, Bowden essentially stays within himself.

"He seems to have thousands of pals," one says, "but I don't know of a single really close friend."

Bowden earned his privacy by working hard enough out front. He is among football's better-paid coaches with $52,000 in salary, a guaranteed $55,000 from a TV show and a 10-year, $1-million annuity set up by the university.

FSU did not lightly convey these presents upon Bowden. Its last two coaching choices wound up costing more than $100,000 for them *not* to coach. Jones was fired with a payoff of more than $50,000 after winning only 15 of 34 games from 1971 through '73. Mudra, 4–18 in 1974–75, took his $60,000 payoff and relaxed out the two unfulfilled years of his contract.

"I could have gotten a job," Mudra laughed, "but I didn't want to save FSU any money."

Thus, on November 5, Seminole authorities wrote into Bowden's self-perpetuating five-year contract what is now known as a Washington State Clause.

Should Bowden leave without official sanction before his contract expires, he would have to repay Florida State at least the equivalent of his salary for the remaining years.

Nobody here looks worried.

"Folks think Bowden handled the job situation pretty well," said Jeff Cairnes, who pumps gas in an Appalachee Parkway station. "The man wants security. That's only proper."

Bowden's ideas on properness have conquered this territory where skepticism to newcomers is as thick as kudzu.

Jess Yarborough is a believer. Yarborough, 73, has lived in retirement here since serving on the Public Service Commission. He head-coached Miami High from 1932 and lost only one game to an in-state team in 10 years.

"Bobby has put together a fine football team." Yarborough said. "But what impressed me most was when he brought his players down to the church we both go to, First Baptist. I've never seen so many gentlemen on one college team."

The deepest mark of Bowden, though, is all the ways he finds to be both proper and funny at the same time.

Before one road game, the Seminoles were being served snacks at a poolside by waitresses clad only in swimsuits.

"We each ordered a dozen shrimp," says Bowden, "and told 'em to bring 'em one at a time."

THE MAN WHO WOULD NOT SWEAT

DECEMBER 15, 1980

Howard Schnellenberger weighed 10 pounds the first day of his life 46 years ago. Even as a child, he never had the face of one. A picture at his first communion at age eight shows adult purposefulness.

He hiked his 6-1, 230-pound frame out of his head-coaching chair a few days ago and pointed to the state college football championship flag flying in front of the University of Miami's Hecht Athletic Center.

"Come on, wind! Blow!" he murmured. He wanted a visitor to see UM's state football championship flag in full swirl.

In mind's eye, Schnellenberger was seeing more.

A *national* championship flag.

"Jack Harding . . ." he said softly. Harding was the football coach and athletic director who put the Hurricanes on the map in the late 1930s. "I would like to leave something like Jack Harding did."

Neither gregarious nor spontaneous by nature, he hesitated. Every word emerging from beneath Schnellenberger's bushy mustache has been considered.

Life with Schnellenberger has so little to do with ego and the flash and dash that go with egoism. He measures satisfaction in terms of familial and professional progress. The two things that have touched him most in his two years at the UM have been, in order, 20-year-old son Steve's resurgence from serious illness, and applause rising from fans at last Monday night's Dolphin-Patriot game who recognized the coach and his wife.

"Steve was pretty sick," he said. "He was stronger than I could have been. And then the fans at the Dolphin game . . . to see them respond that way to what we've tried to do at UM. It means a lot."

His Hurricanes' 8–3 record and appointment with Virginia Tech in Atlanta's Peach Bowl did not happen over a night or weeks or even months.

There was, however, one day in July when the full measure of Schnellenberger "really sank in" on Billy Proulx.

The head coach and Proulx, his administrative assistant, flew to Gainesville to scout accommodations for the Florida game. "At one motel," Proulx said, " he was so demanding about every little facility that I couldn't believe it. Here it was midsummer and he had on a three-piece suit and was telling off the manager, and Howard wasn't even sweating. He wasn't sweating because he simply refused to sweat."

That deal was concluded. Two months later, Miami handed Florida State its only loss, 10–9. Nearly four months later, Schnellenberger walked back into Gainesville and wiped out the University of Florida, 31–7, the first time since 1962 that the UM had beaten both teams.

Another week passed, and a friend mentioned a trip to Tallahassee.

"What's happening up there?" Schnellenberger asked solemnly.

"Don't you know? Florida and Florida State are playing."

"Oh," Schnellenberger half-whispered. "Playing off?"

"What do you mean, playing off?" he was asked.

"For second place in the State," he said, deadpan.

Schnellenberger has a sense of humor. "But there aren't many funny stories about Howard," his wife Beverlee says. "He is just such a *right* person. He cares and shares."

Schnellenberger's life story can be largely summarized by what Raymond Sokolov, the biographer of A.J. Liebling, calls "deferred gratification . . ." even today when he arises at 5:30 a.m., is at his desk before 7—if he has not spent the night on his office couch—and seldom returns home before 9 p.m.

"A good kid," his mother, Rosena Schnellenberger, recalls of Howard the boy, "and a busy guy."

He had to be. Father Leslie borrowed money to buy a tractor-trailer and hauled freight and worked other jobs while Rosena alternately worked as a waitress and pouring gunpowder into sacks in a munitions factory in World War II.

By 16, a Louisville Flaget High junior, he starred as a receiver on a team whose 1950 programs lists "Paul Harnung" as a sophomore quarterback. That was *Hornung*, who would win the 1956 Heisman Trophy at Notre Dame.

Schnellenberger says he "may have been the player responsible for the expression, 'He could catch the ball in a crowd.' I was always catching it in a crowd because I was so slow, I never could get out of the crowd."

He looks wistfully at a photo of himself in full gallop with an entire Covington High team chasing him. "The guy on the left caught me," he says. "Story of my playing career."

He wanted to go to Notre Dame. "A Catholic kid from Louisville? Where else would you want to go?" The Irish did not want him.

He intended to sign with the UM in '52. But when Bear Bryant, the man who was to exert the heaviest male influence on Schnellenberger's youth, offered a scholarship, the boy chose Kentucky. He remains unimpressed by his '55 All-American selection. "A tribute to our press agent, Ken Kuhn," Schnellenberger says. "I wasn't that good."

The Marines thought he was very good. He spent two college summers in training at Quantico, Virginia, and emerged from platoon leaders' training with a phenomenal leadership rating. He never became an actual Marine "because when it was time to commission me, I wanted to play pro football for six months, and the Marines don't do things that way."

He chose a $9,000 contract with Canada's Hamilton Tiger-Cats over a $6,000 offer from the Washington Redskins, was cut just before the '56 playoffs and promptly drafted into the Army where he served 21 months "as a clerk-typist and a damned good one."

He returned to Canadian football with the Vancouver (British Columbia) Lions. The worst thing that happened to him there was preceded by the best. Three thousand miles from his home, he met a lovely tourist named Beverlee Donnelly, 3,000 miles from her Montreal home.

"Canadian girls are aggressive," Beverlee says. "After Howard was cut, he invited me to his home in Kentucky. Of course I went. We were married May 2, 1958. I didn't know that nobody in Louisville ever gets married on Kentucky Derby day. But we did."

Tim Tam won the Derby. Big deal.

Thus began Beverlee's life as what Howard fondly refers to "a social chameleon."

He coached two years at Kentucky under the still-revered Blanton Collier before a call came from old paraclete Bryant at Alabama.

"Talk about a trip. Our car was so beat up, I had to borrow my dad's Ford to drive from Lexington to Tuscaloosa with two baby boys less than a year old." They were driving through Birmingham's Bessemer suburb when Beverlee was startled by a man in a white sheet motioning cars into a large field.

"Whatever do you suppose that is?" she asked.

Schnellenberger laid it out for her: a Ku Klux Klan rally. They drove on. Fast.

Schnellenberger helped Bryant produce national champions in 1961–64–65. He recruited Joe Namath and Ken Stabler and coached them before moving on to work under George Allen with the Los Angeles Rams from '66 through '69.

Don Shula called Schnellenberger when he took over the Dolphins in '70. The lineup of Shula, Schnellenberger (offense) and Bill Arnsparger (defense) sounded like a Cincinnati law firm at first. It sounded more like a Super Bowl championship company two years later.

Schnellenberger's career on paper shows only one period that might be considered a failure. But he was not allowed to succeed as Baltimore head coach in 1973–74. After his first Colt team had gone 4–10, owner Robert Irsay stormed the sideline during the third straight loss of the next season, demanding that Schnellenberger play young Bert Jones ahead of veteran Marty Domres.

"I told him to clear out," Schnellenberger says cryptically, "and he fired me."

End of chapter, but not of story.

"That was a terrible thing, Howard getting the boot like that," says Shula. "But I was glad to get him back."

When Lou Saban precipitously resigned from the UM, January 4, 1979, sports writer Henry Seiden called UM Vice President John L. Green's attention to Schnellenberger. He was hired four days after Saban walked.

Pretty good hire.

BACKFIRE IN FLORIDA FIELD

NOVEMBER 30, 1980

GAINESVILLE—Florida's fans and ABC-TV used the Miami Hurricanes for target practice, but most of the arrows were sticking out of Gator hides by dusk.

Goaded by a bush-league minority of missile-flinging UF fans, UM rubbed the Gators' noses in a 31–7 rout.

These weren't representative University of Floridians. The real ones were in too much shock to throw the garbage these sleazoids did.

But then, to make it worse, TV commentators got all pious, and hardly anyone at home had the vaguest idea of what really was happening.

"That's a strange call," TV's Frank Broyles said when Miami Coach Howard Schnellenberger called for a 35-yard field goal by Danny Miller as the clock ran out. "I wouldn't do that even if my kicker was going for some kind of record."

Broyles was once a good coach, but he wasn't the one catching the garbage from these few idiots in the Florida Field stands.

Schnellenberger was. He had a point to make. He was dead right.

"I didn't call for that field goal for any record or any other reason but one," Schnellenberger said angrily. "I did it because fans in back of us were hitting us with oranges and tangerines and ice and water and cups and goodness knows what else. After three hours of that, I decided we might need a little field-goal practice.

"I don't blame [Florida Coach] Charley Pell. It isn't his job to police the crowd. But it was the rudest, unruliest crowd I've seen in 30 years of football. And I've been around the roughest fans anywhere—from the Chicago Bears to the Buffalo Bills to the San Francisco 49ers when they were in old Kezar Stadium, to the University of Arkansas."

Arkansas, incidentally, is where Broyles used to coach. They must not have morons out there like these garbage chuckers.

Al Michaels, ABC-TV's play-by-play announcer, followed Broyles' remark by asking, "Wouldn't that stick in Florida's craw somewhere down the line?"

Neither Schnellenberger nor his coaches or players were thinking about "down the line."

"Chris Vagotis [a UM assistant] got hit in the head with what I thought was an orange," Schnellenberger said. "But he went to one knee, so I have to wonder what it was. I didn't say anything to Coach Pell because, as I said, it isn't his responsibility. I went to the linesman on our side and talked to him. He said he would say something to the referee and they would have the public-address system bring the situation to the attention of the entire crowd and the authorities. But they never did it."

The poor fools throwing stuff out of frustration just made it worse. The Gators never were in it onfield after the Hurricanes went up, 16–7, in the second quarter

Miami quarterback Jim Kelly controlled both lines of scrimmage, guarded like mother bears tending a cub and kept constant pressure on Florida's fine freshman quarterback Wayne Peace.

One indelible lesson was left for Hurricane fans who plan to take in the 1981 UM-UF opener: Let the players take all the target practice.

TAKE CARE, JIM KELLY

JUNE 12, 1983

Mr. Jim Kelly
Cloud Nine
Over Houston, Texas

Dear Jim:

Anybody with five brothers and a mom and dad as close as yours probably has had enough advice. Besides, wise men don't need it and fools won't take it. But if poor little Charlie Brown in "Peanuts" can stand out there on the pitcher's mound thinking, "The world is full of people anxious to function in an advisory capacity," you can figure how much more advice you'll get after banking the first million of your $3.5-million contract in the United States Football League.

I'm going to offer you some, anyway, and hope it's taken the way it's meant. Just like Donnie Anderson, one of the original bonus boys, meant what he told those who came after him: "Stay out of bars, stay out of cars and, if you're a field-goal kicker, always buy cigars for your holder."

Donnie Anderson realized early that the parasites who attach themselves to the young rich are interested in them only until the riches run out. That's why he stays so successful in business in Texas, instead of in a detox center or the corner saloon raising glasses to what might have been.

The first thing is so obvious, it has to sound stupid: Don't change.

You're a decent, level-headed man who has brought only honor to your family and hometown and your schools in East Brady, Pennsylvania, and Miami. If you could say even before your junior season at UM, "I've got so much to be thankful for," you must be yelling it now.

116

Remember? "People think he's lucky, having six boys who got football scholarships," you said of your dad, "but we're the lucky ones. Dad was raised in an orphanage, and he and my mom have an extra appreciation for children."

God collected a special bunch of molecules to make you what you are, Jim. He gave you an arm that can knock the eyelid off a chigger at 50 yards, and a brain wired right into your fingertips.

He did the same thing for Tommy Kramer and Joe Gilliam and Dan Pastorini, and they're still fighting off the demons that take particular aim on such gifted people.

Some others—Sid Luckman, Archie Manning, Ken Anderson, Roger Staubach, Bob Griese, to name a few—used plain common sense to hold off the dopers and boozers who try to saddle up every champion for their own venal rides. You can, too.

They'll try to sell you $60,000 cars and $5,000-a-week coke and $100 chips. And all of that will vanish faster than the years will if you fall into that I-can-do-what-I-please-as-long-as-it-doesn't-hurt-anybody-else vortex, the way Art Schlichter and Hollywood Henderson and Don Reese did.

That's a dirty lie, Jim.

Every time you hurt yourself, you hurt somebody else.

Look after what you have—head, heart and arm—because if you don't, those leeches surely won't. They'll steel your teeth and come back for your gums. Watch them.

Or, better yet, *don't* watch them. Ignore them. And pay attention to the people you can help who really want to help you, too.

I once said that your exuberance makes you like a steam-kettle, bubbling until you whistle. We all want to be able to say the same thing 20 years from now.

Sincerely,

Edwin Pope

GATORS ROAR, BUT HERE COMES KOSAR

SEPTEMBER 4, 1983

GAINESVILLE—Miami lost a football game and found a quarterback.

If that sounds a little dippy, saluting freshman Bernie Kosar after the Florida Gators had just chewed him and his Hurricanes into 28–3 bits, well, we could argue. And I'll still say UM lost despite Kosar, not because of him.

Florida won laughing because it had college football's fastest draw, Wayne Peace, going against a patchwork defense. The loss turned into a rout when a bagful of fumbles gave the Gators so many extra chances.

The thing for UM to remember is that a 19-year-old-freshman who never threw a varsity ball before moving into this record 73,907-fan madhouse outpitched Peace, 223 to 146.

And one of these fine nights, Kosar isn't going to have to catch up from so many goofs.

Kosar himself goofed when he lobbed a hope-to-heaven pass that Tony Lilly recovered to stop a UM drive late in the second quarter. Bruce Vaughan and Vito McKeever stole two more from Kosar long after the issue was settled.

But Kosar stood in there like a soldier. He's going to win his stripes yet.

Howard Schnellenberger left Kosar in although he admitted that putting in Kyle Vanderwende or Vinny Testaverde "crossed my mind several times." Schnellenberger finally decided, "The situation we were in, it was good practice for Bernie."

That's the ticket. Kosar is the man. Staying with him will mean winning down the road.

Conversely, I wouldn't give Charley Pell any vote for Coach of the Week for leaving Peace in there when the score was 28–0. Here's a splendid athlete just two months past a spine operation, and you're going to run a chance of putting him back in the hospital just to run up a few more points?

That's more than vindictive. That's dumb.

This, though, you can take as gospel: Offensively, defensively, all around, Pell has put together some team.

Usually, when one big-league team beats another by 25 points, there isn't really that much difference.

There was this time. Florida's immense talent and vicious opportunism made it so.

Miami was far from "an outstanding football team" against Florida, notwithstanding that sort of compliment from Pell.

It still can be, because when you have two freshmen like Kosar and Alonzo Highsmith in the same backfield, things can only get better. Fast.

BUSY GUYS, MARINO AND KOSAR

AUGUST 26, 1984

Dan Marino Sr. would—still will—do anything with Danny Jr.

Except fish.

"Danny's dad couldn't stand to sit still that long," Danny's mother says.

So, when 8-year-old Danny decided he just had to teach one of his parents how to fish, his father suggested, "Why don't you take your mom?"

Veronica Marino "didn't know one end of a fishing pole from the other." But she finally consented. She even packed a lunch for Danny and sister Cindi, 5, and 3-year-old Debbie. They got up at 4:30 a.m. Mom fixed them breakfast and Dad drove the gang over to Pittsburgh's Panther Hollow Lake.

"We could have walked, it's only a few blocks," Veronica says. "But it wasn't daylight yet, so Dad insisted on driving us. He let us off at the top of the hill. Danny and I and the little girls walked down a hill to the lake. Danny went over to the boathouse and got me a pole. He and Cindi already had theirs. Debbie was too little to fish."

Danny and Cindi put the worms on their hooks. Then Danny said, "OK, Mom."

Mom said, "OK, *what?*"

"OK, put your worm on your hook," Danny said.

"*Alive?*" his mother asked.

"Sure, Mom. If you're going to fish, you got to do it right. All of it."

Mrs. Marino put the worm on the hook. "Somehow," she says, "I managed to survive it."

They wound up catching a mess of pan-fries. She still treasures the tiny trip as "one of the most precious moments of my life. Danny was so proud that he'd taught me how to fish."

About that time, 65 miles away in Youngstown, Ohio, Bernie Kosar Sr. wouldn't take his son fishing, either.

"We were hung up on baseball," says Kosar Sr. "At least I was."

Instead of taking 6-year-old Bernie Jr. and 5-year-old Beth and 2-year-old Brian fishing, he hustled them off to baseball games.

"They were games to me," Kosar Sr. says, "but they were just one big carnival for the kids. I'd buy them popcorn, peanuts, candy, anything, everything they wanted, just so they would keep quiet and let me watch the ball game. We all loved it. I was getting my baseball and they were getting their carnival."

Then, somewhere along the way, little Danny and Bernie both told their fathers to throw them a ball, and all their lives changed.

Daniel Constantine Marino Jr. of the Dolphins is coming off the best rookie quarterbacking season in the NFL.

Bernard Joseph Kosar Jr. is hurtling out of a freshman QB year that led the University of Miami to No. 1 in college football.

No city has busted its buttons over pro and college quarterbacks so simultaneously hot since, well, since Terry Bradshaw led the Steelers through the 14th Super Bowl and the freshman Marino was helping the University of Pittsburgh to an 11–1 record and No. 7 national ranking in 1979.

Marino and Kosar: Just the way you would figure it for two QBs who grew up only two years and 65 miles apart, their rookie pro and college numbers came close.

Marino crashed the Dolphin lineup in the fifth game, very nearly the way he did his first year at Pitt. Of the nine games he started during the regular season, before Seattle sprung that 27–20 playoff surprise, the Dolphins won eight.

Kosar bounced back from an opening seven-turnover, three-interception, 28–3 loss at Florida to lead Howard Schnellenberger's flaming young'uns to 10 straight victories. That was even before the Hurricanes' 31–30 Orange Bowl Classic riot over Nebraska, when he threw for 300 yards, including two touchdowns.

Busy guys, Marino and Kosar.

They also keep putting the lie to that old saw about the tree being inclined by the way the twig is bent.

Neither Marino Sr. nor Kosar Sr. played college football. Neither forced his kid into the game.

Bernie Sr. even refused to let Jr. play football until he was in the seventh grade: "I thought he would be better off playing cowboys and Indians like normal kids." Nothing has proved pa Kosar wrong yet.

The Marinos knew early on that Danny was going to do *something* with a ball. "He even called light bulbs 'balls,' " Veronica says, thinking back. "Everything that looked remotely like a ball, that's what he'd call it."

They were dissimilar as toddlers.

Bernie was brisk and serious. A scholarly sort, if you can imagine a scholarly infant, Bernie gave almost embryonic indication of the 3.5 average he holds today.

Bernie adored sister Beth, now a rising sophomore at Hiram College, and brother Brian, a 3.825 student at Boardman High.

"Bernie never liked to stay up late like most kids," says pa Kosar. "When he got his play or his work done, it was right to sleep to get ready for the next day."

Little Marino wouldn't hit the sack until they made him. "He'd put it off until the last possible minute," his mother says. "His father was working nights even back then, and Danny was great company for me."

Kid Kosar pounded the books from day one. He came home from his second day in the first grade threatening not to return "because they haven't taught me how to read yet."

Danny spent more time singing than studying. "He did good in school," Mrs. Marino says. "We considered anything above C good. Danny got them when he had to get them."

Danny loved to watch *Happy Days*. Mother Marino says, "He went around singing that song that Ronnie Howard did, 'I found my thrill on Blueberry Hill.' When Danny was real, real happy, which he seemed to be most of the time, that's what he'd sing. He was off-key, but he didn't know it. It didn't matter. It made *us* happy to see him so happy."

Both Marino and Kosar were sensitive.

Danny's mother remembers him crying whenever Lassie got

in trouble on TV. "He couldn't understand why we couldn't keep a bullfrog he brought home to live on the back porch."

Both Bernie Sr. and Geri recall kindnesses of their son. "We loved every minute of raising him, just like his sister and brother," pa Kosar says. "Hey, it wasn't all perfect for his mother. She still dresses both Bernie and me, because we can't even pick out a pair of pants. But it was a house full of love, the same impression I've gotten of the Marinos."

Both Kosar and Marino are one of three siblings. Each grew up fiercely protective of younger children. Each is a curly haired brunet. Both were excellent baseball players as well. Marino was drafted by the Kansas City Royals in 1979. He said no, of course. But his sister Cindi just married Pitt's Bill Maas, a nose tackle who this year was the first-round draft choice of—right—the Kansas City Chiefs.

Both went to Catholic schools. Marino made All-American at Pitt. Kosar may at Miami.

For two giants always under attack by even larger predators, their parents fretted inordinately over the chance of injury.

The Kosars showed their concern by holding Bernie out of football until he was 13.

Veronica Marino thought about one of Danny's childhood incidents when his knee was hurt last season and again when the forefinger on his right hand was dislocated in Dolphin training camp this summer.

"When we lived in an apartment, before we bought our own house, this old, warped, unpainted fence ran along behind our back yard. Danny was playing out there when he was about 22 months, and suddenly he came yelling into the apartment. His hands were so full of splinters we could hardly see the skin."

Mrs. Marino fetched peroxide. She gently explained what had to be done. Then she cleaned her little boy's hand.

After that, she noticed Danny was reluctant to mention the slightest scratch. "When he'd cut his hand or something, I would explain all over again what I had to do, and he would say, 'All right, Mom.' But when I'd get out the cleaning stuff, he would start saying, 'Wait a minute, Mom.' He'd start backing away. He would be halfway across the table before I could finally get to him."

Even younger, Kosar had a football hero before Marino did.

"Bernie was reading the sports page straight through when

he was halfway through the first grade," says Kosar Sr. "I had been reading it to him, but when he started school I told him it was time for him to do his own reading. That's when he complained, the second day of the first grade, that the teacher hadn't taught him to read yet."

"Well, Bernie read the sports section. Straight through—the *Youngstown Vindicator*. Then, the first day he comes home from the second grade, Geri and I ask him the name of his teacher, and he says, 'Miss Lamonica.' It didn't sound right, but he kept saying that."

The next time the Kosars went to church, Bernie blurted, "There's my teacher! There she is—Miss Lamonica."

Her name, in fact, was Monica.

"Bernie was so crazy about Daryle Lamonica, the Oakland Raider quarterback who played in six AFL title games through '69, that he had just *wished* Lamonica's name into Monica," Kosar Sr. explains.

Mom Marino remembers one special day.

"When we first moved from the apartment to the house where we live now, there was this little mom-and-pop store up a hill and around a corner. Danny was in kindergarten then, and he loved to run errands to that store for me. Naturally, I worried all the time he was gone.

"One day there was snow all over the ground and he wanted to go to the store for me, and I said OK. I wrote out a little note telling the storekeeper what I wanted. Danny put his boots on and went out with the note and the money. From our window, I watched him go up the hill. Then I called the store to tell the man to watch out for Danny.

"I waited and waited, and Danny didn't come back. Then suddenly I see him. He has a little bag in one hand. The other is holding the fence. He's coming very, very slowly down that snowy hill. He's being so careful to make sure he doesn't slip and drop whatever is in the sack. Just a tiny little figure outlined against the snow.

"When I see him out there now with those huge men going after him, I think about him outlined against the snow, holding on to that fence, so very, very careful.

"They grow up," Veronica Marino says. "They have to spread their wings. But you never forget a picture like that."

LOSE A GAME,
FIND A VINNY

SEPTEMBER 8,1985

Some day, Miami's Hurricanes will find Saturday night one to remember.

For Vinny Testaverde. For a gang of other reasons.

Just not this morning. Not while Florida's NCAA-slapped Gators snap and growl, defying the world and looking very much as though they can get away with it for a long, long time.

The monsters from the peninsula's northland are contenders for a national championship they could win even though they are ineligible for either a bowl or the Southeastern Conference title.

They were fifth-ranked nationally even *before* they overran Miami's Hurricanes, 35–23, in the Orange Bowl.

Or overpassed them. Miami could not stop four-touchdown-thrower Kerwin Bell.

But this was an evening to remember for more than that.

For a UM team left in shreds late last season and then left flat by pro-turning QB Bernie Kosar, it also turned out as a super-charged concatenation of excellent plays by Testaverde that will remain long in the memory.

One of those plans could last as long as George Mira's famous left-handed touchdown pass against the Gators 24 years ago.

This was the game, rout though it eventually became, in which the UM welcomed a new quarterback, a near-walkout to rival walk-on Bell.

The name is Testaverde, and mark it well.

It was just four months after Bell came to 1984 autumn practice as the Gators' seventh-strong QB—a walk-on—that Testaverde was about ready to walk out of the University of Miami. Testaverde had sat for three years behind first Jim Kelly and then Kosar. Then, last December, he was so sick and

tired or merely sitting and wishing, he was ready to split altogether—until Kosar dropped a hint that he might pass up not
just one but two more years of college eligibility.

Kosar indeed split. Because he did, it was Testaverde rather
than Kosar who was in there when the Gators led the Hurricanes, 20–7 in the third quarter, and Testaverde came up with
one of those moments that stamp college football as magic.

Pinned down a dozen yards behind the line, Testaverde
shifted the ball to his left hand and shoveled an under-handed
pass to Melvin Bratton.

Earl Anthony, the southpaw bowler, couldn't have done it
better.

"He [a Gator defender] grabbed me on the right side," Testaverde said. "It was just a natural reaction to try to throw with
my left hand. I never had done it before."

Neither have many others.

On the sideline, UM linebacker George Mira Jr. must have
blinked. It was his father who had done just that in Gainesville
in 1961.

The difference was, Mira's throw went for a touchdown, and
Miami won. Testaverde's went for no gain, and Miami lost.

For all that, it was the same difference. The picture was
etched in history, for a QB who could become history.

Testaverde couldn't do what he needed to do the whole game
Bell is too smooth, too deadly. But there will come a time, very
soon, when Testaverde has the same kind of command, and we
will look back at that left-handed, under-handed pass and say
that was the beginning.

PHOOEY ON NOTRE DAME

DECEMBER 1, 1985

Too bad about CBS-TV's ratings going down the tube with Notre Dame Saturday at the Orange Bowl, 58–7.

Too bad about Miami's Hurricanes knocking commentator Ara Parseghian's old football team (he coached Notre Dame from 1964 through '74) for its biggest loop since Army did it to the Irish, 59–0, in 1944.

What is this? Notre Dame of the Little Sisters of the Poor?

Phooey on Notre Dame.

Phooey on all those dear Celtic hearts bleeding from coast to coast for the "Fighting Irish"—fighting Irishmen named Beuerlein, Figaro, Kovaleski, Andrysiak, Francisco, Furjanic and Plantz.

Notre Dame was scooping up the cream of America's talent crop for nearly four decades before the UM even threw up its original Cardboard College.

And now sympathy-stricken souls who have been looking down their noses at Miami throughout modern history want us to feel sorry for Notre Dame not being able to hold up its head.

What are the Hurricanes supposed to do?

Should they call off the fourth quarter and even their second and third teams after socking in a 44–7 lead against a team that gave us the ghosts of Knute Rockne and The Gipper and, to be sure, Parseghian—and gave up when things got a little warm out there?

Phooey on Notre Dame.

Phooey on you, too, Ara, just for today. You're a good man; your memory's just a little short. I *know* you were a good coach, but mercy wasn't your strong suit.

As I recall, your teams ran up a few scores. Say, on Pitt, 69–13, in 1965, and Duke, 64–0, in '66. On Iowa, 56–6, in '67.

On both Illinois, 58–8, and Pitt, 56–7, in '68. On Pitt again, 56–7, in '71. And on Army, 62–3, in '73.

Philosophically, it's hard to justify running up a score on anyone. But it's even harder to call off your players when they have been taught from day one to do their best.

"We've talked all year about playing our very best game of the year in the last game against Notre Dame," said Miami Coach Jimmy Johnson.

Now he's supposed to turn around and tell them to stop?

It was just a year ago that Johnson watched Maryland come back from a 31–0 halftime deficit to overrun the Hurricanes, 42–40.

It was just about an hour after Saturday's slaughter that J.J. began to start burning about the backlash from Notre Dame sympathizers.

"If it had been me on the other side rather than Faust," Johnson said, "there wouldn't have been a word said about it."

He referred, of course, to Notre Dame Coach Gerry Faust, who resigned last week when it became publicly certain that Notre Dame would not renew his contract after five seasons with a 30–26–1 record.

"Nobody apologized to me when Oklahoma did it to me in 1980," Johnson said. In his second year at Oklahoma State, the Sooners buried the Cowboys, 63–14.

That's one way Oklahoma and Nebraska usually finish so high in the polls, beating up on helpless Big Eight opponents.

Parseghian took his first shot at Johnson just before Miami jacked its lead up to 50–7. The Hurricanes had built their 44–7 lead largely on starting quarterback Vinny Testaverde's 356 yards and two touchdowns passing.

"I think this is the time for Johnson to show some compassion and run the ball," Parseghian said. "This game is over with."

I guess those Notre Dame-Pitt and Notre Dame-Illinois and Notre Dame-Army and Notre Dame-Duke games weren't over quite as soon, right, Ara?

Then, when Miami made it 55–7 on a blocked punt, Musberger jumped on the case. He was "surprised" Johnson would "humiliate a coach on the other side of the field."

So UM might have gone to one extreme, with an end-around near the end.

Overall, though, it wasn't Johnson humiliating Faust. It was

Faust humiliating himself, and the Irish humiliating themselves.

Faust was just lucky he worked for Notre Dame. Anybody else would have fired him at least two years ago. Notre Dame kept him because it won't fire anyone who sticks to all the moral terms of a contract.

And the Hurricanes are, as Musburger mentioned, still shooting for No. 1 when they play Tennessee in the Sugar Bowl.

I doubt Tennessee will give up in that game as the Irish did in this one.

Give up against these Hurricanes, and the next thing you can look for is shovels full of dirt hitting you in the face. Flying shovels full, in the UM's case, with Testaverde and then Geoff Torretta.

"You stay in the offense that you run," Johnson said. "We're a passing team. Everybody knows that. We school our quarterbacks to take advantage of what defenses the opponents run, not to be governed by the scoreboard. What am I supposed to do, tell Torretta not to score when he gets one of his few chances to play?

"We didn't even have a punt-block in our game plan. We had punt-return-left and punt-return-right on. We had two men rushing the punter and that block for the touchdown just happened."

Notre Dame will remember this score for a long time. It hasn't much else to remember from this 5–6 season. But some Miamians also remember similar situations in reverse.

Remember 1980: Coach Dan Devine called time with 2:06 left against UM in South Bend so Harry Oliver could kick a field goal that finished off a 32–14 rout.

No doubt J.J. will keep catching flak. But most of the weeping and wailing had to be on behalf of Faust, whose coaching was as ignoble as his conduct was otherwise noble at Notre Dame.

The Hurricanes shouldn't have to lie down and play dead just because the Irish reached such a state of incompetence under him.

VINNY SCRAMBLES SOONERS

SEPTEMBER 29, 1986

When a quarterback throws a noose around the Heisman Trophy in September, it seems simply too surreal that the one play that would be remembered most is a 10-yard scramble in the second quarter.

Yet that play may stay with us longest from the day Vinny Testaverde really won the 1986 Heisman, and the Hurricanes became No. 1 by burning No. 1 Oklahoma, 28–16.

What we shall most cherish is not the four touchdown passes Testaverde threw. It will not be his 261 yards or 14 straight completions.

Nor will it be the stricken looks on Brian Bosworth's usually open yap and other slapped-down Sooners' faces when they realized that Testaverde was going to keep going flat-out crazy all day long.

What will remain frozen-framed in our minds is not even the phenomenal number that Testaverde's defensive teammates did on the Sooners—holding them to 30 yards in six possessions over one stretch.

What we *shall* recall is a vision in slo-mo when the owner of the best arm in college football let his feet and heart and head do the running through the Sooners.

Basically, Testaverde ran 10 yards late in the second quarter when the game was still a scoreless tie.

The Sooners were giving up lots of room—amazing amounts of room—partly to try to steal Vinny's deep strikes and partly because they know he can beat most blitzes. This time, they gave him so much room Testaverde simply could not resist.

"I wanted to run," he said. He took off to his right and then cut back up the gut, "and I got a couple of blocks, so I kept going."

People wearing white jerseys and high levels of frustration were diving at Testaverde's feet all the time. He never even seemed to see a hand stretched toward him.

This is the mark of a *quarterback,* forever looking downfield no matter what threatens. Unitas, Starr, Staubach, Fouts, Marino, all have specialized in this.

That so elegantly controlled scramble will do more to capture the imaginations of Heisman Trophy voters than any of his 10 touchdown passes in four games, or any of those to come.

"Have to keep 'em honest," Testaverde said. "They see you looking down for receivers, it holds them back a little."

You want dough, see a baker. You want honesty, see Testaverde.

That scramble was so much more than a 10-yard run. it was a show of fearlessness and leadership, by a fearless leader.

Will this guy wear the Heisman hat well? Does the Boz get a haircut?

This is more than the earliest Heisman-clincher in years. This is a true-blue guy, and you can't believe what a pleasure it is to do business with one like him in the sordid turn sports so often takes today.

That's why we shall remember that scramble: Superstar exposing himself for common cause; feet so quick they move automatically, so his eyes can linger downfield and hold the defense at bay; then, at scramble's end, anger that people mistake for exhaustion.

"I wasn't winded," Testaverde said. "I was mad I didn't get a couple more yards."

VOLUME AND DOOM IN THE DOME

JANUARY 3, 1986

It isn't fair to Tennessee to blame noise alone for the Volunteers mauling Miami, 35–7, in the Sugar Bowl.

These Vols would have beaten any college team in the country—Oklahoma, Penn State, Michigan, name it.

Nonetheless, the UM's problems started with the incredible decibel level generated by Tennesseans who must have toothed on hog-calling.

"I know it was awful noisy at the Dolphin-Bear game in the Orange Bowl," said UM runner Alonzo Highsmith. "But it couldn't compare with that racket bouncing off the Superdome roof."

And the noisier the joint turned every time Miami tried to run an offensive play, the more problems the Hurricanes developed.

Worst of all, Miami *could* have turned down the volume that, along with Tennessee's fierce blitz, bewildered quarterback Vinny Testaverde.

Unlike the pros, college football teams *can* be penalized if their fans make it impossible for opposing quarterbacks to be heard.

Rule 3, Section 3, Article 3 of the NCAA Football Rules and Interpretation Book:

"When the offensive team cannot hear its signals because of noise," a quarterback may appeal to a referee for quiet. The ref then decides whether the noise is loud enough to interfere. If he believes it is that loud, he will grant the QB a rehuddling.

On a second rehuddle grant, the ref may ask the defensive

team to quiet the crowd. If the noise is not lowered then to what the ref considers fair, he may assess the defense a time-out. Each subsequent noise violation is grounds for another timeout penalty. When the defense has used all its timeouts, five-yard penalties may be levied for delay of game.

That's a long way to a solution, but veteran officials say it works.

However, the Hurricanes had made up their minds they would not let the noise get to them.

Offensive coordinator Gary Stevens said, "We had told Vinny not to back off from the ball, to go ahead with the play. We know how the noise in the Orange Bowl intimidates opposing quarterbacks, and the more they hold up play, the louder the crowd gets, and they can't be penalized for it.

"We just didn't know it was going to be this bad. It was twice as bad as Florida or Florida State. When we first walked on the field, the UT band started. I heard the noise crashing down and I said, 'Oh my God!' And when we got to the press box where we work the phones, it was so loud I would have to turn and shout each play to [running game coach] Joe Brodsky after I spoke the play into the telephone to the sideline."

UM thus was damned if it did and damned if it didn't.

It feared riling Tennessee supporters into even more raucousness. Yet it couldn't pick up any offensive continuity because many Hurricanes couldn't hear Testaverde's audibles when he smelled blitz.

Part of UM's offensive chaos derived from failure on several long passes early. Head Coach Jimmy Johnson pointed out Thursday morning that he sent his team out with Testaverde throwing long "because we thought we had to put points on the board to get the crowd out of the game."

Instead, the lack of UM points hauled the massively pro-Tennessee crowd even further into the game.

The problem first appeared when Testaverde called time in his first time under center, because he was shaken by the noise. He didn't have to take a timeout. He could have complained to the referee.

Miami seized a 7–0 lead, anyway, on Testaverde's 18-yard touchdown pass to Michael Irvin. But things turned sour on the next Hurricane series.

Two illegal procedure penalties (at least partly caused by

UM's inability to hear), a Testaverde overthrow deep for Irvin and a sack set the pattern for the rest of the game.

That sack was the first of seven. From then on it was all potholes for Miami and rockets for Tennessee. The Vols' Johnny Majors also outcoached old buddy Johnson on the simple premise that his people were better prepared psychologically. The UM seemed more occupied with Oklahoma beating Penn State in the Orange Bowl than the difficulty of their job.

Of course, a lot of master coaches have been outcoached in bowls. Michigan's Bo Schembechler has had his troubles. Alabama's Bear Bryant once endured such a fearful postseason streak that a joke went around that Bryant quit eating soup because he couldn't handle the bowls.

But rarely has any coach been put through such a brain-rattling auditory ordeal as Johnson's in the Sugar Bowl.

If the British had fought as hard at the Battle of New Orleans in 1812 as the Vols did in the 52nd Sugar Bowl, we would all be paying taxes to the crown. But the outcry wouldn't be any louder than Tennesseans made the Sugar Bowl.

BAD TASTE FROM TEMPE

JANUARY 4, 1987

TEMPE, ARIZONA—The headline in the *Phoenix Gazette* read, "Class beats crass."

The football Hurricanes' reputation continues to spread—in most of the wrong ways.

You can put on these jungle-fighter monkey suits and play soldier and yell and holler at your opponents and their fans, and as long as you win, it's more or less fun.

But when you lose, especially as messily as Miami lost this Fiesta Bowl to Penn State, 14–10, the actors tend to come off like a bunch of, well, jerks.

I'm sitting here amongst the cacti and suddenly humble Hurricanes, and I'm trying to figure out how much all this off-stream jazz has to do with the strictly football.

I am tempted to say, "Nothing at all—not when you commit seven turnovers against a team as solid as Penn State."

But it does have something to do with it. Football, as everyone from Socrates to Jim McMahon has observed, is emotion at work, and how the players act off the field usually reflects how they act on it.

Miami might have won the Fiesta Bowl even after four Vinny Testaverde interceptions and two fumbles, if it had just run, particularly the way Alonzo Highsmith was running, instead of passing with second and goal at Penn State's six and half a minute to play.

We're not supposed to root. However, when you spend as much time around a team as some of us have with this one, complete objectivity is palpably impossible.

So, when Vinny tricked out that pulse-busting last drive to the six, I heard myself mumbling, *Don't put the ball up anymore. You got down here on one miracle. Don't press your luck on another.*

135

Miami pressed its luck. Testaverde was sacked. Then he had to throw on third down from the 13, and that fell incomplete, and the last desperation pitch settled into Pete Giftopoulos' hands shooting out from under that blue jersey, and that was all she wrote.

Does that really tie into "crassness?"

Does it actually relate to soldier suits, or all the tempests, some in a teapot, that have marked this Miami season so otherwise glorious until Friday night?

Yes, it does.

Some of these Hurricanes just seem out of control.

Coaches had to calm Highsmith after he fumbled. "We had to tell him exactly that, 'Calm down!' " said offensive coordinator Gary Stevens. "He was a madman out there."

But Highsmith rushed 18 times for 119 yards. His madness produced.

And defensive tackle Jerome Brown, the mouthiest of all the Hurricanes, played a strong game. You could say his mouthiness produced, too.

But when it came down to brass knucks instead of combat fatigues, Penn State had them. Doesn't that say something for the Lions' buttoned-down, all-business approach?

The Hurricanes went into last year's Sugar Bowl underpsyched. They went into this one over-psyched. They went in to kill. They learned to their shock that they could be the killees. When that dawned on them, everything started going underwater right out here in the middle of the desert.

Testaverde pressed. "I wasn't very happy with my game," he said in massive understatement.

Michael Irvin, his surest receiver, pressed.

The harder those furies in Penn State's secondary hit Miami's receivers, the less sure the catchers became. When catchers get the shakes, it rubs off on the QB. Testaverde was short-arming the ball, taking sacks when he should have gotten rid of the ball, throwing to some of the wrong people.

George Mira Sr., who was once a sawed-off sort of Testaverde himself, stood looking dazed in the lobby of the Hurricane hotel headquarters afterward. He was extra-dazed because his son plays a ton of linebacker for Miami.

"If our defense had been any better, they would have had to

be pros," dad Mira said. "How can you outgain a team 445 yards to 162 and lose?"

Good question.

It leads back to the boys-will-be-boys excuses, when 11–0 turns this clammily 11–1.

It also leads back to another question: After blowing two consecutive chances to win a national championship, how likely are the Hurricanes to get another chance anytime soon?

Staff and players put together the most happily memorable of all Miami seasons—up to the last crunch. Players and coaches worked their tails off.

But that last crunch is what will linger. I can't help believing the afterthoughts would have been so much more pleasant if the mock jungle-fighters' toy trains hadn't been allowed to run so unchecked, and finally off the rails.

POETIC JUSTICE LANDS HARD ON GATORS

SEPTEMBER 6, 1987

As a contest, Miami's history-hammering 31–4 rout of Florida ranked somewhere below a faceoff between Hulk Hogan and Michael Jackson.

Way below.

As a show of sheer defensive brutality, it was enough to turn a Gator's stomach.

Not to mention his direction.

The river of orange humanity that flowed at ebulliently high tide into the Orange Bowl at midday Saturday began washing wearily homeward by the end of the third quarter.

The Gators had just managed to double their total in the weirdest of ways—two safeties on high snaps by UM's Willis Peguese. And quarterback Kerwin Bell was reeling like a punch-drunk fighter under the Hurricanes' merciless, four-interception siege.

Maybe Florida's following was thinking, *Just wait until 1992.* That's the next chance the Gators get to avenge their worst loss in the 49-year series.

One takes no honorable pleasure in kicking a Gator when it is down. The University of Florida represents the highest echelon of higher education in this state. Its football teams have entertained and even inspired millions since 1906, two decades before UM even took root as a modest "cardboard college."

And still there was an undeniable element of poetic justice in this terrible pounding.

The unfortunate part was that players such as Bell and coaches such as Galen Hall, who played no part in the buildup of vengeance, had to be its victims.

Florida's administration, not its players or coaches, made the choice to delay the continuation of this series until '92.

Charley Pell, not Hall, was responsible for the latest payback for wholesale recruiting violations. NCAA penalties knocked these Gators down to 79 scholarship players.

On the other hand, why should Miami let up after so long fighting the harvest of those Florida illegalities? Especially, why should the Hurricanes let up after being dismissed like school-children from Gator schedules the next four years?

"You could see their problem right away," said Bill Hawkins, one of the defensive linemen who raged into poor Bell all the steaming afternoon. "They didn't have enough good players to prepare properly, at least for a defense like ours."

Hawkins was not commenting on this game as a morality play. He was talking in the most pragmatic terms about one team's brain-rattling physical superiority over another.

"How many times do you see a QB get penalized twice for grounding the ball?" Hawkins asked. Bell was.

Hawkins was penalized for roughing Bell amid a melange of emotional late hits. "The referee told me, 'I know it wasn't intentional, but I saw you hit him in the head,' " Hawkins said. "And I guess I did. We were just into things so hard. And you could see Kerwin getting more and more discouraged. I don't want to sound arrogant, but our secondary is so good it makes it so much simpler to get pressure on a guy even as great as Bell. If he's worried about interceptions, he's going to be easier to get to."

Linebacker George Mira Jr. nodded. "Those guys up front beat up on Kerwin so bad, he was getting up slower and slower," Mira said. "We took away their running game. Then, with the defensive-line pressure, we could sit back there and wait for [four] interceptions."

Between their own diminished manpower, UM's terrifying defense and peck-away passing offense with new quarterback Steve Walsh, the Gators were flattened from the beginning. Flattened beyond the rosiest dreams of even the wildest-eyed UM fans.

"By the third quarter," said single-interceptor Bennie Blades, "it was like Bell was just saying to himself, 'I can't do nothing.' "

Double-interceptor Donald Ellis added, "Both times I had my man covered, and Bell threw it anyway. I guess he figured he didn't have any choice the way our defensive line was pressuring him."

Ellis celebrated early. When Danny Stubbs sacked Bell on the first series, Ellis "must have been 40 yards downfield, and I just ran up as fast as I could so I could high-five Danny. That hit Danny made on Kerwin gave us the fever, and we never lost it."

Florida's last loss this ignominious was a 44–0 wipeout by Georgia in 1982. That also was the last time the Gator offense was shut out.

"How'd you like to have been Bell playing against you out there today?" a man asked Stubbs when the UM dressing-room riotousness had dwindled to a few glassy-eyed grins.

Stubbs laughed. He seemed to want to avoid boasting, but he had been in Bell's frantic face all day, and there was no use denying it. Finally, he said, "It wouldn't have been a good job."

No one would have agreed any faster than poor Bell, head ringing and right shoulder separated.

Baseball

HE PULLED CLEMENS TOO SOON

OCTOBER 26, 1986

NEW YORK—John McNamara never should have pulled Roger Clemens.

Do you pull Howie Long? Carl Lewis? Danny Marino? Wade Boggs? That's what it amounts to.

But what Met fan cares? The Red Sox might never have given up their 3–2 lead in the Mets' 6–5, sixth-game victory if the Red Sox manager hadn't taken out Clemens after seven innings.

And if they hadn't given up the lead, all those other weird things wouldn't have happened.

I don't care how many pitches Clemens had thrown—135 in this case. He was still strong. He had given up only four hits.

And then McNamara pulled him. He left first baseman Bill Buckner in to help lose the game, but he pulled the best pitcher the Red Sox have had since Lefty Grove. You figure it.

I don't care if Clemens had a blister. He was the best, and when you have a chance to put a World Series opponent away with your best, you take it. Period.

The Sox had the Mets down and then out came Clemens and all hell broke loose. For the Mets, all *heaven* broke loose.

When it was over on Mookie Wilson's grounder through first baseman Buckner's legs—the elusive bounding ball that scored Ray Knight—the Mets were winners and back tied at three games apiece.

Thanks to McNamara.

They will be second-guessing this one for a long time. The Sox stood grinning on the edge of their first World Series championship since the year World War I was over, and they blew it.

It was a spectacular ballgame. It had everything—questionable managerial decisions, close calls, a tautness absent from any other 1986 World Series game.

It didn't seem possible the Mets could even stay in the game the way Clemens started. He was masterly, a mastiff shaking a mouse, a red-hot razor slicing through snow. Oh, he weakened just a little midway, but he was bringing it when McNamara yanked him.

Then, in pandemonium to match any since the sixth game of the Red Sox's last Series, 1976, the Mets tied the score at 3–3 and the Sox went out front again on Dave Henderson's homer and Marty Barrett's double and the Mets were back in it.

Maybe the Mets messed up when manager Dave Johnson didn't bunt with Howie Johnson in the ninth.

It didn't matter in the end. It didn't matter because McNamara was too quick with the hook for Clemens.

McNamara may yet get over it, if his Sox can somehow re-seize the momentum he turned over to the Mets in this game.

I doubt it, though. In the end, the Red Sox always seem born to die. They just don't usually need any help from an over-manager.

Dear Mom, A Rookie's Letters Home

A LONG WAY FROM BLUEFIELD

MARCH 21, 1976

Dear mom

I'm getting this in the Miami p.o. fast so you can say you got a letter from a real big-league Baltimore Oriole, and they aint no guarantee Ill even be a Oriole by the time you get it the way the mail generally speeds back to Jonesville.

Just dont mind my punctuation as I have not yet got the hang of it but frankly it is not bothering me near as much as my control.

Anyway most of us rooks are staying in the Dupont Plaza Hotel. Very high class eh mom? Only some of the old gents on the Orioles told me I better wear my batting helmet if I went over to Flagler St after 6 oclock at night. This is one rough town. I keep reading about POLICE BRUTALITY but from all the patches I see on the polices faces Im wondering whos doing the brutality.

Anyway I aint complaining. The Oriole mgr Mr Earl Weaver has been pretty nice to me. That is he aint said nothing except that I could come to camp with the big league Ps and after that it would be in the laps of the gods the way he put it. So Im enjoying it long as I can before they decide to ship me back to Bluefield WVA where I was last yr or whatever.

At least they got a real handy setup for shipping out rooks. The Miami Stadium where we practice is right next to a train depot. Ha ha.

Whilst Im at it mom I wish you would thank Mr Thombs the principal for giving me my diploma in 75 just so I could get out with the other 6 and get on into Organized Ball. Maybe I will thank Mr Thombs by becoming Jonesvilles 1st big leaguer. After all Babe Ruth come out an orphan asylum didnt he? Course he wasnt 22 yrs old when he come out but thats just academic as we scholars say ha ha.

Anyway dont worry about me now. I aint started drinking yet and from the prices I dont think theres no danger. I was setting in the lobby of our hotel and seen one guy come out of the LOUNGE moaning about a drink costing him 1.40. Pa was born 30 yrs too soon. He could have made a fortune selling his stuff down here.

Yrs in love
Wilbur

THEY NEVER EVEN SEEN OVERALLS

MARCH 22, 1976

Dear mom

Boy am I bushed. Only please dont tell nobody down to the store that I said nothing about bush. I am hearing enough about bush rooks from the old gents on the Baltimore Orioles.

However all of them aint all that smart. From the looks they give me when I come into the Locker Room youd think none of them ever seen overalls before.

Anyways they are noticing me. Mr Billy Hunter the coach looks over at me and then says to Mr Jim Palmer the P you better watch yourself Palmer this rook Wilbur can do it all he pitches righthand and has got a lefthand head.

I am glad they see I am versatile because they are just so many spots on the roster and frankly the lefthand hitters are hitting me over the fence like they are all standing in CF so I may have to take up lefthand pitching if I am to have any chance of GOING NORTH as the older gents put it.

You just got to be sharp all the time here mom.

Speaking of which I had to get sharp with one little wise apple vet. It seems about the only thing I got as a rook P is I am the biggest guy here. I don't want to mention this wise apples name for fear of retribution as they say on TV but he knows Im from Jonesville. Anyway he is only about 5 foot 8 to my 6 foot 4 and he says to me hey Wilbur I heard about Jonesville they don't raise nothing there but shady ladies and football players.

Well mom I know rooks are supposed to keep shut but I couldnt let that go by. I grabbed him by the neck and sed Mr you better watch your mouth because my mom and my girl live in Jonesville. Then I tightened up on his neck and he turned real red and said oh yeah what positions do they play?

I guess I done the right thing because he shut up.

Thats it for now. We are off tomorrow and Im going to ride a bus up to see the Yanks practice in Fort Laud. I heard Mickey Mantle is there helping them. Would I like to get a shot at him. Course he is 45 years old ha ha.

Keep your fingers Xd for me mom and if you see Mrs Fedge my old English teacher remind her I am still attempting to get straight on this punctuation business she was such a bug on although I dont know why.

Yrs in love
Wilbur

HELP FROM MR. BILLY MARTIN

MARCH 23, 1976

Dear Mom

Well this was an adventurous day for the rook from Jonesville as the Oriole stars respectively call me. I caught a bus to Fort Lauderdale to see the Yanks and I think they got more coaches than they got players. I told you Mr Mickey Mantle would be there and he was. So was Mr Elston Howard and Mr Yogi Berra. You remember how much pa thought of them before the thresher got him.

Speaking of threshers mom I seen where Mr Billy Martin the NY mgr made them all get haircuts. Well if them are haircuts old Wallace in Jonesville would be turning out 100 cuts a day. I seen Mr Dick Schaap the TV star from NY taking his 6 year old kid in the park and somebody yelled hey Schaap you better not let Martin see the kids hair or he will run you back to the barber shop. The kid was about the onliest one in the whole NY camp that looked human. The rest look like they just broke out of a chain gang.

Mom I pulled a sneaky one on Mr Martin. I hollered for his autograph and he come over nice. I sed Mr Martin Id like to get into Ball—I couldnt tell him I was a Oriole because Mr Weaver probably dont want me giving away no state secrets ha ha—and I asked Mr Martin could he advise a young P. He says sonny just keep the ball down. He adds you might as well try to shave a doberman pincher with a dull razor in a phone booth as try to make it without keeping the ball down.

So I hung around awhile watching the Ps and then hitched a

ride back to Miami where they let me off on Biscayne Blvd a couple of miles north of the Dupont Plaza and I got quite a laugh whilst walking the rest of the way. Mom I cant believe city girls can be as dumb as these are. They are always coming up right on Biscayne Blvd asking for directions and smiling. From the numbers that come up for directions there must not be none of them that know where nothing is. But I am always polite mom count on it.

I will have bigger news for you sooner for better or worse as it is getting close to hog killing time. By that I mean the rooks are skating on thin ice which includes

Yrs in love
Wilbur

MR. EARL WEAVER DROPS THE AX

MARCH 31,1976

Dear mom

Well I said I would have news only it is not any better than my punctuation. In short the ax has fell.

Today Mr Weaver calls me off to 1 side and says basically Wilbur yr problem is that your arm is in overdrive when your brain is in low gear and vice versa. So I am giving you 1 day to clean out your room at the Dupont Plaza Hotel and then go up to the minor league camp at Biscayne College and may the Lord have mercy on the Miami Orioles if you wind up in A Ball. Mom you can see Mr Weaver is a charitable man at heart.

All this come about right after I was pitching Batting Practice and almost beaned Mr Lee May the 1B. Mr Weaver give me the curly index finger meaning he wants a word with me and he says Wilbur I cant have you killing my hitters before the season even starts.

Then Mr Weaver sez Wilbur in your case a brain operation would be minor surgery and he informs me of my next destination.

Frankly mom it is not a complete surprise. The other day I am pitching a B game and Mr George Bamberger the P coach come out and says Wilbur just relax I know you can get the ball over I got confidence in you. Then Mr Bamberger starts back to the Dug Out and about halfway there he turns and says Wilbur just dont deliver the pitch until I am safely in the Dug Out as I do not want to get hit in the head.

Well mom as pa used to say the bitterest pill is when you have to swallow your own medicine so now I am reaping the harvest of not working hard enough on my control.

I then went into the Locker Room and Mr Mark Belanger the SS says Wilbur cheer up theres one good thing about unemployment you cant beat the hours. And Mr Brooks Robinson the famous 3B who has sort of befriended me says dont take it so hard even Mickey Mantle once got cut from the NY Yanks.

So its back to the bushes where it seems Fate has destined me to be 1 more year before I crack the great P rotation of the Baltimore Orioles. I wont be writing for a while as I am going to use every spare minute working on my control and also as you point out my punctuation can use some practice although frankly mom I dont see how that is going to help my earn run average.

> Yrs in love (and A ball)
> Wilbur

MR. COFFEE AT AGE 67

FEBRUARY 10, 1982

Joe DiMaggio whistles through 67 summers that have dried out so many others like beef jerky. He stands straight as bamboo. Not a silversilken hair strays from its place above his handsome tan.

"Geez," a visitor says, "can't a guy get a cup of coffee around here?" He suddenly realizes what he has said to whom, and turns red.

"I wish I could help you," DiMaggio laughs. "I can't."

DiMaggio hunkers back against a Fort Lauderdale Stadium fence. Hardly a New York Yankee has checked in for spring training, but the greatest pinstriper since Babe Ruth drops by anyway.

He likes the quiet. DiMaggio freezes up in crowds. John Travolta never drew the mobs that DiMaggio did. Nobody who knows DiMaggio's deepest heart ever mentions Marilyn Monroe, but three words he uttered about crowds will endure as long as any picture of this acme of baseball grace.

When Monroe came back from entertaining troops overseas, she said, "Joe, you never heard such cheering."

He said, "Yes I did."

That was all. "Yes I did." Never any overkill for Joe DiMaggio, hitting, running, catching, talking. Just "yes I did."

DiMaggio even refused to play in celebrity golf tournaments for years because the swarms around his tee made him fear he would skull someone with a drive.

He relaxes here in the lazy day outside Fort Lauderdale Stadium. He talks golf with old pal Nick Nicolosi, who is putting on the Yankee Greats tournament.

"I'll play, if you could call it that," DiMaggio says. He flexes his right shoulder. "Little sore. Seen pitchers who say they can't get their arm up to comb their hair? I got a little of that."

DiMaggio wanders into the almost empty dressing room outside Manager Bob Lemon's office. Lem fumbles around trying to turn on his air conditioner. "Hell," Lem says.

DiMaggio grins from the doorway. "Don't look at me."

Lem calls for Nick Priore, who is assistant clubhouse manager to Pete Sheehy, who saw more of DiMaggio's 361 home runs and 51 World Series games than anybody else. Priore flicks a switch. Out pours air.

"Maybe I should have been a mechanic," DiMaggio says.

"Sure," a man says. "Sure, Joe. Sure you should have."

Nicolosi tells DiMaggio that George Selkirk and Charlie Keller are coming to the golf tournament.

"I bet a lot of people will remember them," DiMaggio says.

"*Them?*" Nicolosi echoes.

DiMaggio shakes his head. "I'm only famous for one thing. You know what happened the first time I went to Boca Teeca."

"Yeah," Nicolosi says. "This little old lady comes out of a back office and goes up to Joe and says, 'Mr. DiMaggio, there's a tiny wire broken in the coffee machine.' "

"See what I mean?" DiMaggio says. "I get that all the time. I said, 'Ma'am, I just do their commercials. I can't fix them. But I'm sure if you call the company they'll take good care of it for you.' "

TALKING SEASON

MARCH 15, 1983

Whitey Herzog tips his chair back to where he is almost re-clining. He pulls the flaming-red St. Louis Cardinal cap down over his eyes.

"Ain't no doubt," Herzog rasps. "Best thing for a manager who has had some success is to get his butt fired.

"Look at Billy Martin. Fired by Oakland. Comes up smelling roses with the Yankees. Bill Virdon gets canned at Houston and he's making more in Montreal. How about Dick Williams, ain't he making more at San Diego than he was in Montreal? Hell, I ain't complaining. I didn't know we would win the World Series when I signed a new three-year deal last year. But it's true. Get yourself fired. Make more. Simple."

Herzog says "Huh?" now and then. He has a tiny hearing defect. But he talks so readily and intriguingly, people don't have to ask him much.

"Huh? What's that? How much the World Series mean to me? Forty-three nine [$43,900, the winners' share]. Could have made more doing speeches, but who wants to fly around in snow? I did go to Binghamton up in New York. Told 'em I left for Binghamton in '51 and it took me 'til '83 to get there. The Yankees assigned me there in '51, and I wound up in Norfolk instead."

This is The Talking Season of The Summer Game. Little happens to change what will happen in April. But it *sounds* important to people who watch men play children's games in the springtime. It is important to them in the way that Sinclair Lewis wrote in *Babbitt*: ". . . a sensational event was changing from the brown suit to the gray contents of his pockets. He was earnest about these objects. They were of eternal importance, like baseball or the Republican Party."

Few managers sound the same. Kansas City's Dick Howser rarely goes up even a decibel. A tiny smile never leaves the craggy mug of Baltimore's Joe Altobelli. Detroit's Sparky Anderson is electric, animated. Atlanta's Joe Torre thinks before he answers, and makes sense. Virdon comes on straight with bare-bones answers. The Mets' George Bamberger philosophizes. Pittsburgh's Chuck Tanner doesn't have to work to be pleasant. That is pure Tanner.

At Fort Lauderdale, Martin sometimes shakes off questions by proffering a sheet of prepared answers. Martin almost sneers as a writer speculates aloud on the Yankee infield.

"Thanks for making out my lineup," Martin snaps.

All across spring training, double-knits moving against outlines of royal palm and oleander and Australian pine, the older and more adventurous mercenaries swap nervous whispers over the latest juice. It isn't orange.

The wives of ex-pitchers Jim Bouton and Mike Marshall have written a book, *Home Games*. It is supposed to be the distaff answer to Bouton's best-selling *Ball Four* of 1970, which opened bedroom doors all over baseball.

Bud Furillo quotes an advance copy on his nightly radio show from Dodgertown back to Los Angeles.

"At the counselor's," Furillo reads from a Bobbi Bouton passage, "Jim said I didn't dress sexy enough . . . He had tried to get me to go bra-less. But I wasn't comfortable."

Furillo goes on in Bobbi's words: "Some days Jim would talk about how when he made it back to the big leagues, he would be the *Time* magazine Man of the Year."

Home Games is one "record book" no player wants to make.

Herzog's phone jangles in St. Pete.

"Clubhouse!" he barks.

A woman is calling for a player. "He's on the field," Herzog says.

Pause. "No lady," Herzog says, rolling his eyes, "I can't call him off the field."

Herzog hangs up and says, "I find out more about some guys by just answering that phone than watching them play nine innings."

But the only things that matter to the Herzogs are what take place on the field. Even in The Talking Season of The Summer Game, it is all *now*.

"Now," Herzog says. "we go to beautiful Vero. Then beautiful Bradenton. And then beautiful Cocoa."

They *are* beautiful when talking is the game. They only turn ugly two weeks from now when pressure closes in like 100 per cent humidity on the too young, too old or/and too untalented who won't make the 25-man rosters.

"Neal Heaton, remember that name," Bob Quinn says in Tucson. Heaton is the $100,000 lefthander from the University of Miami. Quinn runs the Cleveland Indian minor-league system.

"Heaton is the best lefty to come up through our system in the 10 years I've been there," Quinn says. "He could be the best since Sam McDowell in the '60s. Heaton's going to be right up there."

Down in Pompano Beach, the Rangers' Mickey Rivers bangs three bats against the ground and rattles on as snowbirds wearing sunburns try to make out at least one of every five of Rivers' words tumbling one over another.

"Ugliest big-leaguer I ever saw was Dan Napoleon, the Met outfielder," Rivers babbles. "Dan was so ugly, when a fly ball was hit at him, it would get almost there and then curve away— just to keep from hitting him."

The Talking Season may be the best season of all.

AUTOGRAPHS AND CONSCIENCE

MARCH 22, 1974

As surely as the Brooklyn Dodgers had their Boys of Summer, all baseball has its Children of Spring and Summer.

These are the young spectators, not the players. The kids in torn T-shirts and hole-spattered jeans. Four to 14. Angels with dirty faces. Moppets brandishing pencils. And, among the extremely well-organized, autograph-pads.

The luckiest autograph-hounds live in Florida where most of the big league training is done. Players are more relaxed in springtime. They are more apt to slow down for a signature in Miami Stadium in March than, say, in Baltimore Municipal Stadium on a hot and hitless August night.

True, some players are unforgivably rude to seekers of signatures. Just as truly, some tykes are as insulting as their favorite players, returning a cold stare with an epithet. *Yes, dear hearts, sometimes a compound.* Baseball is the most profane of sports but even some of the mightiest cussers run a Sunday-school second to urchins shunned in quest of autographs.

Then there are the country kids who never get near a big league ballpark until they are in their teens. We did our autograph-collecting my mail. That was when you could send a self-addressed postal to the Cincinnati Reds in, say 1939, and a couple weeks later it would magically reappear in your mailbox.

Those marvelous inscriptions: "Frank McCormick. Lonnie Frey. Bill Werber. Eddie Joost. Harry Craft. Mike McCormick. Ival Goodman."

Some names straight up and down, some with flourishes and curlicues. But all nectar! To a boy, what wonder in simple

157

penmanship! "Bucky Walters. Joe Beggs. Jim Turner. Paul Derringer." Even the manager: "Bill McKechnie." Deacon Bill!

And that is why, as a onetime collector of scrawls from even the most unlearned of baseball players, I sympathized with—and delighted in—a boy who wrote this letter on March 15, 1972.

"My name is Keely Andrus. I am 11 years old. Today me and three of my friends skipped a half-day of school so that we could watch Johnny Bench play at Miami Stadium and get his autograph.

"Well, we got all the other ballplayer's autographs but his. In fact, he ran me off. And he yelled at me like he was my big brother—or father.

"And all I did was ask him for his autograph.

"Please would you tell him that when he gets old no one will want his autograph?

"P.S. But right now I would like to have it."

Again this spring I mentioned that as my favorite letter, an inspired mix of outrage and whimsy.

Then, the other day, I got another letter from Keely Andrus in Bardwell, Kentucky. I give it to you and to Johnny Bench without comment:

"We have moved to Kentucky. In the last few weeks I have received about 15 copies of *The Miami Herald* with your article. I even received some mail from some ladies in Miami.

"Now comes the time to tell you the real reason why Johnny Bench didn't give me his autograph.

"He ran us off because we were jumping up and down on the dugout. He told us to quit but we didn't and that's the real reason why he didn't give us his autograph.

"Now that you know the truth I'll be able to sleep better at night."

MARK TWAIN'S WORLD SERIES

OCTOBER 19, 1985

Persons attempting to find a motive in this narrative will be prose-cuted; persons attempting to find a moral in it will be banished; persons attempting to find a plot in it will be shot.

'The Adventures of Huckleberry Finn'

KANSAS CITY, MISSOURI—Mark Twain would have loved this World Series—if it didn't break his heart the way the rest of the world did.

It will be seen on TV by more people on any night than read all of the Missourian's works in his lifetime.

Many of the St. Louis Cardinals and Kansas City Royals earn more in a single year for throwing and catching a ball and striking it with sticks than America's greatest writer did in his career. He spent most of it broke.

What that says about our values is not very positive.

What it says about the World Series' grip on America and its place in Americana is inarguable. Too bad the World Series was only seven years old when Twain died in 1910. He would have wrung a million laughs out of this one. And no one could have appreciated more than Twain the intrinsic adventure of every Series.

The World Series motive is pride, not the relatively inconse-quential winners' or losers' shares that would have represented a fortune to Twain.

It has no moral. Outfielder Willie Wilson is the last remain-ing Royal of four who did time on drug charges. Other Series legends—Willie Stargell, Willie Mays—have been touched by scandal, and remain scarcely less heroic in the public mind for that.

The World Series plot changes every day, as Twain might

159

never have known whether a book would contain four chapters or seven until it was done.

Even Twain's pen name was taken from the Mississippi River that runs by the St. Louis stadium. "Mark twain!" was shouted to indicate that a boat stood in two fathoms of water.

And here we have the unfathomable twain meeting for the first time—old, tough, intense St. Louis against up-to-date Kansas City, so formal that some Royals' fans actually wear suits to the games.

But geography does not make a World Series. The World Series is the World Series because it is the World Series. It knifes into the long-drawn-out football season like Huck Finn himself blurting, "Well, I catched my breath and most fainted."

If the Super Bowl is the exclamation point of the winter, the World Series is the classic figurative verb of autumn.

It answers, for unbelievable numbers of fans, the ultimate test of absorption—what would you rather be doing than this?

The World Series is not one player or two or even 200, any more than Twain was only Huck and Tom, but an endless, moveable feast.

The World Series runs and runs and runs, and stays totally singular in our lives. Many of us can no more remember our first Series exposure than our first hot dog or first haircut. That is because it is an experience woven and rewoven into so much of our existence.

True, for some players, the World Series represents as much misery as ecstasy. They are the superstars who never played in one. For 300-game winners Phil Niekro and Gaylord Perry and that marvelous hitter Ernie Banks never to have made a Series is as dismaying as the idea of Joan Benoit never running in an Olympics or Muhammad Ali never fighting for a title. Or of Mark Twain never writing a book.

For a great many, the Series brings comfort as much as thrills. The Series scoreboard brings certainty to an uncertain world. There are no abstractions in a final score. But until it goes up, the scene can be as wild as a passage from *The Adventures of Tom Sawyer:* "They sprang away, stumbling over roots and among vines in the dark, no two plunging in the same direction. A furious blast roared through the trees, making everything sing as it went. One blinding flash after another came, and peal on peal of deafening thunder."

And this World Series is showing the world the Show-Me State.

Missouri's famous saying originated with a congressman named Vandiver telling a banquet in Philadelphia in 1899, "I come from a state that raises corn and cotton and cockleburs and Democrats, and frothy eloquence neither convinces nor satisfies me. I am from Missouri. You have got to show me."

I know there are fans who would rather read a box score than see a game. This does not apply to the World Series. This must be shown every October.

"October," said Reggie Jackson, "that's when they pay off for playing ball."

Just like Tom Sawyer conning the kid into painting the fence for him.

PETE ROSE AND TY COBB

SEPTEMBER 12, 1985

Two hotel rooms and a fury of contrast.

That's what I thought about when that 4,192nd hit thudded off Pete Rose's bat, this baseball era's ashwood equivalent of Excalibur.

Sure it's an odd reaction. But that's what rolls back to me: The quintessential Rose and the quintessential Ty Cobb, revealing themselves in person and by phone in hotel rooms in Atlanta, Rose at 1 a.m., Cobb at noon, 16 years apart.

I was *told* to interview Cobb in 1950. If you were growing up around there around then, especially if you were growing up just 40 miles from The Georgia Peach's home and had heard all the stories about his meanness, you had to be ordered to go near him.

I had met him once before at, of all things, a Rotary Club lunch where an adult hauled me along for what was supposed to be the thrill of my 14 years or so. I had no reason a few years later to think his charm would improve with age. Cobb made people feel as welcome as the Washington Redskins in Dallas.

Cobb flung open the door of his Atlanta hotel room, telephone tucked between chin and shoulder. "Sit there!" he snarled. "And be quiet! I'm doing business!"

He did business, as he did everything else, in exclamation points. "That's the price for Coca-Cola, that's idiotic!" he shouted into the phone. "General Motors! That can't be right!"

He cursed and slammed the old black phone into its cradle and bellowed a description of stockbrokers that couldn't be printed in *Rolling Stone* to this day.

"Make it fast!" he snapped at me.

Terrified, I murmured some inane question about that year's Detroit Tigers trying to gain ground on the New York Yankees.

"I don't keep up with that *bleep* any more!" he yelled. I would learn later that, then, at 63, and right on up until he died 11 years later in a black vortex of bitterness and alcoholism, he kept up with two things, money and booze. Those interests alone did not make him Godzilla. They didn't make him Dale Carnegie, either.

I managed a semi-question about how he had remained such a great player for so long.

"Hunting! Walking through the woods every day of the off-season! Resting! Don't these players today ever do any training in the off-season!" A statement screamed; not a question asked.

And then he rasped, out of nowhere: "I don't go to cocktail parties, even to this day, do you know that! I went to a cocktail party! And when it was over, I said, 'Well, is this what it is!' And I tried it one more time, and that was the same! So I figured they were all the same and I never went to any more!"

He shoved me toward the door. The "interview" with Tyrus Raymond Cobb was over.

And then, altogether by accident a decade and a half later, a friend told me that a young Cincinnati Red named Tommy Helms was good copy. The same Helms who was the Reds' first base coach Wednesday night, providing a shoulder for a weeping Rose after the record-breaking hit. My friend said it didn't matter when I called Helms, he would have all kinds of interesting things to say. So I tried calling him in his hotel room in Atlanta right after a night game in 1966, and just kept trying every 15 minutes, hoping to catch him just as he hit the door. Instead, his roommate, Peter Edward Rose, answered.

Pleasantly enough, Rose said Helms hadn't come in quite yet. I apologized and tried to back out of the conversation as gently as possible. But Rose was chattering away as though it was high noon.

I don't remember everything he said. I hadn't prepared for questioning Pete Rose. How was I to know what he would be doing a summertime 20 years later? But he was intense, as incorrigibly *up,* over that phone at 1 a.m. as he was the night he busted Cobb's hit record.

Even then, Rose was saying things like, "I was so surprised, I didn't know whether to scratch my watch or wind up my butt."

Even then, he was the irresistible set upon catching the irascible.

No two men could have been any more different.

I make no claim that Rose is the ballplayer that Cobb was. But I don't like Rose being dismissed so offhandedly by comparison.

If Cobb didn't have the lively ball to hit, he didn't have to hit that dead ball at night, either. If Cobb didn't have artificial turf to skim hits over, neither did he have to spend his playing career in even the subliminal apprehension of climbing on and off airplanes.

And very seldom did Cobb have to deal with hordes of media. There was little radio, no TV, and none of that voracious demand for quotes from even the most moronic of "superstars."

They were vastly different ballplayers as well as vastly different people in vastly different eras.

As one example, you hardly ever heard old-time players says, as so many of today's do, "They can't take that away from me."

Well, who's trying? But Cobb thought that way long before it was common in baseball. He talked that way at least in the glorious imagination of the blank-verse epic *Ty Cobb Poem* written in 1976 by one William Packard.

The poem often speaks to the largely unmentioned biographical fact of the Cobb "whose mother took a shotgun and blasted his father's head off when this player was only 18 years old."

One story said Ty's mother mistook her husband for a burglar at a window of their home in the dark of night. Other stories said Ty's father suspected her of infidelity, and was trying to catch her at it. None doubted one thing. Ty's mother shot Ty's father, his idol, dead.

The poet Packard believes that episode held the answer to a question forever asked, "Why did you fight so hard, Ty Cobb?"

And then Packard ends the poem the way Ty Cobb might have said it if he had not died crazed.

i was the first man
voted into the Hall of Fame

i was the first man
i got 222 votes
all the others got less
than i got

Walter Johnson got 189 votes
Christy Mathewson got 205 votes
Honus Wagner got 215 votes
Babe Ruth got 215 votes

i got 222 votes

i was the first man

I think we should not diminish what Rose has done just because Cobb was first and still has most of the numbers.

I like the way the statistical master, Seymour Siwoff of Elias Sports Bureau, puts it. "I don't care what or who, a record is a record," Siwoff says. "A triumph. Something to be cherished."

RINGMASTER RON FRASER

SEPTEMBER 19, 1985

"Gainesville!" Ron Fraser barked. "Ugly fans. Nasty fans. You never beat them. They only *let* you beat them. Gainesville! That's really where the University of Miami won the 1985 national college baseball championship!"

Fraser was talking in front of a luncheon the Greater Miami Chamber of Commerce pitched for his Hurricanes' second College World Series title in four years. I mean, this is the *king*. No one around here has won major national titles back-to-back since the Dolphins' Don Shula in the seventh and eight Super Bowls.

And Ron Fraser was talking *Gainesville*.

He was talking that way because it's more fun and that's what Fraser is all about. Fun. And show business.

This may be the best coach of any kind the University of Miami, or any university in the state of Florida, ever had.

This is the man who puts in so much time at "little" things— begging and pleading money for United Way, leukemia, abused children, March of Dimes, muscular dystrophy, diabetes, children's genetic diseases, Miami ballet—he has to coach almost as a sideline.

Not to mention the time he spends cajoling money for UM baseball. But he doesn't talk about that.

This is the man who put heat in The Light, who turned Mark Light Stadium into a county fair picnic. This is the man who has won 930 games, second only to Southern Cal's Rod Dedeaux, who has coached more than twice as many as Fraser's 23 seasons.

Fraser doesn't talk about that either.

It's a bigger kick to talk about the morning in Gainesville after the UM beat the Gators, 11–0, last April. It's *a heap* jollier, if you're a University of Miami man who feels about the University of Florida as most UM people do, to talk about that historic morning's multiple ripple effect.

Imagine a boulder being dropped in a dead calm pond. That's it.

"Eleven-zip," Fraser said, all but drooling at the memory. "We beat nine players, all those nasty fans, and three umpires up there, 11–0, in the first of a two-game series. And then it happened."

"Then" actually started with some celebrating after the victory. Fraser returned to the team hotel about 1 a.m. after having dinner with a daughter.

As he walked down a hall, he heard "metal raining out a window."

Four players were trying to get rid of the empty cans before Fraser discovered them. Too late. And everyone, not just the four culprits but all 30 players, would pay.

Fraser roused the team at 6 a.m. A bus drove them to Florida's field.

"Four knew why, and about 26 didn't," Fraser said. "Nobody else was up around there at that hour. You know, Gators don't wake up early. Gators lay around a lot."

Fraser began his own small party at UF's baseball field with "a bit of distance-running. Like five miles apiece. Then a few wind sprints. Then a few hundred bear walks, cartwheels, grass rolls. Some of the guys who had been up a little late—ah, eating pizza—had a little problem about then."

Of course, the story is slightly exaggerated. More fun that way. But no UM player will ever concede that Fraser exaggerated one single thing about that moaning morning.

"After about two hours," Fraser said, "I had the air turned on in the bus, and we all got back on. I reminded the guys that we had set a goal of winning every series all year.

"I said, 'But we're only going to split this one, because we;re going to lose tonight, because you're going to be dragging your tails so bad we can't possibly win. But that's all right. This one's on me, for what I'm making you do.' "

The players listened, tongues like cotton. And listened. And listened. Finally, Fraser shut up.

"That it, Coach?" one Hurricane asked. "Now we go back to the hotel?"

Fraser shook his head.

"No. This is what you might call halftime. Now get back out on that field."

Again they ran. Again they bear-walked and grass-rolled. Again Fraser sat back and smiled.

Then it was, when Fraser figured they had put in about 28 miles apiece, that he heard whistling.

"They had picked up Julio Solis, our catcher, whose legs are wider than they are long. They were carrying him. They were whistling the theme song from *The Bridge on the River Kwai.*"

At noon, Fraser dismissed them. But not back to the bus.

"Coaches ride," he said. "Ballplayers run. Every step. Five miles back to the hotel."

And that night, "we came back to score four runs in the ninth and beat the Gators again, 6–4."

That's when Fraser knew.

Even then, even before not one opposing coach or any one of 36 writers in Omaha picked the Hurricanes, Fraser knew the College World series was his.

OK, so it's more like a mile or two—not five—back to the hotel from the field.

That's show biz.

That's Ron Fraser, for the fun of it, which is what it's still supposed to be all about.

Horse Racing

THE WORLD'S GREATEST JOB

MAY 2, 1986

LOUISVILLE, KENTUCKY—Charlie Whittingham, 73, gymnastically dodged a thoroughbred's heels and skipped over to a barn rail. It was a tick past 5 a.m. Even the ocher pre-cast of sunlight would not strike Churchill Downs for nearly two hours.

"Borrow your comb?" Whittingham asked a bleary-eyed visitor. Then he threw back his cueball-smooth head and brayed in merriment.

"Seen a lot of jackasses out in the desert," Whittingham said. "But I never saw a baldheaded one yet."

Whittingham ambled over to swap a few lies with Woody Stephens. Woody is 72 and the acknowledged master of aiming a horse at a goal and hitting it dead-on. Like four straight Belmonts.

Together, the two men with a combined century of training behind them smiled across bluegrass.

"Ain't this fun?" Whittingham said.

It was a statement, not a question. Stephens has no colt in this Kentucky Derby, but he won with Cannonade in 1974 and Swale a decade later. Whittingham has taken seven national training championships but never a Derby. He's in from California for his first Derby in 26 years, with a bull of a colt named Ferdinand.

"Fun?" Stephens echoed. "Nothing in God's world like it. Take a block and tackle to get you out. I saw too many farmers wringing water out of those hills up yonder. Hoed cotton for $2 a day up there myself. Uh uh."

The candles on Whittingham's and Stephens' birthday cakes pour out more flame than a night in Belfast. No matter. They work like mules, yet live in ongoing rapture.

They are horse trainers. This is the best job in sports and

maybe anywhere else. Trainers are often underappreciated and underestimated, but the engines inside them never seem to burn out. How many trainers making a decent buck ever quit for some other job and make it stick?

Their engines run on expectation. They are riding the rainbow and they love it.

A man poked a microphone into Whittingham's wrinkleless face. "Mr. Whittingham, you're ... ah ... 73 ... what do you think of these young trainers?"

Whittingham baited the hook. "I like 'em."

"Why?"

"If there weren't no young ones," Whittingham said, "there would't be no old ones."

Life is a natural upper for good trainers. It is true that there are some bad trainers who don't feel that way. They have either had horrendous luck or they are so dumb they couldn't tell time in a clock factory.

Nobody can keep a bad horse going good. A good trainer can keep a good horse going good for a while. The horses' engines always burn out or run down. Good trainers ride the rainbow forever.

Down shed row, D. Wayne Lukas bobbed his head in sheer joy. Wouldn't you, if you collected 10 percent of $11 million in stakes winnings last year? And owned some of the horses to boot?

"It's a business," said Lukas, whose Badger Land will go off as second choice to Mel Stute's Snow Chief. Lukas trains more than 200 horses and pays almost that many employees.

"But I get goose bumps," Lukas said, "just thinking about how lucky I was to get out of basketball coaching and into racing. Only thing is, you can't call time out at the quarter pole."

Lukas, 50, *never* calls time out. Neither do his "people," including trainer/son/partner Jeff, 27. Wayne seldom frowns, either. "If you're not up, the horses sense it." Work for Lukas, smile or cut out. "Upbeat, that's the answer, every day. I don't want to know what you did yesterday."

Lukas is a millionaire many times over. And looks it. Six feet of ramrod straightness, dressed from the hide out.

Most of his ilk are millionaires. Most just don't dress like it. LeRoy Jolley, who won here in '75 with Foolish Pleasure and

'80 with Genuine Risk, togs out in subdued shades, no thread out of place, never showy.

Jolley, 48, can talk art, literature, history as well as bloodlines. His wit is self-deprecating. "Trainers are supposed to be tough guys. A few years ago some people in Paris gave me a very elegant party. But it was during the worst heat spell they had had in something like 200 years. I fainted. Passed right out. I was so embarrassed. They must have thought, 'These American trainers are the world's biggest wimps.'"

They aren't. They are vigorous, plain-walking, plain-talking men, romancing every minute of their work.

"Happy? Oh, hell yeah," Snow Chief's Stute, 58, said quietly. "How could I *not* be happy? It would be the greatest life even if I never made a Derby. But to bring Bold 'n Rulling here in '80 and have him run sixth at $68.70 to the dollar and bow a tendon and never run again . . . and to come back now with the favorite in Snow Chief. Happy? Brother!"

Much of the glow written on trainers' weather-blasted faces may spring from the pride of honesty. As surely as certain trainers would skin a flea for its hide and tallow, the best are dead on the square.

"It's a shame," says 73-year-old Johnny Nerud, a brilliant conditioner for a half-century and now owner-breeder as president of Ocala's Tartan Farm, "that the public perceives trainers as people who wear striped suits in the daytime and steal chickens at night."

Other sports should be as clean, Nerud insists. "Pro athletes are medicated to the gills," Nerud said. "But in some states, if you use Lasix, the anti-bleeding agent, or Butazolidin, an anti-inflammation drug, they say trainers are hopping horses. That's not fair. There's always some skulduggery where money is involved, but most of our trainers run an honest game."

Riding the rainbow makes up for those perceptions and then some.

Trainers do put in hours that would stagger a Sherpa mountain-scaler. The standing joke is that they only work half a day—from 6 a.m. to 6 p.m. But the hours are healthy. They leave so little time or energy for dissipation.

That time factor also rules out philandering, even if a man had a mind to. Unless he wants to ape one more or less famous trainer who used his stall as a boudoir. Most of the best stay married forever.

There *is* time to bet, which is some of the fun.

Bill Kilmer, the old quarterback who now owns horses, is tight with Stute. "One of the reasons I love Mel is that he likes to bet as much as I do. Any afternoon he's running something, he bets every race. When I die, I'd like to come back as Mel Stute."

Most trainers would like to come back as themselves. And bet. Even ultra-conservative Sunny Jim Fitzsimmons sent it in pretty good. Mr. Fitz won three Derbies—with Triple Crown champions Gallant Fox in '30 and Omaha in '35, then with Derby victor Johnstown in '39. He made standing bets of $50 across the board on every horse he raced in younger days.

"But I'll never forget my biggest single bet," Mr. Fitz said not long before he died 20 years ago at age 91. "I put down $100 on Man o' War—not that I trained him, Louis Feustel did—at Saratoga. I'll never forget the exact date, either. The 13th of August, 1919. Man o' War went off at 11 to 20. I figured if ever there was a sure thing, that was it."

Mr. Fitz sighed. "Only race Man o' War ever lost. Horse named Upset did it. You hear about upsets now? That's where the word came from."

Another relentless optimist, Johnny Campo, isn't running anything in this Derby. But Campo won $70,000 in the Las Vegas winter book with Pleasant Colony in the 1981 Derby winter book. He sent out $1,000 at 25–1 in February and dispatched $2,000 more when Pleasant Colony's odds fell to 10–1 after he ran away with the Wood Memorial.

That, too, greases trainers' engines for the long haul. Their juniors love it just as much.

Cam Gambolati, 36, sipped coffee on the Churchill Downs backside and said, "I keep remembering something that happened when I got back to the barn after we won last year's Derby with Spend A Buck. The first guy I saw was Angel Penna Jr., a good buddy and a good trainer. The first thing Angel said was, "How do you feel? Tell me how it feels to win the Derby!"

Gambolati told Penna, "It's the greatest feeling of my life. But I feel so sorry for Roger Laurin, he's so dejected after Chief's Crown ran third."

Roger Laurin's father Lucien retired 11 years ago at age 62 after winning Derbies with Riva Ridge in '72 and Secretariat in '73 and the Triple Crown with Secretariat. Lucien couldn't stand it. He's been back training seven years now.

They whistle when they work, *and* when they cash a bet.

"That keeps the owners happy, too," Nerud said. "And when the owners stay happy the trainers stay happy. You know William L. McKnight was one of the richest men in the world when he died eight years ago at 90. He was worth at least a billion dollars long before he bought Tartan Farm and helped build the Calder track. Well, the happiest I ever saw him was over just a few hundred dollars."

McKnight stood beside Nerud at old Tropial Park nearly 30 years ago when the trainer hoisted Herb Hinijosa up on a claimer and told the rider, "When that gate goes up, get his ass!"

McKnight looked quizzically at Nerud. "What did you mean by that?" McKnight asked.

"I meant, 'Put him on the lead and let him chuckle!' " Nerud explained.

"Oh," said McKnight. "You think I should bet $20 across on him?"

"If you can spare it," Nerud said.

The horse won. McKnight collected $260. "And I don't have to give the government one red cent of it!" McKnight gloated.

"The next day," Nerud said, "Mr. McKnight's wife called me and said, 'John, I don't know what you did, but you've made a new man out of my husband.' "

Gambolati trained Spend A Buck to last year's Derby title. Gambolati came up from Florida this week to accept an award.

If Gambolati did not become a millionaire out of Spend A Buck's racing, he could through a lifetime breeding right to the colt now standing at stud in Versailles, Kentucky.

This year hasn't been as kind. In the first four months, Gambolati has won exactly *one* race.

"And I have the best job in the world," he said.

STOOPING TO PROFIT

FEBRUARY 1, 1963

They call them stoopers but it is a misnomer. The good ones hardly ever stoop. The old dodge has evolved into almost a science. It is surprising the number of gimmicks a man who does not work for a living can think of.

The stooper is a person who walks around racetracks looking for cashable parimutuel tickets that have been thrown away by mistake. It is hard to imagine anyone discarding a slip of paper worth money but it happens all the time.

The best stoopers are well dressed. Often they are more presentable than the wealthiest customers. They operate in clubhouses where they are apt to find discarded tickets of large denominations. There they simply blend in with the scenery of $150 suits and $35 brogans.

A stooper has to have a head for figures. He must memorize the numbers of the win, place and show horses or dogs in each race. In a stooper's mind, numbers run endlessly and seldom are confused.

The aristocrats among the stoopers drive tiny tacks into the sole of the right shoe, near the toe. They hold a program or Racing Form in their left hand and look downward as though they were reading it. Actually they are reading the tickets on the floor. If a ticket is lying upside down, they deftly scoop it over with the tack, so they can read the numbers.

An accomplished stooper can read thousands of tickets, almost every day, between horse tracks and dog tracks and jai-alai. He has enormous odds going for him. One score and he has made his daily bread.

Backaches would seem to be an occupational hazard for stoopers but the truly outstanding stoopers never stoop at all. They place a gummy substance—sometimes flypaper—on the sole of the left shoe.

After kicking the ticket over with his right toe, the stooper reads it, and if it is good he plants the left toe atop the ticket. It sticks. The stooper meanders to the men's room and removes it. From there it is only a short and glorious trip to the cashier's window.

The top brass of the stoopers have nicknames just like regular crooks. The fraternity was delighted some years ago to discover a member named Hooper. Of course he quickly became Hooper the Stooper. Another whose first name is Paul became Paul The Pointer because he wears shoes with pointed toes, like a real sport.

The tracks discourage stoopers by cleaning up tickets as fast as possible periodically during a program. But the stooper soon learns the routine of the clean-up crew and usually is one kick ahead of them. The war between the cleaners and the stoopers is eternal. They consider each other poachers. A lot of the clean-up men are amateur stoopers themselves.

The stooper revels in his cunning, and one of the favorite stories of the breed concerns an arrogant man who boasted he never blew a good ticket. One day he found a ticket worth $100, and cashed it, and bet the $100 on a horse. The horse won but in an unexplainable mental lapse the stooper threw away his ticket. A fellow stooper spotted it and cashed it for nearly a thousand dollars.

The arrogant stooper never was much good after that. His spirit was broken, and now he works the grandstand instead of the clubhouse. For a stooper there is no humiliation quite like getting out-stooped.

SECRETARIAT AND HISTORY

JUNE 10, 1973

NEW YORK, NEW YORK—Anybody who held one ticket on Secretariat and cashed it Saturday had to be hard up. The $2.20 payoff was peanuts compared with the scrap of history they held in their hand.

The Belmont Stakes was history, all right, a compellingly emotional moment in a sport deeply in need of such a brain-reeling performance.

It was simply the best race by maybe the best racehorse of all time.

Not for competition. Just for class.

Secretariat actually turned the Belmont into two races—his own riotous record-blasting rush over the mile and a half, and another, in which Twice A Prince, an incredible 31 lengths back, beat three other horses.

Even Secretariat's Triple Crown achievement, first in a quarter-century, was almost diminished in importance by his time of 2:24, which was 2 1-5 seconds faster than any 12 furlongs ever run on a dirt course in America.

When New Yorkers leap and cheer at anything, that is history in itself. The 69,138 customers watching Saturday knew they were seeing a once-in-a-lifetime tableau. They honored it by shrieking themselves hoarse and hurling papers and hats and finally themselves into the air in a demonstration unseen in New York sports since the 1969 Mets made madmen of ordinarily sedate spectators.

Thirty-one lengths! This would be a heavyweight champion knocking out a formidable opponent in the first 12 or 13 seconds. It would be a nine-second 100-yard dash or a National Basketball Association championship margin of 40 points or a National Hockey League title margin of six goals. It would be Don Larsen's 1956 perfect World Series game all over again.

I'm awfully glad I got to see it. I'm not sure I can wait another 25 years for a Triple Crown, and no colt may ever run a mile and a half this fast again.

Eight colts have won Triple Crowns and seven more have missed by the heart-tearing length of the Belmont, but none of the eight came close to doing what this fantastic chestnut son of Bold Ruler did.

So classically superior was Secretariat's journey that rider Ron Turcotte had time to look at the fractional times on the toteboard and make a deliberate attempt to ride him out to the record. The toteboard was closer than the opposition.

The *Daily Racing Form,* in a nugget of understatement, called the performance "tremendous." Trainer Lucien Laurin, "no weight pushing down on me now," was less restrained: "The greatest horse I've ever seen, without a doubt," thus dismissing his last year's champion, Riva Ridge.

Chick Lang, the general manager of Pimlico, where Secretariat had won the Preakness after the Kentucky Derby, had summed up the colt about as well as anyone. "Every once in a while, God decides to make a perfect horse," Lang said, "and Secretariat is one."

Drawing away before unbelieving eyes Saturday, he looked it. Sham had run a respectable second to Secretariat at both Louisville and Baltimore. But Secretariat's marathon sprint on this steaming, hazy day so broke Sham's spirit and stamina that jockey Laffit Pincay and Sig Sommer's good colt finished a pathetic last, 45$^{1/4}$ lengths back.

Two hours almost to the minute after the race, a brutal thunderstorm hit the track. Nature's timing was as beautiful as Secretariat's. Two hours earlier for that rain, and golden history would have been prevented.

"I had times from Gallant Man's 1957 Belmont record written on my program just for fun," said Pimlico's Lang, "and I saw that Secretariat after a half-mile was 3-5 of a second faster than Gallant Man. I said to myself, 'Somebody's either got to drop dead or slow down right here.'

"Then I heard the crowd roaring, and the only time I ever heard a racing crowd make that kind of noise was when Canonero II won the Preakness two years ago. I knew I was looking at something that no one ever expected to see."

SEATTLE SLEW'S TRIPLE CROWN CRUISE

JUNE 12, 1977

NEW YORK, NEW YORK—He did it.

Seattle Slew, the poor folks' Secretariat, the people's horse, did it in spades. The 109th Belmont Stakes and the 10th Triple Crown belong to the brown bomber who cost less than the monthly wine bill of old August Belmont, for whom both this track and race were named.

The original Belmont was a German immigrant who laid out $20,000 a month for the bubbly at his Fifth Avenue manse in the late 1800s.

Seattle Slew, also an original, cost $2,500 less than that—$17,500 precisely—at a 1975 auction. But skimming over Saturday's 1½ miles of mud he looked more like the $15 million price that will be hung on him now.

Should Slew wind up worth that much for breeding purposes after he hopefully runs through 1978, the owning families of Mickey Taylor and Dr. Jim Hill will show a return of $857 on every $1 they put in.

Anybody bucking a mortgage may not believe this but I don't think the owners really care. They love him for the ebullience he has brought back to racing for the first time since Secretariat's flaming 1973 Triple.

So Karen Taylor can be excused for saying, "He's the greatest horse there ever was," minutes after jockey Jean Cruguet stood up in the saddle waving his whip in his right fist just before the finish.

That was the only bad moment Trainer Billy Turner had after needing an extra five minutes to thread Slew through a traffic jammed barn area to the paddock. "I was afraid Jean might fall off," Turner said.

Numbers ultimately fail to support Karen's contention that Slew is the "greatest." His time of 2:29 3/5 while finishing four lengths ahead of Run Dusty Run and six in front of Sanhedrin looks like trotting-horse stuff in contrast to Secretariat's record 2:24 when he won by 31 lengths.

But this is a pro who does what he must when he must— "Enough to win while staying sound enough to keep running," the way Mickey Taylor put it. So who is to say that he may not be even a bigger name and better attraction than Secretariat somewhere down the line?

Slew is the first unbeaten Triple Crowner. Nine out, nine in. It cannot stay that way.

But so far, except for a crock-sided start in the Kentucky Derby that he won by 1³/₄ lengths anyway, nobody has even made him strain.

Especially this hazy Saturday in the Belmont.

Everybody knew what was coming. Most of all, Cruguet knew. He was walking into the jocks' room early in the afternoon when a groom asked him how Slew would do. "Slop or mud, grease or blood," the 37-year old Frenchman said in his painful English, "he is going to run like hell today."

Except he didn't have to. Three times they came to him— Spirit Level, Sanhedrin, Run Dusty Run. Three times Slew shook them off.

An old superstar named William Shakespeare said it for all of Slew's new millions of idolators in his own *The Taming of the Shrew*: "Now is the day we have so long looked for."

Now came Cruguet and Slew, flying as one, putting a continuing lie to the myth that the Belmont is made for stretch-runners only. Slew was the 32nd of the last 41 Belmost champions to be leading at the eighth pole, and not one of the other nine was farther back than third.

"I knew the stretch wouldn't bother us," said trainer Turner, the most thoroughly likeable face in racing today. "I also knew we wouldn't come close to a record. This is not a record-breaking horse.

He's good enough.

THE WOLFSONS, HAND IN HAND

JUNE 9, 1978

NEW YORK, NEW YORK—Hand in hand, Lou and Patrice Wolfson walked away from watching their colt Affirmed work out for Saturday's Belmont Stakes. Then trainer Laz Barrera fell into step. He made a jocular reference to Wolfson's wealth.

"My wife here has all the money," Wolfson said. "Laz, you should have married a rich woman. Perry is going to take care of me the rest of my life."

Patrice—"Perry"—smiled. She always does when her husband speaks.

She is 41 with the freshness of 21. He is 66 and Hollywood-handsome. It is a beautiful mating.

They are forever touching each other. The way people in love should. Her husband of six years will stand behind her with his hands on her shoulders. She leans against him. And when their eyes meet, which is often, Cole Porter should be there to write something that could be sung about the two of them together.

The one disconcerting note is Wolfson calling his wife "Perry." Washington lawyer Edward Bennett Williams gave Patrice that nickname, short for Perry Mason, "because she is always defending Lou."

The reason she feels she must defend him is what keeps this week from the possibility of perfection for them.

In short, it is a long way from jail to a Triple Crown.

And the man the bluebloods of racing maybe never really wanted is precisely 1½ miles and roughly 2½ minutes from completing the incredible journey through the championships of Kentucky Derby and Preakness and Belmont Stakes.

His full name is Louis Ellwood Wolfson. He once played end on the University of Georgia football team, and bought and sold junk in Jacksonville, when junk still meant scrap metal, and became the scourge of Wall Street as a corporate genius.

And he is one and the same Louis Ellwood Wolfson who did time for selling unregistered securities.

Most convicts would call it "soft time" because Wolfson did it at Eglin Air Force Base, Florida, hardly the harshest of prisons.

Wolfson would call it hard time because nobody before him ever went to prison for simply violating of Securities and Exchange Commission regulations.

He served nine months, from the April before Majestic Prince won the 1969 Derby to the next January.

Today some ask how a man with a prison record is allowed to race horses. In a way it is a peculiar question because so many of racing's most revered names made their millions through sweat-shops and paupers' blood, while Wolfson made his through proxies and numbers.

But I suppose it is a fair question, since they didn't go to jail and Wolfson did.

Pat Lynch, assistant to president Jim Heffernan of the New York Racing Association, has a fair answer: "Mr. Wolfson wisely did not apply for a license between the time of his conviction and the completion of his sentence. When he did apply to New York in 1971, stewards decided that he had paid his debt to society and also had served racing well for many years. Just because a man has gone to prison doesn't mean he is forever barred from racing, unless the offense is of such heinous nature that society forecloses on him."

So now in semi-retirement Wolfson has bred and financed and nursed Affirmed to the edge of a Triple Crown reached only 10 times since 1919.

"I will be glad when it is all over," Wolfson said. Mostly he will be glad because of Patrice, or "Perry."

By nature she is shy and self-contained. She grows defiant when the unpleasant side of her husband's past comes up.

"Lou's life is an open book," she said. "If someone asks him, he answers. We did dread the Triple Crown because we were afraid it would give too many people chances to ask questions."

It has done that, all right. "Why can't people just let us enjoy the horse?" she asked. "The horse should be the center of attention."

Now Wolfson was urging her into their car. "Dear," he said softly, "you're getting indignant." His tone was droll.

With Patrice at the wheel, they drove away. To be alone.

'BEST RACE
IN 50 YEARS!'

JUNE 11, 1978

NEW YORK, NEW YORK—Acreage prices in Ocala start shooting through the roof after the hairiest two minutes 26⁴/₅ seconds in thoroughbred racing history.

The chestnut flame named Affirmed—that Ocala baby— ran down his favorite uncle Alydar by a bobbing head in the 110th Belmont Stakes and thudded in as the first Florida-bred colt among 11 Triple Crown champions.

If these two had been playing a World Series, it would have been over three games ago. Affirmed now has shaken off his star-crossed shadow Alydar seven times in nine confrontations, including three straight through Kentucky Derby and Preakness and Belmont.

But none was like this. Nothing in racing was ever like this.

"Fifty years I've been around this game," said trainer Woody Stephens, leaving the horseyard, "and never saw the beat of this. Absolutely the BEST race in at least 50 years."

Believe it.

Alydar chucked his old hang-back battle plan and hooked Affirmed halfway through the brown loam of the 1¹/₂ mile track. From there it was hands and boots and horses in pumping tandem, an immaculate coupling of men and animals.

And in the end, man-child Steve Cauthen, barely 18, threw up his left fist, clenching his whip, in a victory salute reminiscent of Jean Cruguet's on Seattle Slew in last year's Triple Crown.

The dramatic difference was that Cruguet had it made with Seattle Slew so early that he signaled triumph yards before the finish.

Cauthen was so busy whacking his golden king just inches

inside Velasquez, one wasteful movement would have cost him the day and the Triple.

My mouth had gone dry with Secretariat's wild 31-length runaway in 1973, restoring a Triple Crown after 25 years. I rooted for Seattle Slew, who was so good he was not even extended through the Triple.

But I never had a race twist my innards like Saturday's Belmont.

And still, hours after it was over I could only believe that if these magnificent beasts ran another 20 miles or 200 miles, even given the indomitability of Alydar, his little nemesis of barely 1,000 pounds would be in front at the finish.

The ultimate horse race also was ultimate testimony that the Belmont is a tournament of both stamina and strategy.

The Derby over a clamorous mile and a quarter puts the first meaningful test to a three-year old's heart. The 110-yards-shorter Preakness is to the swift *and* the clever around tight turns. But the Belmont across 12 furlongs is the next thing to life-and-death combat between horses.

It is as much in the jockey's head as the animal's legs.

When Cauthen, 14 years Velasquez's junior, saw the Panamanian move Alydar even at the 6½ furlong pole, he coolly urged Affirmed ahead. They went flank to flank from there to the 3/16 pole, where Alydar's flaring ears may have gone inches in front of Affirmed's nose.

Then, right-handed, Cauthen slapped Affirmed's shoulder.

No response from Affirmed. Alydar was holding. Cauthen was trapped. He could not whip Affirmed on his right flank. Alydar was in too tight. And Cauthen had never hit Affirmed left-handed.

Would Affirmed swerve out from the rail because of a virgin sting on his left side?

Cauthen made his decision instinctively. Moving almost invisibly fast, Cauthen switched his whip to his left hand.

Two jumps before the eighth pole—220 yards from racing's Holy Grail—Stevie Wonder slashed downward, left-handed.

Affirmed popped a head back in front and they careened the last 20 yards in stomach-churning proximity.

The toughest race since *Ben Hur* was over.

SURE YOU WANT TO BE STEVE CAUTHEN?

JUNE 13, 1978

NEW YORK, NEW YORK—You look at Steve Cauthen, whose face is soft as a baby's behind and who needs a Brinks truck at an age when other kids are just starting to zap their old men for motorcycles.

And you think, "What I wouldn't give to be him!"

If you were Steve Cauthen, you would be the youngest jockey to win a Triple Crown. You just walk Affirmed around the Belmont Park paddock and women throw you notes with telephone numbers written on them.

You were on *Time*'s cover a few weeks after Anwar Sadat. The last guy to have a book written about him at 18 was Mozart. You're *The Kid*, which is the name of Pete Axthelm's book about you. You can't lose for winning. You made more than half a million dollars last year. That was *before* the Triple Crown.

You even win playing cards—thousands—against jocks who were dealing "racehorse rummy" before you were born.

You've got the touch. You know nobody can be as good as you're supposed to be. But people want to believe you are. You're going to argue?

You've got it made. That's what you think. Now hear the other side.

You can afford pheasant under glass three meals a day. But you can't take three straight bites in a restaurant without somebody wanting you to sign something or just to talk.

Or to buy you a drink. That's the worst part. Eating is bad enough for a race-rider. Drinking is worse. When you worry about weight so much, it's too easy to keep drinking and put off eating.

Men with cameras and microphones and pencils come in waves. One TV crew wanted to film you getting out of bed the morning of the Belmont. *Getting out of bed.*

After the Belmont, you had to take off through the crowd like Reggie Jackson running off the field after his three home runs in the World Series wind-up. It was split or get split like a wishbone. Fat ladies and corporation presidents were grabbing at you from all sides.

You wonder how long people will keep carrying on around you like this. The worst of that is, when it stops, you're in trouble. And the longer it goes, the more you're apt to insult somebody.

You can't lose. But you can't win either. And not much in life is going to be new to you when you're 20 years old.

Are you positive you'd give anything to be Steve Cauthen?

BEN SENDS
IT IN

FEBRUARY 6, 1986

"Don't worry," Ben Cohen tells Sonny Hine when the trainer's brow curls in concern just before a horse race. "It's in the hands of the monkeys now."

Cohen is talking about jockeys. "What do you expect?" he will ask Hine after a particularly disappointing ride. "We never had a five-foot president."

Jocks don't care to be talked about this way, but what can they do? Cohen is 86 years old and does as he pleases. Doing as Ben Cohen pleases means betting horses. Fast, uninterruptedly and all out.

He can afford it for several reasons. He makes it both ways. He owns Baltimore's Pimlico Race Course along with his 91-year-old brother Herman. Benny has made money owning horses, too. Not long ago he paid nearly $400,000 for an Alydar colt.

Whatever he makes, though, he will send plenty of it back in.

"He's incredible," says Hine. "He's always got a story. If they come in 10-5 in a perfecta, Ben will say, 'I had the 10, why didn't I have the 5? Everybody knows 5 goes with 10.'

"I don't know where Ben gets those theories. He'll say, 'A 7-1! Should have had it! I got the 7, and 1 always goes with 7!' "

Most of what Cohen says has to come through Hine. Cohen makes his own life easier partly by never giving interviews. I don't blame him. If I were 86 and didn't have a care except the winner of the next race, I wouldn't give interviews either.

"The only thing Ben cares about is the next race," Hine says. In a game of dreams, Cohen is a realist.

Hine, 55, has been Cohen's trainer for a dozen years; Cohen says Hine will be his last. Sitting by his Gulfstream Park barn in that pleasant patch right off the French-fry frenzy of U.S. 1, the trainer loves to talk about the owner.

"I tell Ben I made him a millionaire," Hine says, "and Ben says, 'Yeah, I had 10 million when I met you. Now I've got one. You made me a millionaire, all right.' "

Cohen winters here, but the pattern of his life does not vary much from the rest of the year in Baltimore. Zelda, his wife of 50-odd years, walks three miles every morning. Ben leaves shortly thereafter for the track. He does not wish to be disturbed by anyone who does not have "information." But he is not invulnerable to the basic struggle in a business where there are as many busted hearts as busted bones.

Hine recently bought a horse for himself. Cohen wanted half of it. Hine politely demurred.

"Look at it this way," Cohen told Hine. "Half of something good is plenty. Half of something bad is too much."

Looking at it that way, Hine sold Cohen half the horse.

Cohen hangs in there. Even after winning a stake, he refuses customary drinks in the directors' room. "It's more important that I play the last race," he says.

Cohen spotted Pimlico General Manager Chick Lang rushing down a hall early one afternoon. "What's your hurry?" Cohen asked.

"There's smoke in the grandstand!" Lang blurted. "I got to call the fire department!"

"Wait until after this race," Cohen pleaded. "I'm alive in the double."

CHARLIE WHITTINGHAM AND HIS DOG TAR

MAY 3, 1987

LOUISVILLE, KENTUCKY—You wished for a sound camera for this moment.

With three hours' sleep, Charlie Whittingham rolled his red-rimmed eyes under his glossy dome like a road map imprinted on an egg. He looked at his Kentucky Derby champion Ferdinand and said, "I like the way Ferdinand looks coming out of the race, but I don't know if he likes the way I look. Took us a long time to get dinner last night and you know how that is—you order a shooter and wait for dinner, and then you have another shooter, and maybe a few more to boot."

Hard sunlight beat through Churchill Downs' oaks and played off Ferdinand's chestnut snout and Charlie's 73-year-old mug and dust-crusted rubber shoes.

"Funny," Charlie said. "Lots of times when I think about dinner, I think about my old dog. Labrador, name of Tar. This horse is smart, but that dog was half human. I'd take Tar to dinner with me and he'd lie down under my chair. If I had a few too many drinks, he would hang down his head when we walked out. *Ashamed* of me. Tar usually slept right by my bed, but when I drank to much he'd go way over to the other side of the room."

This was one of those Sunday mornings when most Derby winners' hearts beat in their eyeballs.

For Charlie, who had just won the Derby in his first try in 26 years, it was not Sunday morning coming down as Johnny Cash sang it. Whoever thought he would give the Derby this kind of flogging, coming in with Ferdinand just two for nine and then 54-year old Bill Shoemaker riding like an avenging angel?

"I did," Charlie said firmly.

He blinked against the sun flying in through the skylight of the green-roofed barn. He peered out at a sea of garbage in the infield beyond that loam where he had made his biggest score in three score and 13 years, and you would never have guessed he was born April 13, 1913.

"Oh, I was counting my money all week," he said. "My heart sank a little when Shoe got pinched on the break. But Bill picked him up and got him going and made that move inside at the top of the stretch.

"I know, I know, I've been saying the horse loafs on the lead, and you know what? The last part, from about here to that barn over there"—Charlie flung out an arm—"Ferdinand was trying to pull himself up. Bill had to pump to keep him going, God bless the both of them. If I'd had any hair when the race started, I wouldn't have had any when it was over."

The other day, Charlie was staring at a bushy-headed writer named Michael Katz from *The New York Daily News*. Katz has so much hair he tells a story on himself that he went into a barber shop and the barber took one look at him and said, "Not here, buddy!"

Anyway, when Katz came around to Charlie's barn last week, Charlie surveyed Katz's great mop and said, "This must be a big race—they're sending Russians to cover it."

Now, Sunday morning, Charlie was still wagging his bowling ball of a head and saying groggily, "Sleeping's overrated. I usually sleep four hours and get up at 3:30. I never had a headache in my life, not even in the Marine Corps when we used to butt heads for fun. That smarted a little. That would ventilate you. But I never had a headache. I'm just a little peaked."

Peaked, but definitely pumped up.

So would you be if you were in his shoes after all those years away from the Derby after running eighth with Gone Fishin' in 1958 and ninth with Divine Comedy in '60.

Charlie is big now.

Real big.

It wasn't that long ago, in the 1950's, actually, when he couldn't even afford a car. He was bumming rides to the track.

And one day up in Northern California an owner walked into Charlie's stable and told him he was turning over all the horses to another trainer. It nearly wiped him out. But Charlie came back, and now when you ask people all over the world who's the world's best, they say Charlie is right there with Woody Stephens.

A reporter asked, "Do you think a lot of folks will just now think you're a great trainer since you finally won the Derby?"

Charlie suddenly cocked an ear. "Sounds like a seagull over yonder," he said, "Ever been a seagull in Louisville?"

Charlie has to have his jokes. "You know I'm Irish?" he half-whispered to a man at his side. "And you know what the Irish do? Ten percent of them work and 90 percent of them criticize the work."

Then he looked at the person who had asked the question about how good people thought he was or not, and he said, "It's not important what other people think. It's only important what you think yourself. I know I've been a good trainer."

So do I.

Fishing

LIFE AND DEATH FOR 'BIG WATER'

APRIL 22, 1984

OKEECHOBEE, FLORIDA—This is about the Four Horsemen of fishing. They are lies and humiliation and storms and
death.

I hope it does not come out quite as serious as that sounds
although God knows it is serious enough when a specter of
utter destruction hangs over the 700 square miles of freshwater
that is Lake Okeechobee.

But this also is about the Two Puppy Dogs of fishing. Those
are, first, fathers and children being together alone, and, second, out of reach of the most abrasive and unadvertised pollution of all. Noise pollution. Telephones. Television. Portable
stereos. Dogs baying in the night. All the sounds that afflict the
human condition.

Let's start at the beginning. Which is, fans of David Woodley's quarterbacking will swoon to learn, I am an even worse
fisherman than columnist.

So it was that I made the fatal mistake at the end of a day on
Lake Okeechobee of asking an adjacent angler the oldest fishing question: "Do any good?"

"Yeah," he said expansively. "Got 32 specks."

It took only a few seconds to realize that I had wedged myself
into a crack too small for both book-learning and common
sense.

I knew the man was referring to *Pomoxis Nigromaculatus*,
more commonly recognized as the speckled perch and sometimes as black crappie.

Somehow I had forgotten that, in asking the question, I was

inviting the last one that my son and I wanted in return: "How 'bout you guys?"

I attempted a blase look. "Several specks," I said.

The man knew he had his 33rd fish of the afternoon. He bore down and reeled in. *"How many?"*

"Three or four," I said.

My 14-year-old son's glance nailed me. I have taught him not to lie for a lot of reasons, the most practical being that it is easier to remember the truth.

"Ahh . . . three," I finally amended.

The devil of vanity forced me to amend brilliantly, "And one *big* catfish."

The man in the other boat cast one contemptuous look and took off.

Well, it was worth whatever humiliation is involved. How often do a father and teen-age son get to spend 24 hours a day with only each other for five days?

The boy's mother is marvelous in every way that a mother and wife can be. But, as the boy himself tells her every time she mentions the possibility of making a threesome out of an extended fishing trip, "Mom, some things a son should only do with his father."

If that comes off as sexist or chauvinistic, so be it. It could go just as well for a daughter and father. If anybody ever finds something better than fishing with one's child for restoring the soul and cleansing the spirit, they can bottle it and become an overnight millionaire.

In all our lives, boredom is the No. 1 enemy, the loose board at the top of the stairs. It is simply impossible to be bored on the water with one eye on a pole and the other on a son or daughter or both.

What my boy and I truly know of each other, we have learned at the ends of fishing poles from the threshing tides of the Keys to the serene backwaters of Vermont. It was only a year ago that we discovered the magnificent solitude of Lake Okeechobee.

Sadly, just this year it also came to us that these tender, silent days are imperiled for my son with his own children, and if not them surely his grandchildren.

Humans die.

Lakes should not.

Especially, Big Water should not. This is how the Hitchitai Indians named Okeechobee. *Oki* for water. *Chubi* for big.

They thought it would live forever.

So do too many people today who, out of ignorance or indifference or greed or all three, are inviting the death of Lake Okeechobee.

We are talking about a lake that yields a virtually incomprehensible crop of food and pleasure. That's an average of 450,000 sportfish a year. Seventy percent speckled perch (black crappie), 15 percent bass and 15 percent bream.

Death has its eye on Lake Okeechobee. It has happened before on a far smaller scale. Lake Apopka died. Lake Tohopekaliga is hurting.

And now Okeechobee.

The process is at once savagely simple and as complicated as trying to maintain balance in a 700-square-mile swimming pool.

It can be stopped at a certain point. The problem is, not even the wisest scientists know that precise point. They do know that once that point is passed, restoring a lake's vibrancy is all but impossible.

Manure and other nutrients from cattle and dairy and muck farms work in disastrous concert with discharges from sewage stations and points as small as individual homeowners' septic tanks.

Feeder lakes such as Kissimmee once acted as natural filters for Okeechobee. However, the channelization of Kissimmee resulted in discharges being more or less *shot* into Okeechobee, with commensurately injurious effect.

These wastes spark the growth of plants. The overgrowth of these plants robs the water of oxygen fish need. Fish die.

Certain varieties of undergrowth even multiply every time an outboard propeller hits it. A snakelike plant called hydrilla is by far the worst. It is even more deadly than even the water hyacinth.

You can't mow a lake.

My son, 14, and I think about these things every time we get out of our boat and go off to eat in Lightsey's Restaurant ("We cook what you hook"). A framed clipping there salutes one Johnny White, who won the last two World Catfish Skinning Championships in Crescent City.

My son noticed a man at a nearby table ingesting catfish about as fast as you figure Johnny White could skin them.

"That looks like the man in the clipping," my son told the boss at the cash register, Andy Arrants. "Is *that* him? Is that Johnny White?"

My boy was so excited he might have been asking if it were Danny Marino, or at least Thomas Edison.

"Naw, it's his brother Jackie," Andy Arrants said. "Jackie can't skin 'em like Johnny, but Johnny can't catch 'em like Jackie."

Jackie had just arrived with 1,200 pounds of catfish off his trotlines. We noticed another trotliner at a nearby table. His face was burnt to the consistency of alligator skin.

"How long will the lake keep coughing up catfish like that?" I asked the man.

"Them cats are tough mothers," the man said. "Tougher'n specks, bass, bream, anything except gar. But if them hydrilla keep twistin' up in there, chokin' the life out of everything, well, there won't be none for Jackie to catch *or* Johnny to skin."

The truly terrible treacherousness of hydrilla is that it offers great natural cover for fish just before it takes over everything.

Right along that horrifying delicate ecological line, Lake Okeechobee is a fisherman's paradise today.

My boy and I found sanctuary from a thunderstorm one afternoon in a marina called Okee-Tantie on the Kissimmee River.

"Tellin' you," a weatherbeaten fisherman was regaling a waitress, "them fish just jumped right into my cooler. Hey, honey, you want to clean some fish for my supper?"

"Got no time for that foolishness," the waitress snapped. "Run your mouth someplace else."

The fisher sighed. "Guess I should have just held up a filet knife when them fish were jumping into the cooler, and then they'd have been fileted by the time they hit the cooler."

Experts say only the toughest sanctions against runoffs will stave off the day when no such stories are possible.

It will be a sad day when no father, or son, will even be able to answer, "Several speck."

True, the day may be a long time off. Okeechobee is a big sucker for anything to kill.

It is a big sucker to be on when a storm hits, too. We were lucky to be on the Kissimmee River when a big one struck. Rain fell so furiously that three fishermen in a small skiff had to use a pocket compass to find their way back in.

"I don't mind the rain," one said upon reaching safe haven. "But I don't want to be no lightning rod out there."

My boy said he didn't either.

Then the storm cleared, and one day we were sitting in the majestic quiet of Okeechobee, and my boy said, out of the limitless optimism of a 14-year-old heart, "I don't think people would ever kill this lake."

How do we explain to him and his children to come that it could already be happening?

TED WILLIAMS FISHES FOR LOVE

JUNE 4, 1967

ISLAMORADA—The living room in Ted Williams' home is capacious, but bare of baseball ornamentation. It is today's room, not yesterday's. The room of a fisherman, not a Baseball Hall of Famer, the last of the .400 hitters. Two plastic-encased Atlantic salmon flies are the major decoration.

Williams sits in an easy chair beside a telephone, the bane of his life. A visitor who smokes is politely asked to swap seats so Williams will be on the lee side of the smoke. He has never smoked and the scent of certain brands annoys him.

That is, the visitor is politely asked *once*. The second time is not so polite.

Williams spreads himself out in crimson walking shorts and oversized T-shirt and talks fishing, fishing, more fishing. Two guides, Jack Brothers and Bill Grace, are chewing the fat with Williams before the daily search for tarpon. Brothers is an engaging raconteur as well as guide and he was telling a fancy story about the orca, or killer whale. He has barely finished his tale when Williams stalks to a hall closet and pulls out the *Wise Encyclopedia of Fishing* to check Brothers' story.

"For crying out loud," grouses Brothers. "A guy tells a fish story and you pull an encyclopedia on him!"

This is 48-year-old Theodore Samuel Williams, his mind as geared to absolutes as it was during a Hall of Fame baseball career when he conducted extensive studies on sleep and diet.

Fishing is no game with Williams. It is a life, a totality of joy. "Get serious," he admonishes companions. He may make a federal case out of the way a guide ties a certain knot. His friend Brothers suffers a continual needling. If Brothers asks

199

where the clippers are, Williams retorts heavily: "Right here. Right where they're supposed to be. Oh, aren't we LUCKY? Aren't we LUCKY?"

Williams has a well-developed sense of humor, if ribald. He enjoys Brothers' stories like the one about a guide named Cecil Green. "Ol' Cecil had some city fellows out tarpon-fishing and they're goofing up everything, and finally Cecil says, 'Gentlemen, be seated. To catch fish, you must present the bait properly. You are presenting it improperly. Gentlemen, there are two ends to a fish. There is the eating end and there is the . . . . . end. CAST YOUR BAIT TO THE EATING END!'"

Williams roars at that. But there are not many such idle moments when he is chasing the cunning *Tarpon Atlanticus*.

One afternoon he drove to Long Key, about 10 miles south, whisking over narrow bridges, steering with his knees while using his hands to make a conversational point.

He raised one tarpon there, but it got off the hook on the first jump. After two hours Williams directed the party into the back country off the Buchanan Keys. Darkness was closing in when the tarpon began shaking themselves out of the mud and running along a sandbar.

In quick succession Williams had three tarpon on his hook. "When they run by here," he had warned, "you might see a flash that looks orange or black. You only see about 1/20th of the fish." Williams' eyesight still is almost perfect, although he dismisses as fiction the old story that he could read the label on a moving phonograph record.

His first tarpon off the Buchanan Keys quicksilvered up out of the water, flung its head angrily and was gone. "Spit out the buck!" Williams grimaced. "Nothing you can do about that."

The second tarpon hit hard. Almost too fast to see, Williams pumped the rod upward three times. Then it was pump-pump-pump to the side, a swishing sound like three knives whirring through the air. The fish went into the air a half-dozen times as Williams played it around the boat. "When they act like they're going under you, you better loosen the drag quick," he said, still manipulating the rod. But this one got away, too.

It was after 9 p.m. before Williams sat down to eat in Manny and Isa's Restaurant—out of loyalty to old friends Manny and Isa, he ignores a more fashionable eatery.

Here, as well, everything eventually comes back to fishing

with Williams. But the range of his mind and the catholicity of his tastes are staggering.

Williams discusses photography in technical terms that baffle professionals; his home is lined with pictures he took of his daughter.

"What do you think of Vietnam?" he blurts. "Does Miami have a chance against Notre Dame? Were those Cassius Clay fights with Sonny Liston in the bag?"

Williams had not been with the Red Sox more than eight hours in 1939 (when he was 20) before he was confounding the erudite Moe Berg with scientific queries. Berg spoke nine languages but Williams stopped him with a legal question.

He skips from a question about Miami Beach's chances of landing a political convention to a sudden interest in a friend's recipe for a dish made from coconuts. "Did you read Hotchner's book on Hemingway?" he asks a moment later. "Good stuff."

Always, though, it comes back to fishing. He has fished for them all, and he regards tarpon and Atlantic salmon as the best. "The tarpon," he said, "is a tackle-buster, spectacular and exciting. The Atlantic salmon is very romantic, very edible and anything else good you could say about a fish."

To hear tough-hided Ted Williams talk of romance seems strange. But this spells out his feeling for the Atlantic salmon he catches near his cabin in the Canadian province of New Brunswick. "After they are spawned, they might go back down a river more than 200 miles to grow up. Then they pick a mate and fight back all the way to the original spot, by instinct alone, to spawn. They fight off nets, natural predators, fishermen. They're magnificent. I suppose if I had just one fish to fish for the rest of my life, it would be the Atlantic salmon."

But the tarpon is his quarry here. All else is sublimated in the search. It was nearly 11 when he left the restaurant. "We want to catch that same tide," he said. "So we'll meet at my house for breakfast at 5 o'clock and be out at Buchanan by 7."

By 9:30 the next morning, he had his tarpon, a 95-pounder.

A photographer was there and got the picture. Williams told him what camera-setting to use.

THE LADY IS A BOMB

JULY 10, 1978

JEWFISH CREEK, FLORIDA—By love's atlas, it was a strange place and time to meet such a beauty. I never even had time to tell her I was married. If this meeting has a moral, it is that you should never offer an *hors d'oeuvre* to an exquisite stranger unless you want to lose your heart as well as your tidbit. Especially if she is underwater.

A layer of black cloud hung like a bowler hat over Blackwater Sound. In our skiff, my son and I rocked with the chop. The lady, still hidden, must have been contemplating barging in without introduction as I pondered questions that only an 8-year-old can ask.

Can fish read?

They can read a menu if it includes live shrimp.

Does catching fish hurt them?

Not as much as not catching them hurts me.

How do fish hear without ears?

I don't know.

What makes clouds?

God.

When will the fish come?

Only God knows.

Are there any more Fritos?

No. Hush now. Fish.

Suddenly the peace of this speck of Upper Keys was shattered: cathedral invaded by bongo. My fishing rod went double in the shape of an upside-down horseshoe.

We had turned the drag to light tension against just such an explosion that had cost us another lulu here a year ago. Line peeled off the reel in that *zziinngg* that bonefishermen know.

Twenty yards. Thirty. Forty, without pause. But we weren't on the flats that bonefish favor. This was too deep for bonefish.

Besides, a bonefish strikes like Chuck Foreman, power plus speed. Our visitor obviously was smaller, although as fast, a submerged Walter Payton.

Quicksilver flash broke the brine. A slim back arched straight up, again glinting silver even on the sunless day.

The boy shouted, "Is it a shark?"

I said it might be a ladyfish. Expert Erwin Bauer once wrote, "The ladyfish is the only fish I know which can run while jumping and jump while running."

This was a lady and she was flying with the line. "I never saw a lady go that fast," the boy said.

A bonefish will go and stop, run and gun. He will feint and maybe stop altogether. Even turn and come back at you, to slacken your line, then take off and pop it.

The ladyfish fights continually after the initial racking stab. She is a lithe and lissome princess, the miniature Wonder Woman of the sea except she is all bones and no meat.

The ladyfish is pygmy cousin to the tarpon in that she can throw a hook before it is firmly set. This one came out of the water again, desperately shaking her slim head, gyrating faster than the eye could follow. But once the hook is inbedded in a ladyfish's spiny jaw, it is as firmly fixed as though caught between three layers of Levis.

Elops Saurus is her scientific name. Not very romantic. Even the name could not kill this love affair.

Finally the lady came alongside the skiff, heaving, exhausted. I saw a glint in the eye of my son, who refuses to look at any 8-year-old girl. But a three-pound lady*fish?* That's different.

"She's . . . she's beautiful . . ." the boy breathed.

We slid Ms. Elops Saurus gently back into the water, to lift more hearts and then break them.

NO MORTGAGES ON A TARPON

AUGUST 25, 1979

I first fell in love with fishing about the time Caesar got his first close-up of Cleopatra. I caught absolutely nothing. I didn't get stabbed, either.

My fishing luck has changed little except for one extraordinary day when I out-caught the self-described world's greatest angler, a former baseball player named Ted Williams. More accurately, by blind luck, a large sailfish impaled itself on my hook. My pleasure was undiminished by skipper Ray Hathaway's remark that "a 6-year-old could have caught the same fish." Any time any adult can approximate any feat of anyone 6, he is ahead of any game.

Cynics describe fishing as a delusion surrounded by liars and smelly clothes. It is no use trying to impart the ecstasy of fishing to, say, a confirmed cosmopolite like the late and brilliant columnist Jimmy Cannon.

Once, Cannon became so annoyed by rival Red Smith's paeans to fishing that he wrote of extensively interviewing bartenders and waitresses who concluded that fishermen were the cheapest tippers alive. Smith responded to the effect that Cannon surely must have interviewed a lot of waitresses, but if they were discussing fishing, the conversation should be preserved in the Smithsonian.

For one thing, Cannon was a lifelong bachelor. His impatience with anything more than five miles from the center of Manhattan was matched only by his indifference to children.

Cannon in his meteoric prime may have been the best newspaper columnist ever anywhere. I don't think it is unfair to say he died a poorer man because he was so well off financially that he never experienced the richness of peace fishing can bring to a man whose house has more mortgages than paint on it.

Nor could he have heard a 10-year-old son, as I did, plead one night, "And, dear God, please let the tide be high tomorrow."

After my Master Charge balance began to resemble Bert Lance's overdraft account, I spent the latter part of this vacation fishing with my boy.

Fishing is one of the last recreational raptures that can be handled without a promissory note. Our most expensive expedition stood us $13.85—$3.85 for breakfast and $10 for two Zara Spook lures.

I would be delighted to detail the location, but for the advice of an Everglades guide who stiffed his own cousin by telling him a certain fish-lode was barren. "When it comes to fishing holes," the guide told me, "I ain't got no kinfolks." Amen.

My son's lure hardly had struck the surface when a silver-sided chunk of ferocity arched out of the water. The tarpon turned a twist to shame Nadia Comaneci. And spit out the Spook.

Overharshly, perhaps, I mentioned keeping the rod-tip high and the line taut.

When Somerset Maugham in *The Bread-Winner* observed, "Children are always rather bored with their parents," he was not talking about fishing trips, or today's children who read newspapers.

Mine murmured something about "child abuse" and invited me to take my best shot.

Tarpon Atlanticus attacked my Spook like Jack Youngblood going for a quarterback's gullet. It pirouetted up against the sky. Power-dove. Then split for the mangroves. I was trying to turn him when the line snapped with the sound of a firecracker.

After a bit the tarpon departed and so did we.

"You had the drag too tight," the boy said gently. "But it's all right. The thing is just seeing them jump like that. It's like something out of *Moonraker*."

He thought for a moment, sorting out a child's fantasies. Then he said, "No. It's better."

Boxing

GIFT FOR SUGAR RAY

APRIL 7, 1987

LAS VEGAS—Sugar Ray Leonard caught lightning in a bottle, a "Las Vegas decision" in his favor and history in his hands.

Marvin Hagler got robbed.

Hagler threw the big punches and tore up Sugar Ray inside for by far the biggest part of the 12-round route.

In the end, though, in the kind of verdict for which Vegas is justly notorious, Leonard was awarded the middleweight championship of the world.

Two judges' scorecards to one said ego outslicked hatred. They figured flash—the flash Leonard was supposed to have lost while fighting only two nonentities in six years—outfoxed fury.

Those clowns. It was all *HBO'S* Larry Merchant could do to keep a straight face when he greeted a friend a few minutes past the thievery.

"Sugar Ray stole it fair and square," Merchant said, eyes twinkling.

Those two judges must have had their eyes closed.

I scored Hagler a winner, 116–112. I never figured Leonard would make it even this close. The old saying that close only counts in horseshoes and hand grenades doesn't go out here. Close does count, on what the officials did to Hagler.

Leonard threw a lot of strikes, but so many were pure junk they shouldn't have counted. Hagler was the punisher, and still the victim.

The jury still hasn't even been seated on one of the big prefight issues—Leonard's eyesight. But Hagler inflicted no visible damage on Leonard's left eye, which was repaired for a detached retina.

That doesn't mean Sugar Ray is home free visually. It means only that the worst did not happen immediately.

Instead, Sugar Ray detached Marvelous Marvin from the title he has held for eight years.

He did it with cunning, finishing rounds with bursts that impressed but didn't hurt.

Most of all, though, he did it on the name of Sugar Ray Leonard.

A Hagler right uppercut staggered Leonard at the end of the fifth round. Leonard was almost helpless on the ropes. Ready to go. But the king who hadn't lost in 10 years still couldn't put away the glamour guy who had fought only two piddling "opponents" in six years.

If Leonard truly won—and this debate could go for ages—it was in large part because of the generalship in his corner.

He was working with the premier team of Angelo Dundee, Janks Morton and Dave Jacobs.

Coming down on a Caesars Palace elevator just before the fight, Dundee winked at a Miami acquaintance and said coolly, "We're going to clean this guy's clock."

When the rounds ended, the triad of the corner talked some more. Leonard listened, and delivered the best any 30-year-old so long out of the ring could possibly deliver.

The cornermen not only convinced Leonard that he could win but that he *was* winning.

I never thought so. I gave Hagler eight of the 12 rounds.

Hagler hurt Leonard several times. Leonard never hurt Hagler.

But that's show biz, and if ever a fight was pure show biz, from Leonard's craftiness to Hagler's rage, this was.

NO MAS, NO MAS

NOVEMBER 26, 1980

NEW ORLEANS—Swift as inflation, sweet as sugar, Ray Leonard ran rings around the bearded rakehell named Roberto Duran and reclaimed his World Boxing Council welterweight championship in the one way nobody though he would.

Duran quit.

Suddenly, starkly, barely four minutes after Leonard had mocked and ridiculed him with a rhumba and a shuffle in the seventh round, the passionately proud Panamanian threw up his hands in either disgust or pain.

He turned to walk back to his corner. Leonard rushed in and landed a left hook to Duran's side. Then referee Octavio Meyron of Mexico strode between them and made the end official at 2:44 of the eighth round.

"No mas, no mas, no more box," Meyron said Duran told him. I was sitting barely five feet from Duran's stunned corner when the single thing that couldn't possibly happen did.

"Why did he quit?" I asked Duran's 73-year-old co-trainer, Freddie Brown. "What did Roberto say to you?"

"He didn't say anything," Brown said, shaking his head. "He just quit."

There will be some fast hell raised about *this.*

The first public reaction will be that Duran chucked the fight to create a third and bigger rubber match. Even bigger than the first two that brought Duran some $10 million to Leonard's $17 million.

I don't know.

Only Duran's heart knows.

Until this thunderstruck evening in the Louisiana Superdome, there never was the slightest reason to doubt Duran's heart.

I tend to think that Duran quit as much from humiliation as pain. His soul must have shrunk when Leonard, the one man he seems to detest above all others, made fun of him in the seventh round.

"Do you still think you're a better man?" someone asked Duran when he reached his dressing room.

"A thousand times better," Duran said.

Strange, strange way to show it.

Leonard was just beginning a full takeover when Duran, who had swaggered into the ring smiling and spent most of the first three rounds grinning devilishly at Leonard, made his shocking decision.

This time, unlike Duran's victory in Montreal, Leonard set the tempo, skipping, jabbing, ducking, slugging, baffling Duran altogether.

I had Leonard ahead, five rounds to two, with one even, when the so-called Super Fight ended in a chaotic fizzle.

Duran had constantly referred to Leonard as a TV-created "baby." But those weren't rubber duckies Leonard was throwing at Duran. They were fists inside eight-ounce gloves, and they landed with such thudding regularity that Duran was well on his way to defeat long before he chose an easier termination.

Leonard was fighting *his* fight, not Duran's.

By the third round, Duran's smile had turned to a grim mask and Leonard was laughing. Sugar Ray took a Duran right hook in that round and laughed in Roberto's face.

It gets dreadfully lonesome in there when the man in front of you has a left hand on a swivel and a pair of rollerskates for feet.

The idea in any fight, as in most athletic contests, is to avoid direct confrontation with an opponent's strength. Leonard's game plan was easier to say than to execute. He was supposed to do just what you would do if you saw a large truck bearing down upon you: Get out of the way.

Duran originally planned a steady encirclement to his own left. That would maintain a suitable gap between himself and Leonard's jab. Then Duran would turn and bull in, all elbows and head.

Duran never could do it. Leonard made it too hard.

Most champions keep trying no matter how hard it gets.

Not Duran.

No mas, no mas.

ARMSTRONG'S GHOST STALKS ARGUELLO

NOVEMBER 14, 1982

The first man in 42 years to try to win four separate boxing titles suddenly saw that last man in front of him.

On a silken November Friday night in the Orange Bowl, Alexis Arguello faced the literally spitting image of Hammering Henry Armstrong of the 1930s.

Aaron Pryor turned into an all-too-live ghost of the old, perpetually moving Hammer.

Armstrong lost his 1940 bid to win a fourth crown. So did Arguello when Pryor, Armstrong's modern Xerox, sprang again and again for a technical knockout at 1:06 of the 14th round.

Not one of the estimated 23,800 viewers in the Orange Bowl could doubt from the opening minute that they were witnesses to a classic. At fourth round's end, The Associated Press' veteran boxing writer Ed Schuyler turned to a friend at ringside and said, "This may be the greatest fight I've ever seen even if they don't throw another punch all night."

Only two matches of recent history could hold a candle to the crackling express that junior-welterweight king Pryor rode to the finish in this Saturnalia of sight and sound:

• The 1975 Thrilla in Manila when a Joe Frazier drained from 13 tumultuous rounds could not answer the 14th-round bell against heavyweight champ Muhammad Ali.

• Or, maybe—*only maybe*—Roberto Duran's 1980 seizure of Sugar Ray Leonard's lightweight crown.

It was fitting, if unimportant in the larger context, that Armstrong and Ali and Duran and Leonard were all right there.

This Friday in the so-often-maligned old bowl was at once a

212

night for the ages and one that aged Arguello as nothing else in his 30 years ever had. The unstoppable Pryor finally left Arguello unconscious for minutes in which it seemed that he might not ever regain his feet.

Until that end so brutal that many turned away in horror, the night had turned the world's eyes again, through both HBO cable TV and closed circuit, toward a pulsating and picturesque Miami. A large part of the city for a few precious hours became a carefree carnival again without either the stigmatic label of crime or tedious political bickering. Magic came back to the Magic City.

It happened that way because 11 Latin-American businessmen believed that Miami would respond to the twin-siren call of gloves and glamour tied into the Armstrong saga.

Archivists may make only footnotes of these 11 names, but they are worth remembering: Walter Alvarez. Jorge Luis de Cardenas. Al Cardenas. Roberto Cambo. Dr. Tirso Del Junco. Manuel Gonzales. Pedro Lopez. Jose Arriola. John and Jaime Goudie. Pedro Nelson Rodriguez.

Alvarez put up the drive and ingenuity. The other 10 put up their money to join Top Rank as promoters.

This night, though, Pryor's was the only name that mattered.

Pryor's name.

And Armstrong's ghost.

Pryor became a soaring efflorescence who hardly even blinked at the best punches in the Arguello arsenal considered boxing's all-around best. No fighter who misses four of every five of his punches can go non-stop for 14 rounds, but Pryor did.

All the time, Pryor was coming, coming, coming.

Benny (Kid) Paret used to do this.

Once, I heard a man tell Miami Beach promoter Chris Dundee that Paret was catching an awful lot of punches. And Dundee replied, "Yeah, but he catches and comes home."

Paret died in the ring because he caught blows full-on. Pryor's out-of-ring biography indicates he is susceptible to more injury in social activity than fighting for cash purses. He's the only fighter who needs to wear a bulletproof vest *at home*.

Inside the ropes, though, Pryor attacks with such raging, side-to-side speed that he seldom absorbs any punch's full impact.

His corner attacks at the same time. At 1:10 of the 10th round, after trainer Panama Lewis had repeatedly charged referee Stanley Christodoulou with allowing Arguello to hit below the belt, the South African official half-ran across the ring to Lewis, who was pounding on the canvas in violation of the rules.

"Now, you cut that out." Christodoulou shouted, "or I will send you away from the corner yet!"

Lewis finally let up.

Neither Pryor nor Armstrong's ghost ever did.

A RAGING BULL IS NOT A HERO

JANUARY 8, 1981

When Jake LaMotta was doing time, a friend called me. "You want a column," he said. "You want to talk to Jake in jail?"

I did want to. But then my friend said, "You got to promise me one thing. You got to write nice things about Jake."

"Nice? About a guy convicted of selling a 14-year-old girl?"

He said, "Then the deal's off. If I take you out there and you write anything bad, Jake will kill me. He's the only guy I ever been afraid of."

The deal was off.

I thought about that during *Raging Bull,* the movie about LaMotta. I didn't go to see it for a while because I figured it would glorify Jake. Several people said it didn't. So I went.

It is some movie. *Rocky* was uplifting in its soaring flights of fantasy. *Raging Bull* is hard, brutal, masterfully shot in black and white, evoking a far more honest picture of the way boxing's people talk, which means every other word has four letters in it. But it was taken from Jake's own book. There is a certain element of sympathy there, as though saying, "This man was sick."

I can't say what he is now. What he was then was pure louse.

The movie has to stand on its own merits because most people under 40 don't even remember LaMotta. He was a barrel-shaped guy who held the middleweight championship from 1949 to 1951. He quit in '54. I saw Danny Nardico beat him almost senseless two years earlier in Coral Gables, and still Jake wouldn't go down.

Watching the movie, I also thought of Roberto Duran. LaMotta would never have turned and quit cold as Duran did in his second fight against Sugar Ray Leonard, no matter how badly he was hurt. But Duran wouldn't have thrown a fight as LaMotta did against Billy Fox in '47.

A lot of fight people forgave Jake for that. Even as mean-spirited as boxing is, though, it has a code, and the code says you don't brag about tanking. LaMotta did.

I have some trouble buying the movie scene that shows him crying after going into the water against Fox. Most wife-beaters aren't so sensitive about principle. Jake's wife Vikki used to show up now and then wearing purple welts under her makeup. "You know Jake," she would say. "He keeps me in stitches."

Another story came down about Jake after he quit and opened his bar on Miami Beach. A busted-out ex-champion of a lower division would come into the joint. Call him Billy. That's not his name. One night he told the bartender, "You better watch yourself, going into that till. Jake has some mirrors rigged up where he can see you from the office."

As the story goes, LaMotta found out what Billy had said. Jake was mad. He found Billy and asked him if he would like to pick up some money by driving his car to New York. Jake would pay all expenses and pay him a little extra.

"Sure," Billy said.

Jake gave Billy about an eight-hour headstart and then called the cops. He told them his car had been stolen. Billy was picked up heading north. Police laughed at his story. Billy finally talked them into calling Jake. "He'll tell you the truth," Billy said.

Jake answered the phone when the police telephoned. "Who?" he said. "Naw, I ain't seen Billy in months."

And Billy stayed right there in jail until he somehow convinced the law of the truth.

The world hasn't much conscience left. Sports has done its bit. We excuse some obscene conduct in the name of winning. That being so, a movie that falls even a shade short of painting LaMotta at his gutter worst may make a big man out of him again.

He shouldn't have to wear a hair shirt all his life for things he did a quarter-century ago. But he shouldn't be made a hero, either.

CHRIS DUNDEE RATES THE HEAVYWEIGHTS

FEBRUARY 6, 1979

Tenderly as a mother lowering her baby into a crib, Chris Dundee placed his 18-year-old poodle Brandy in the Bayshore Golf Club lobby.

"Been around 10,000 fighters," said Dundee, entering his 51st year in the most bestial of sports. "Never seen one as game as Brandy here. He's blind. His heart's bad. His liver's shot. Three times they almost pull the plug on him. But he always fights out of it."

Dundee tied Brandy's tiny leash to a chair-leg. "I'll be right back," he told the dog. "Just going for coffee."

Brandy could count on it.

Dundee is the antithesis of the movie prototype of the boxing mogul. He prizes his word. Countless plaques attest to that in his offices at Miami Beach Convention Center.

He lives by his wits while denying he has any. "I'm 72 years old," he said. "And I'm stupid. I should be a millionaire. In the 1930s, I was offered wrestling in the state of Florida for three hundred bucks. Turned it down. Liked boxing too much."

He doesn't like all *boxers*. He isn't wild about Muhammad Ali although his brother Angelo has trained him all 19 pro years.

When Ali was training for his rematch with Leon Spinks, Chris spotted him in New Orleans with a toothpick in his mouth. "That toothpick makes you look like a bum," Chris told Ali. "And you better get in shape or Spinks will whip your butt again."

Now, at the golf club, Dundee shook his head. "I'd have sworn Ali couldn't shadow-box 15 rounds, let alone beat Spinks like that," he said. "But Ali ain't going to quit. He'll keep fighting.

217

"He does some bad things. In Las Vegas he insulted Joe Louis. He goes too far."

A man at Bayshore asked Dundee to rate the 10 best heavyweights he had seen since he got into boxing in 1928.

"Ali's the best, no matter what," Dundee said. "I never saw Jack Dempsey fight. I did see Gene Tunney. But Ali and Rocky Marciano were the two best."

Dundee played the part of referee in Murry Woroner's computerized "alltime heavyweight championship tournament" a decade ago. The computer let Marciano win on a KO in the 13th round.

"That hurt Ali more than you know," Dundee said. "Rocky would have had to kill him to beat him."

Dundee ranked Tunney third. "The complete boxer. And Tunney could murder you with a right hand just below the heart.

"I make Louis fourth. Joe was a 'manufactured' fighter. His strength was his left jab. Who's to say the jab could have reached Ali? Joe Frazier would be fifth—all blood and guts."

Dundee had a surprise for No. 6. "Max Baer. Maybe the best ever if he hadn't liked women so much. One morning he calls me at home. Wants a woman. I say, 'Max, don't call me at home. Call me at the office.' And Max says, 'I can't wait, Chris.'"

From there the list blurs between George Foreman and Ezzard Charles and Jack Sharkey and Max Schmeling.

"Ali psyched out Foreman like he psyched out Sonny Liston. Charles was some beautiful boxer, only he was a natural light-heavyweight. Sharkey was underrated. Schmeling is a legend but who'd he ever beat besides Louis?"

Then Dundee excused himself. "I got to take Brandy home," he said. "Poor little thing."

Golf

THE GREATEST TOURNAMENT

APRIL 14, 1986

AUGUSTA, GEORGIA—It was, for all the right reasons, the greatest golf tournament ever played.

What more compelling figure than 46-year-old Jack Nicklaus, our most-loved sports hero of the last quarter-century, to re-Americanize the Masters?

What more searing test than one between the three best golfers of the last three generations?

Jack Nicklaus. Tom Watson. Seve Ballesteros. Throw into that cage of tigers: Tom Kite, whose lack of a major victory is difficult to comprehend; Greg Norman, Australia's Great White Shark; and Nicky Price, who just the day before had withered Augusta National with a record 63.

Score it Nicklaus 65–279, Kite 68–280, Norman 70–280, Ballesteros, 70–281, Price 71-282, Watson 71–283 for a sixth-place tie with Jay Haas.

I just hope America loved it on TV as much as Augusta did in person.

"Unbelievable," Nicklaus said of the massive crowd's response.

No one knows how massive the crowd was. Augusta National Golf Club's books are closed—even to Nicklaus.

"Deafening," he said of the gallery's clamor during the seven-under-par round that gave him a sixth Masters title. "It was so loud I didn't really have a clue what I was doing on the back side."

They knew.

He was making birdies on five holes down the backstretch and an eagle at the 15th, and winning the Masters by a stroke.

Maybe it was just heaven's way of repaying Nicklaus for the joy he has brought us in winning 18 professional majors. That's an incredible seven more than old Walter Hagen won against far poorer competition. That's nine more than Ben Hogan or Gary Player, 10 more than Watson, 11 more than Bob Jones or Harry Vardon.

For his innate class as much as his stroke-making genius, Nicklaus has lived in sports fans' hearts on a historic level with Ty Cobb, Babe Ruth, Joe Louis, Red Grange, Arnold Palmer and, yes, the Masters' own late Bob Jones.

But as a golfer, in all candor, he was just about dead and gone coming into this Masters.

Nicklaus almost agreed to that before he began his magnificent charge down the backstretch where your knees play castanets and every sapling looks the size of a tree and every trickle an ocean.

"It was written in Atlanta last Sunday that I was washed up," he said. "My friend John Montgomery put it on the fridge in our house here to kid me, and I sizzled. Actually, I almost agreed with it. I'm not as good as I was 10 or 12 years ago, but I know I can still play a little, and I wasn't going to quit the way I've been playing lately."

"Lately" was the past two years, since he won at his own course in Muirfield, Ohio, in 1984. It had been six years since he won his record 16th and 17th majors in the U.S. Open and PGA.

Until Sunday, the sweetest golf sight I ever saw was 40-year-old Nicklaus striding into the U.S. Open championship at Baltusrol for a fourth time.

This was better.

If there had been one golfer that people figured Sunday morning had the least chance among the top 15 Masters scorers at the end of three rounds, it would have been Nicklaus.

Julius Boros was 48 when he won the '68 PGA. How often do you believe in miracles?

"Even Jack would admit he's past his prime," said Kite, as heartbroken as Norman.

Yes, he is.

But for four precious hours, he found it all again.

Light a torch. Raise a toast to Jack Nicklaus.

You will never see the like of this again—unless Nicklaus does it.

No one, not even Palmer, ever captured the soul and admiration of a golf crowd as Nicklaus did Sunday.

"The funniest part was, I couldn't even see the finish of a lot of my shots," Nicklaus said. "I can't see that far any more."

He can see far enough. He can see inside himself.

IMAGINE ARNIE APOLOGIZING TO GOLF

JUNE 18, 1976

DULUTH, GEORGIA—Arnold Palmer has gone from hero to curio and it is the saddest thing in golf and sadder yet because Palmer in his pride rejects the inevitability that eventually the body simply cannot keep the mind's promises.

He is pushing 47. He is pushing himself even harder in his 24th consecutive U.S. Open Golf Championship. His breath explodes in a "whoof!" when humidity wraps him like a blanket on the way to a first-round score of 75 at Atlanta Athletic Club.

The heart twists to see him struggle like a tiger whose teeth are crumbling and eyes dimming.

Arnold Daniel Palmer *is* golf.

The other night, I heard Palmer utter perhaps the most touching sentence in sports since the crippled ex-Yankee Lou Gehrig stood in Yankee Stadium on July 4, 1939, and said, "Today I consider myself the luckiest man on the face of the earth."

He was accepting another of those innumerable awards golf rightfully keeps on giving him, and he said, as offhandedly as though discussing a putt that rimmed a hole, "I think about how little I really have done in golf."

How little he has done?

How little he has done!

The sentence is breathtaking in its humility.

Palmer did for golf what Edison did for illumination, what Salk did against polio, what Debs did for labor.

He took a second-rate spectator sport and hauled it center-stage on the strength of his will and the magic of his daring.

"The Lindbergh of the links," promoter Fred Corcoran called Palmer. So right: Palmer made golf fly.

He won the 1960 U.S. Open and finished second in four others. He won two British Opens and four Masters and made millionaires of dozens of other golfers.

How little he has done?

He could strike balls from briarpatches into cups, and putt on ice floes. And he never forgot a face or how to be courteous to the most obnoxious lout on the course.

And now he is No. 126 on tour.

His waist has thickened. He wears rimless glasses. The hair that once flew in the wind—like Willie Mays' cap skittering from his head at his height of speed—is gray and there is less of it.

He has not won a major tournament in a dozen years. "Can it have been that long?" he asks in disbelief.

Throngs around Palmer used to erupt in "Aaiiee!" Now they go "Oooooooo . . ." Ecstatic shrieks become droning groans. His galleries are conspicuously smaller. Like Legionnaires at conventions, the ranks of Arnie's Army thin by the year.

"Still, it's amazing," says Tom Weiskopf. "When a crowd catches Arnie, he comes out with ball-point-pen marks all over his arms and his shirts. I couldn't live with that. Arnie thrives on it."

He used to thrive on putts.

"Now . . ." and he paused at the suggestion of inner fear, ". . . now I'm just trying to get the ball up there close . . ."

Thus, the agonistic turning of a hero into a curio.

But the inside, the core, the most important part of a hero, remains. Who but a hero, after all he has done, could say something like that?

"I think about how little I really have done in golf."

That is more than humility. That is heroism. That is Arnold Palmer.

HONOR LIVES!

JUNE 14, 1982

Inversely, that ruckus about pro golfer Curtis Strange abusing a volunteer scorer and a photographer tells the sorry tale of pro sports more vividly than a safetyman crippling a receiver or a baseball player giving a crowd the bird.

Strange's outburst at Arnold Palmer's Bay Hill Classic in Orlando—obscenely berating both a female official and a cameraman—would rate only passing mention in any other sport. But Palmer threw a justifiable fit in a letter to Commissioner Deane Beman, and Strange's own tour companions are now shouting "Amen!" to Palmer's rage.

"This is a gentleman's game," Fuzzy Zoeller said. "Our players should show more discipline." Zoeller suggested "sending them home for a couple of big tournaments."

Envision such peer reaction in, say, tennis, where John McEnroe curses more officials in 15 minutes than the entire golf troupe does in 15 years. You may take men's heads off or berate honest zebras in football, baseball, basketball, hockey or soccer with no more outcry than an amused giggle.

The mere fact of pro golfers so chastising one of their own underlines a truth that should be embossed in gold: Golf towers as pro sports' last barrier against uncontrolled boorishness.

"A gentleman's game" would come across as hopelessly old-fashioned in any sport except golf, whose practitioners even call fouls on themselves. Witness Tom Kite facing a tap-in putt in the 1978 Hall of Fame Classic at Pinehurst and inadvertently moving his ball one-quarter inch. He penalized himself a stroke that cost him a tie with Tom Watson.

Damon Runyon once wrote of a lovable crook, "He is opposed to lawbreaking, but he is not bigoted about it." Golfers *are,* and proud of it.

Here, now, comes the old question. Should we ask more of sports than we do of the world at large?

Forgive a small man climbing a large soapbox to yell, "Yes!"

Yes, because sports command a unique forum in our society.

How many baseball players even shrug when a Garry Templeton makes an obscene gesture to a crowd? Defensive ends are cheered for spearing men helpless on the ground. Hockey cast off basic decency decades ago. It remained only for Conn Smythe, the old Toronto Maple Leaf owner, to articulate hockey's philosophy: "If you can't beat them in an alley, you can't beat them on the ice." Soccer and basketball have degenerated into travesties of sportsmanship.

Tragically, the same way one lawless day in a city wipes out 10,000 lawful ones, all of tennis' honorable Arthur Ashes and Stan Smiths and John Newcombes cannot make up for one McEnroe.

Cable TV's onsurge means sports' forum will grow ever larger. Golf never will take any TV prizes because its panoramic spendor is impossible to compress into a box, but this sport takes all awards for inner ethics.

Others excuse their excesses by blaming those of fans. Pro golfers reject that cop-out. Hale Irwin said of one unruly crowd, "If they pay their money, they can do what they want. But that doesn't give us the right to act in kind."

Strange's tantrum at Orlando, however inexcusable, would not have raised an eyebrow on any turf but golf's. The reaction of his contemporaries illustrate golf's code better than anything could.

GOLF, WHY DOST THOU STING?

JUNE 10, 1962

I have a problem. Its name is golf. It baffles me, frustrates me, defeats me. I was never any Norman Vincent Peale, but golf is turning me into a hopeless churl. I am completely and inextricably hooked.

You think I exaggerate? Then you do not understand the depth of my misery.

It is not as though I am the world's worst athlete. Maybe I never won a decathlon championship, but I played tailback and shortstop at the Y, and ping-pong at the Variety Club, and I am pretty slick with a hoe in a garden. I couldn't be this bad at golf. But I am.

Explain it to me. I am on a health program. I get plenty of sleep, like Ohio Fats Nicklaus. I practice, like Arnold Palmer. I squeeze little rubber balls and eat proteins, like Gary Player. I read instructional pamphlets. I line up golf balls in the living room and putt until I am cross-eyed.

I feel I am the strongest man in the world until I step to the first tee. Then the strength deserts me. The golf sticks turn into instruments of Satan. The swing that impressed me as so resplendent on the driving range turns into a tragic parody. Some people snigger. The nicer ones turn away.

I have tried all the woods off the tee, and I might as well be using a baseball bat. I had to give up using woods in the fairway. Maintenance men were muttering about trenches.

Water ordinarily doesn't bother me. I don't hit the ball hard enough to roll it down a bank into the water. But on one water hole at Plantation, I had to borrow three golf balls. Partners come equipped when I play.

Another stands 30 feet in front of me when I hit in the fairway. When I censure him for the breach of etiquette, he says it is the safest place on the course.

"I don't understand you," says still another. "The closer you get to the pin, the harder you hit the ball." My chip shots take off like Faith 7. Every trap holds a magnet for me. If they ever shoot me to the moon, I am 3 to 5 to land in a trap.

On the green at last, I remember how Hogan used to line up putts in the Masters. He always chain-smoked while computing distance and rub. I bend down, study the contours and light one cigarette after another. Sometimes the ball winds up in the next fairway. I am the only man who ever lost a ball putting.

I guess I'll keep trying. But don't expect me to be happy about it. I hate you, Nicklaus. Drop dead, Palmer. Get lost, Player. What right have you got to hit a golf ball like that?

Olympics

L.A. DOES IT UP RIGHT

JULY 29, 1984

LOS ANGELES—Sport sent a message to the world.

In hopeful symbolism, church bells tolled open the most ambitious athletic event in the history of what we euphemistically call civilization.

The message was simpler than the opening ceremony of this 23rd Olympics. The message also is just as perilously fragile as the fate of these Summer Games.

But it beamed out with pristine clarity for 3½ heart-pumping hours on an afternoon born in heaven—flags swirling, humans laughing and cheering and weeping for sheer joy in a Los Angeles Memorial Coliseum bright as Joseph's coat.

Sport was telling mankind that men can co-exist. A track lane can be a road to amity. Peace can rest on parallel bars. Even a punch on the nose can be delivered in brotherhood. Sweat is capable of nourishing the olive branch.

Never mind that Russia and a raft of other Red nations were missing. The joint's hopping.

Anybody whose heart didn't jam his throat for this party ought to be checked for a pulse. Norman Rockwell would have been stunned brushless. Part of L.A. actually lost power during the show. Probably blew its mind.

For one afternoon, we were able to sit and believe that nations would never murder again.

The opening ceremony is the emotional Mt. Everest of sport. Never has there been one as kaleidoscopically overpowering, as uplifting to eye and ear and heart as this one.

Not in the sombreroed gaiety of Mexico City in 1968. Not in the Teutonic rigidity of Munich in '72, nor the exuberance of Montreal in '76. And surely not in Moscow in '80, when Lenin Stadium had 16,000 performers but very little of the free world marching.

Grandeur marked the message: Gloves over genocide. Canoes over cannons. Backstroking over bombs. Marathons over missiles.

The church bells reminded us to pray that the Olympic spirit lasts as long and as vibrantly as it whooshed into the consciousness of 93,000 humans in the Coliseum and another 2¹/₂ billion watching on television worldwide.

History says it can't happen. Saturday, before TV sets from Van Nuys to Vietnam, was a time to believe it can.

Terrorism had seemed to be edging closer almost by the day—that McDonald's massacre near San Diego, a motorist mowing down sidewalkers right in Westwood the night before the ceremonies.

But sunlight and sensation and a million chords and colors made it difficult Saturday to believe that Olympism was born in cheating and lives in a steroid miasma.

Greek athletes rounding the track had heard the story of the very first Olympics of mythology.

Back before parking lots took every drachma you had, just to rest a chariot, a mean king offered his beautiful daughter for marriage.

There was one catch. She had to elope. And every time she tried, the king would chase the would-be bridegroom and kill him.

Up finally popped a brainy charioteer named Pelops. He paid off the king's chauffeur to weaken the axle of the royal wagon. This the driver did, and leaped to safety before the king was thrown out and killed.

Pelops then did away with his accomplice. He took the lovely lady as his own and started the Olympics as a reward to the gods for their generosity.

I suppose you could call that democracy.

And so it was, Saturday, that Andorra, a cluster of Pyreneean hills peopled by only 32,000, got to parade just as smartly as representatives of a billion Chinese.

Souls soared and the meanest-spirited of men found their cheeks wet.

My God, if only the world will remember.

FUN AND GAMES IN MEXICO CITY

OCTOBER 19, 1968

MEXICO CITY—The wife of an American television official left a wake-up call for 7:30 a.m. with a hotel switchboard here this week. She awakened at 8, on her own, went into a snit at not being called, and dialed the operator to demand the reason.

"Why did you not call?" she harangued. "You know I left a call for 7:30. This is inexcusable!"

"Ah, Senora," the operator said smoothly, "if you will just hang up the telephone we will be most happy to call you."

That stunningly blase retort summed up the Mexican attitude toward the Olympic Games now approaching midpoint. Mexicans are proud of their 150 million dollars worth of construction and the Games are being run off promptly and efficiently. But around the edges the attitude is still "manana."

In our billet in the Olympic Village, we had two tiny bathrooms for eight people, with an acute shortage of hot water. The other day we returned to the dormitory to find one of the bathrooms reduced to rubble by a pick-wielding plumber probing for what he thought was a defective pipe. Turned out he tore up the wrong bathroom, leaving us with approximately none.

"Oh!" cried one of the six Italians in our section. "They are destroying our home!"

The plumber's answer to this was the typical two first fingers held about a half-inch apart. This means "Poco" or, freely translated, "Just a little longer and everything will be all right, Senor." But the plumber hasn't been back and the bathroom remains another pocket of frustration among the thousands surrounding the Games.

The government thought it had the crime problem licked for the two-week Olympiad when it rounded up 1,125 known undesirables and jailed them for the duration. Obviously some escaped the dragnet. Many visitors have entered the main stadium with their wallets and left without them. Newsmen are cautioned to keep their hands on their press badges at all times.

Will Grimsley, an Associated Press writer who is accustomed to the gentle ways of his native Tennessee, propped up his foot for the usual one-peso (about eight cents) shoeshine outside the village one afternoon. "For two pesos," the shoeshiner volunteered, "I will make your shoes like a mirror."

Big spender Grimsley decided he would spring for the 16-center. A few minutes later he displayed his gleaming shoes to a co-worker and told him the story.

"Oh my gosh," said his friend. "You didn't fall for that one, did you?"

"Fall for what?" Grimsley asked, puzzled.

"That two-peso polish that makes your shoes 'like a mirror' has acid in it," the friend advised him. "Check them in two hours."

Grimsley did. His shoes had virtually disintegrated on his feet.

There is this thing, too, about finding royalty in the strangest places here.

Prince Philip visited the British athletes' cafeteria and stood in line for his steak and potatoes just like a commoner.

Prince Barnard of Holland paid a visit to the local calabozo where an old friend was being held for shooting a man after an argument over a traffic accident. Prince Barnard is a former chairman of the International Equestrian Committee. His jail-bound pal was Mexican Gen. Humberto Mariles, who won a Gold Medal in equestrians in London in 1948.

Mariles said bitterly: "If I were only free, I would have been proud to train the Mexican equestrians." He was not freed because of wave of protests, not the least of which came from the family of the dear departed.

It isn't always fun, but the Games go on. That is the important thing. For all the jokes, the Games go on. Mexico City is laughing loudest of all.

MURDER
IN MUNICH

SEPTEMBER 6, 1972

MUNICH—Terrorism came to the Olympics in bloody irony.

It was visited upon Jews whose persecution was reaching its pre-World War II heights the last time Germany was an Olympic host.

That was 1936, long before these athletes were born.

Thirty-six years went by in a flash of doom.

Horribly, incomprehensibly, some here acted as though it had not happened at all.

An Arab attack upon the Israeli athletic delegation turned what was originally designed as a movement toward world brotherhood into another microcosm of the world as it is—rent and raging, an armed camp.

Some $700 million laid out by West Germany to show the face of the "new" country were pouring down the drain in a torrent of arguments that seemed fairly petty until one turned into death.

"Welcome to the political Olympics," American lightweight James Busceme had said after losing a boxing match. He thought politics cost him the decision.

Now it is costing much more.

German police surrounded the Olympic village late Tuesday. Earlier in the day one could walk close to Israeli quarters where Arabs held hostages.

There I met British wrestling coach Stan Bissell. I thought he knew about the death of Moshe Weinberg, who coached Israeli wrestlers. Bissell had known about the trouble in general but no particulars.

He turned ashen-faced when I told him of the death of Weinberg, who had tried to hold a dormitory door against the Arabs.

"Oh no!" Bissell said. He and Weinberg had been close.

Troop-carriers dumped out load after load of police as we talked.

The eeriest charade went on just below us, near Israeli quarters. Sunbathers lay on the banks of a tiny lagoon. A blonde in a bikini sat and smoked and read, oblivious to the crowds above her outside the village fence. Across the lagoon, a tall man waded unconcernedly at water's edge.

Another gruesome contrast appeared in the huge press center, or "pressezentrum." Manfred Shreiber, president of the Munich police, had come to brief newsmen from most of the 122 nations competing here.

Just before Shreiber took the microphone, decks of TV sets hung throughout the center depicted a rowing match. It was like the Poughkeepsie regatta being conducted beside a battleground.

Police here wear no guns. That has been their theme since the opening of the most widely seen Olympiad ever. Police have been unfailingly polite to visitors. They remained so Tuesday. But they wore puzzled looks and were apologetic in having to turn back those who approached the Israeli residence.

"Nein, nein," they said with smiles. One, with a small command of English, said to me: "Not this way. Perhaps another way around."

In the rear of the village, athletes were told they would have to climb the fence to enter or leave. Some clambered up and went on to practice their sports.

I stopped a Kenyan athlete and asked him what was happening inside the village. "No politics," he said. "We speak no politics." He ran on.

Munchners holding children wandered as close to the scene of crisis as police would permit. German teenagers flew down walkways on bicycles. The curious came in ever larger numbers.

Few had known of the Arab attack before attending a press conference for America's Mark Spitz at 9 a.m.

Spitz, who won a record seven gold medals in swimming, did know. The mustached American refused to go to a microphone because, a translator said, he felt safer sitting in a crowd. His answers were cryptic. Spitz is Jewish.

Communication has been a problem all along. Malaysians

and West Germans swung at each other in field hockey. Fencers exchanged insults. Yugoslavs and Cubans—Communist countries of different philosophies—fought in a water polo game. Drug charges were flung about in swimming and pistol shooting.

Larry Black, the Miami Killian High graduate, referred to Valeri Borzov as a "clown" after the Russian won the 100 meters and 200 meters, beating Black in the 200.

And at night, the 20th Olympics—perhaps the future of all Olympics—hung in the balance.

To many it was far more personal than merely the Olympics.

A Chicago columnist heard of the Arab attack early in the day. His first move was to drive to Dachau, the notorious old concentration camp only 11 miles from Munich.

"I thought, under the circumstances, it would be a good day to visit Dachau," he said.

He went to Dachau, and wept.

MONTREAL '76:
A House Is
Not a Home

JULY 22, 1976

MONTREAL—*Bonjour, ma chere femme:*
Just a touch of old Francais there, baby, to let you know I am really with it in the Paris of North America.

Cherie, you state that you wonder how I am faring at the Olympics. That is something of a long story but not, I fear, as long as the Olympics.

For myself, there is good news and bad news.

The good news is that Montreal must be the most beautiful city in the hemisphere.

The bad news is that I am not quartered in the city.

Most of *les journalistes* – that's us, sweets—are based at the University of Montreal.

But what's to complain? A dormitory room costs only $14 a day—about $1 per square foot. As Tom Callahan of the *Cincinnati Enquirer* says, "Mahatma Gandhi wrote some of his best stuff in a room smaller than this." Must have been writing on the head of a pin.

But the neighborhood around the dorm is picturesque, which it should be after 334 years. We especially enjoy looking at the old stone houses when I take my rat out for a walk.

It could be worse. Blackie Sherrod of *The Dallas Times-Herald* booked a hotel room downtown through COJO (*Comite d'Organisation des Jeux Olympiques,* there I go again, bonzo!) and found out he was paying $50 a day for a room in a Vietnamese bordello. He didn't pay any attention when the cab driver laughed when he delivered him there.

Then, the first morning Blackie got up, he couldn't even unlock his door from the inside. He climbed out a window to shout for his landlady, or whatever they call them here. The walkway was freshly painted. Blackie's the only writer in Montreal with purple toenails.

Dragon Lady solved Blackie's problem. She had the bolt taken off Blackie's door, meaning he had no lock at all, which was less than ideal considering the hallway traffic.

But this is a great spot for nonsmokers and nondrinkers of martinis. They charge $1 for cigarettes in competition sites where "No Smoking" signs are posted. A lot of customers have become sudden non-smokers.

Also, we now know another way Montreal plans to recover some of its $1.5 billion nut. In the Main Press Centre in the Place des Jardins downtown, they charge $2.50 plus 12 percent automatic tip—$2.80 for a martini.

The other side of that coin is, Montrealers may be the politest folks in the world. They patiently direct even the ugliest Americans. Of course, there's always an exception. I asked a lady at the information desk of the Main Press Centre downtown for some copypaper. She said archly, "We only furnish information."

I said, "OK, I'd like some information on where to get some typing paper."

She said, "We do not have that information."

Guess you've been hearing about Montreal Mayor Jean Drapeau. He's the bird who conceived the 1976 Olympics for here and almost blew it at the last minute. By now, though, they've learned not to sell old Jean short. He's a plump little rascal who created Expo out of sewage from the St. Lawrence River. Pretty strong cat for a kid whose mother Berthe told him he was too weak physically to become a doctor. For 16 years as mayor he's been working from 5 a.m. to midnight, six or seven days a week.

As they say in the states, you pay your money and you take your choice. Drapeau chose to be 100 percent politician. In 1968, the year after Expo, he scheduled an anniversary blowout for Expo officials. A few hours before the first cork was popped he remembered his son was getting married that day.

That is what I call a working Jessie, even if his three kids don't recognize him.

Drapeau has the sense of humor of an undertaker. At least Lord Killanin, the boss of the International Olympic Committee, is a jolly one. After all those countries quit the Olympics, Lord Killanin said, "Speaking as an Irishman and not for the 100, I wish that a few more nations would drop out—so we'd have a better chance of winning something."

Yes, *ma cherie*, things just keep happening around Parc Olympique. Did I tell you about the reporter who went up to the top of the main stadium for a story on the unfinished construction? A 100-ton crane fell on him.

He was pretty lucky. He is in Royal Victoria Hospital—in Rooms 101, 102, 103, and 104.

> *Avec mon amour le plus tendre.*
> Edwin

P.S.—That is "With all my tenderest love" in the Francais. Dig?

SNAPSHOTS
OF SARAJEVO

FEBRUARY 21, 1984

SARAJEVO, YUGOSLAVIA—Things I will remember from the 14th Winter Olympics:

Cold breakfast and warm soda pop.

Out-of-school kids sledding down farm hills in more delight than all the tourists' thousands of dollars could bring them.

Scott Hamilton's size 5½ shoes—about the same as Garo Yepremian's—and the $600 his skates cost him.

Phil and Steve Mahre finally showing what they could do in "midget" slalom after giant-slalom efforts that would shame amateurs.

The wrenchingly loveliest moment of all, when Sarajevo Mayor Ugljesa Uzelac simply drew the Olympic flag to him and kissed it while 50,000 opening-ceremony watchers in Zveco Stadium went bananas.

The *Dr. Zhivago* landscape around this modern airport.

Every adult Serbo-Croatian smoking endlessly.

Wondering why East Germany even bothers to call it sport when that nation refuses to send athletes who aren't considered sure to win medals.

Cleaning women working in men's public restrooms without paying the slightest attention to anything around them.

The soul-lifting wonder on 20-year-old "unknown" Debbie Armstrong's face when she gold-plated the giant slalom.

Bob (*Chicago Tribune*) Verdi's line when a waitress in a sub-zero restaurant asked him how much milk he wanted with his coffee–"Two lumps, please."

Feeling so safe in a town of a half million that people don't even have to feel for their wallets every 30 seconds.

Bill Johnson, The Olympian Without a Doubt, calling his downhill shot time after time and then firing it, *bull's-eye!*

British bobsled brakeman Mark Tout holding up a sign, "Hi

Mum," at the finish, and then reversing sides to send the same message in Serbo-Croatian.

So many beautiful children here. If only, like kittens, they didn't have to grow up.

A train-load of passengers in grim, northerly Zagreb never once changing expressions as a stereo player carried through the depot by an American blared three lively tunes from *The Beach Boys' Greatest Hits.*

USOC President William Simon's interminable answers to even the shortest questions.

Crowds as great as 80,000 braving the worst traffic jam of the Olympics and then slogging five miles through the snow of Igman Plateau to watch the 90-meter ski jump, visual king of all these Games.

The local name for dry mouth caused by overheated rooms, also adopted by athletes to denote choking under pressure—"Croat Throat."

Slavs nonchalantly chug-a-lugging 26-proof beer and then chasing it with 120-proof plum-brandy slivovitz.

The last day, and a Sarajevo radio station nostalgically beaming out *Oh Bring Back My Bonnie to Me.*

And Other Trips

RACE FOR THE ELUSIVE 3-PRONG PLUG

APRIL 23, 1985

My most exciting moment in sports? Easy. Los Angeles, 1979. A Dodger fan freaked out and threw a cupful of beer into my friend's computer after the Yankees won their third straight game in the World Series. The explosion when the suds hit the computer made a liar out of Texas Instruments, which had named it the Silent 700.

Most frustrating moment? Simple. Sarajevo, 1984. Yugoslavia was buying extra electricity for its Winter Olympics, and the current went up and down like a candle's flame. The power-surges—spikes, we call them in the biz—caused two fatalities right in my dorm room. Killed a couple of TRS80 Model 100s. Left them like dried skulls beside the trail of the new sports journalism.

You can see sports doesn't always have that much to do with sports any more for some of us. Electronics took over our dodge a decade ago when computers replaced typewriters.

Now, instead of talking touchdowns and women and forehands, it's text streams and word wrap and formats. Imagine Pete Rose out there discussing *motherboards* with umpires.

Up to a few years ago, when somebody asked you how long it took to write a column, you figured how long it took for your back to give out on the little green Olivetti. Computers do it all now, but it's a race to get it into the host computer before a fuse blows. And they thought *sports* was full of jargon.

All the games changed when Mr. Tandy went in for Mr. Royal, when Texas Instruments took over for Texas Leaguers. The circuit clout gave way to the short circuit. Typewriter ribbons just wore out. Computer memories *blow* out. That's when curses replace cursors.

The other day out West, a sports writer in his early 40s asked one in his 20s if he had a carbon of something good he had just written.

"What's a carbon?" the younger man asked. If I'm lying I'm dying.

Sports journalism went from bawdy to baudy when bytes took over for bogeys. Never mind Derbies, I'm hot on delimiters. Remember when K stood for a strikeout by one character, instead of 1,000 characters of computer memory?

Handing copy to Western Union was an adventure, but nothing like the high of dialing an 800 number to the host computer, first making sure the DC modem is plugged into the RJ11 and the modular jack.

I get the feeling that Kirk Gibson and Joe Montana and Marvelous Marvin Hagler and Bernhard Langer and John McEnroe are beginning to lose something in the translation. It doesn't exactly put a roar in your prose, crawling around on hands and knees looking for a three-pronged plug. But electronics is the new name of the game. It only changes for newer computers.

Growing up, my hero was Don Shula. Now it's Thomas Edison. Forget the infield fly rule, let's talk interfacing.

Once I thought I'd give anything for another of those three-day bus-rides with Cassius Clay from Miami to Massachusetts in '65. Now I would sell my mother's picture for a wall-plug.

Dick Anderson intercepting four passes against the '73 Steelers? I would blot it out of my mind for a promise that never again would I have to chase down another modem at a Final Four.

You'll drink to that? Name your poison, pal. J&B or IBM?

ONE AND ONLY WIMBLEDON

JULY 4, 1984

Words lurch out of his Irish-white face like wind-up soldiers.

His left hand, the one that turns a British prime minister's salary to pocket change merely by propelling 2-ounce tennis balls, joins the zigzag flight of his voice. Words and hands stop and restart in semispastic concert.

"I would like, ah . . ." One hand inches to his nose.

". . . to . . . some day . . . ah . . ." A finger darts from nostril to forehead, chalky as skimmed milk.

". . . enjoy playing this, ah, game . . ." The finger pulls at his nose and finally invades it, a bony Magellan exploring a physiognomic Pacific.

John Patrick McEnroe is picking his nose at Wimbledon.

An official gestures: *No more questions.* McEnroe seems lost without an umpire or linesman to badger. How can a 24-year-old earning $2 million annually be so ill at ease, so downright miserable? He would give wrong directions to an ambulance if it carried a tennis official, but he earnestly tries to please in interviews.

McEnroe ducks suddenly through a side door of the pressroom, a child fleeing the principal's office.

"Camera!" a supervisor shouts. "Somebody has a camera!" He rushes from seat to seat among newsmen, all holding palms upward. "Do you have a camera? Do you? You must not have a camera in here!"

Finally satisfied that no film but Wimbledon's very own will frame these magical moments, certified and sanctioned by the All England Lawn Tennis and Croquet Club, the supervisor signals in another player for another interview.

Cramped in a subterranean mix of comic strip and shrine with the insecure angel/devil/patriot/pain-in-the-rear McEnroe, one is entitled to wonder, "This is *Wimbledon?*"

This bloody well *is* Wimbledon, which is to tennis what the Vatican is to Roman Catholicism. Queen Mary so loved it when she visited the All England Lawn Tennis and Croquet Club, she embarrassed her hosts by staying until the last tea bag went limp.

The croquet disappeared somewhere. Lawn tennis, never.

Wimbledon as an *idea*, as much as a tradition, prospers while England's old legs totter. Wimbledon at age 107 steams on, unique, as the boll weevils of life gnaw at London's very vitals— unemployment, underproduction, inflation and labor strife. Not even the scrofulous rebelliousness of young players gone mad as millionaire churls can impede Wimbledon's success. Just last year, it bestowed a record surplus of more than $2 million on the United Kingdom's lower tennis echelons, a yearly gift to the improvement of British tennis that abjectly fails to make British tennis great, or even especially good: No male Briton has won at The Big W since bulldoggish Fred Perry in 1936.

You wonder why Wimbledon even bothers to sail on, an anachronism of propriety against professional tennis' mush-rooming greed and bitchiness. What sustains the steel of authority in this crosshatch of forehands and frenzy, caviling and cheering, backhands and booing, rhubarb and royalty where the Duke and Duchess of Kent are almost daily communicants and even Queen Elizabeth has been known to drop in?

You find out fast.

It sails on because, in The Fortnight of The Big W, England again can bestride the world. It works because *Wimbledon* works so hard, digging in as England's last edge over all the evils besetting this tiny country.

And the All England damned well means to keep it that way, despite intrusions both economic and fleshly, that have turned almost every other mammoth sports event into chaotic asylums run by the inmates. Unlike those others, Wimbledon can still say No! to the 20th Century and get away with it:

One minor Wimbledon official is kicked out when found monitoring the Ladies' dressing room through a one-way mir-ror. Another official—sad to relate, an American newspaper-man moonlighting as a courtside rules enforcer—is sent packing after pinching females bottoms in one of those daily crowd-crushes out by the champagne stand.

Well, Wimbledon did not get to be sport's *grande dame* by saying "yes" to just anyone.

Ask Ted Tinling. He has heard both answers. He has lived both ways, at Wimbledon and away from Wimbledon. Believe Ted Tinling, *at* is better.

"I suffered terribly in the 28 years I was away," says Tinling, now 73 and back as player-management liaison. He was banished for nearly three decades on accusations of "putting sin and vulgarity" into the Big W when he designed "too transparent" lace panties as part of the 1949 uniform of player Gussie Moran.

He was only trying to liven up the scenery, which surely can stand it, with its endlessly green and mauve background and eye-glazing rows of hedges stretching forever, and players commanded to wear predominantly white.

Understand this, to understand the intensity of Tinling's longing for Wimbledon all the years he spent away. Wimbledon stands for orderliness in a disorderly world. History will remember it that way, even as sullenly as some of its playing heroes suffer that condition: McEnroe reacts so vilely on no less than 13 courtside decisions in a semifinal match against Australia's Rod Frawley two years ago, even the future Princess Diana departs the Royal Box.

But Tinling was remembering the true innards of Wimbledon each Christmas during his exile from tennis' great green theater. He would spend those times tormenting himself over memories of the warm and nostalgic teas that the Wimbledon staff would have. And on D-Day (the Allied invasion of France in '44, when Tinling worked as a lieutenant-colonel in British intelligence)," My first thought in that brutal weather was, 'Thank God there is no Wimbledon this year.' "

Wimbledon gets to people that way. It is as much an *attitude* as an event.

Scenic, it is not. Even the famous Members Enclosure rates a zero for aesthetics, if a 10 for exclusivity. It is open only to Wimbledon's constitutionally limited membership of 375. Three hundred of these are men; England yields to no one in male chauvinism. Nobody seems exactly sure how the regular members are selected (Evert Lloyd and Borg still are only honorary members even after eight championships between them, but at least one newspaperman is a full-fledged member), except that neither sheer royalty nor sheer tennis ability will swing it. The single blanket assumption one may make on Wimbledon's members is that they are "for" tennis, free-handed but not wastrels, sociable but not drunken, congenial but not comedic.

The main thing anyone who has not visited Wimbledon should know is, it is nothing like as pompous as it is so frequently painted.

On my first trip, in 1982, I am as intimidated as others by these accusations of officiousness. I begin to buy the feeling when I see a pressroom guard standing tall, shoulders arched as though clipped by a giant clothespin, like those forbidding statues down by Buckingham Palace that seem to leap up every time a man waves a sword or pulls a trigger.

The guard is Sgt. Major William Thompson.

"How do you do, sir!" Sgt. Major Thompson says in a subdued roar.

"Howdy."

A flick of bewilderment, and then he stands even more stiffly for the moment. He relaxes day by day. First, a painful, "Yes, ah, how do, sir!" And finally, by Fortnight's end, "Ah, ho ho! Howdy!" (Smile.)

By that time, I am actually speaking English. I am not only tucking in the tailends of sentences that usually trail off, southern-style. I have even bought a little tweed cap on sale for $12 at Harrods, the humongous department store.

Wimbledon's atmosphere thus is not only contagious, but marvelously casual when not in official session. Other than The Fortnight, Wimbledon comes off as a breeze for anyone not obsessed with seeing the tennis. Sightseers have pretty much the run of the 42-acre club except for the last week every June and first week every July.

I don't realize this until my wife joins me in London the week after Wimbledon ends. She wants to take some pictures. We call the museum, and the lady there says come on out. I figure my wife will get to see the museum and nothing more.

Walking directly in from the street, about 30 minutes by subway from central London, we find Wimbledon wide-open. Not a dirty champagne glass has been picked up after the gastronomic orgy of 2,000 cases of bubbly and whisky, 66,000 pints of beer and ale, 300,000 hot drinks, 126,000 ice creams, 56,000 sandwiches, 14,000 pork pies and other treats.

The Centre Court grass, nursed 351 days a year as carefully as the royal baby, looks as though armies have marched over it. Gone is the almost luminescent green of opening day, grass-blades zapped by thousands of strokes.

Two laborers appear as we stroll into the stadium. This, while 13 per cent of Greater London is unemployed, and strikes bedevil railways both overground and underground, electricians, hospitals, coal mines. The Thames River was polluted so long, it is only now yielding salmon again. Even the queen's bedroom is unsafe from prowlers or Fleet Street's rabid tabloids. GIVE HER A CUDDLE, PHILIP, one paper urges the queen's husband, suggesting he return to the royal boudoir.

In this land of crisis layered atop crisis, we later find the two laborers sound asleep, smack in the Royal Box.

We stroll into the box still littered with invitations and place-cards.

"Hullo," a workman says drowsily. "We're only taking a bit of a nap."

He peers around for bosses. Seeing none, he chats on.

"You're not English, are you? Oh, Florida?" He winks at his co-worker. "I wish we were in Sanibel, with something doing all the time. So bloody dull here."

Pause. "But it does have a certain air about it, eh, mate?"

Amen, and double-amen, when the flags fly ever higher over Wimbledon's surgically manicured (3/16-inch) lawns, where even royalty is told when to sit and when to sip.

". . . Afternoon tea will be served between 4.15 p.m. and 5.15 . . ." the pertinacious invitations to the royal family declare. ". . . It is requested that movement in and out of the royal box be restricted either to the completion of a match, or if during play, the period when players change ends."

CLURE MOSHER WENT FIRST-CLASS

JULY 27, 1966

I thought and thought about how to start this, and finally said, the hell with trying to be clever, just go ahead and say what kind of guy my friend Clure Mosher was. In the kind of words he liked. Short and blunt.

Mosher's death the other day hit me a double jolt because I was supposed to spend next week with him in New York. He wasn't supposed to die of a stroke in his 40s. Mosher never did what he was supposed to. Usually just the opposite.

His invitation was typical. "Come on up and stay with me," he said. "I've got a whole *bleeping* suite at the Drake Hotel." He paused. "You don't think I'd stay in just one room, do you?"

Not a chance. Mosher went first class or not at all. When he left Miami's Channel 7 for New York sportscasting, he hooked into so much more money—he was making more than any of today's Dolphins, which is not a usual thing in media—he figured he needed a business manager.

The manager lasted three months. "He only gave me $50 a week walking-around money," Mosher complained. "I could charge anything I wanted, but that wasn't the point. You know I can't walk around with just $50 on me."

One of his first moves in New York was to rent two apartments and use them as one. A friend told him he was paying more rent than Bobby Kennedy was on his Long Island estate.

"Well," Mosher said, "sure."

A little later, Radio Winer, the Miami Beach restaurant proprietor and Mosher's best pal, wondered about the piano he had loaned Mosher for his home here.

"It's all right," Mosher told Winer from New York. "I brought the piano with me."

Mosher was a big man physically. He played center for the Pittsburgh Steelers before he got into TV. His heart was bigger than he was. He would give you whatever he had on him, and expect you to reciprocate.

That was how it was in his odd traveling circle. Show-biz celebrities, pro football owners and priests, bookmakers and loansharks, automobile distributors and horse-trainers, jockeys and college and pro coaches and athletes. And some gangsters who didn't flaunt it, but were, right on.

Most of them gambled. None more than Mosher. So it was a standoff as to who was giving whom more shirts off whomever's backs.

In the parlance of the gambler, Mosher bet what he weighed—whatever he had on him. Horses, dogs, craps tables, football, anything went.

In the end, the high living, debt-induced hypertension and plain overweight just killed him. The best you could say is that few ever enjoyed it more.

He won $3,300 one night at the old Hotel Nacional Casino in Havana. He was taking in daiquiries about as fast as chips, though. "They were having to strap me to the table to keep me upright," he later explained. After awhile the manager, who liked Mosher, sent two torpedoes upstairs with him to see he got to bed with his bankroll intact.

"I played like I was asleep," Mosher bragged the next morning. "But as soon as they left, I got up and went back downstairs and blew the $3,300. I guess I showed those guys."

We came back C.O.D. the next day. Passing through customs, he asked me how I was going to get home from the airport.

"I wish I knew," I said. "I'm busted."

"OK," Mosher said, "here's $4 for a cab."

That cleaned him out. He borrowed his own cabfare from a customs inspector who loved Mosher's show.

THE 500
SEEMS TO
LAST FOREVER

MAY 29, 1978

INDIANAPOLIS—I couldn't know how this 500 looked on delayed TV. I can only say how it was here. It hurtles at you. Pure explosion. A rush of heat and sound and color, like a suddenly fragmented blast furnace, attacks your consciousness.

They say auto racing began just after the second car was built. It has been going on here literally through the blood and guts of nearly 70 percent of this century. You can watch the race on TV or listen on radio or read about it in a newspaper. But, unlike a World Series or Super Bowl, you cannot begin to perceive the vaguest fraction of its impact on your senses until you have been right beside or over an Indianapolis 500.

It is too overwhelming to put in a box in your living room. My first reaction was numbness. Fear was next.

Finally came wonder. Wonder at the madness of 32 men and one woman driving grenades on wheels, wearing helmets as potential death masks, knowing there can be only one winner, which was Al Unser, the "quiet" Unser, a wink in front of Tom Sneva and Gordon Johncock.

I hung over a rail 40 feet from machines lighter than Volkswagens and faster than some airplanes and noisier than banshees.

I saw—felt, really—Danny Ongais whoosh by after stealing the lead from pole-sitter Sneva.

Heard a gasp rise like a Gargantuan burp from one nearby batch of the 350,000 people here.

"Ongais is crazy," a man said.

"The others aren't?" I asked.

The 500 seems to last forever (by the clock, Unser finished in three hours five minutes 54.99 seconds) but never long enough to fill the hunger of its fetishists.

After a while, the onlooker sinks into a state just short of hypnotic. His head wags like a mechanical dog as one aluminum-clothed projectile after another blurs past.

I saw Spike Gehlhausen hit a wall and get by with it. A Mexican standoff. He lost his car and saved his life.

I thought about what Jimmy Clark said after winning Indy in 1965, before racing got him for good on a German afternoon in 1968, an April day that should have been beautiful for a beautiful little Scot, but was deadly instead.

"The crowd is disappointed if there is no accident," Clark had said. "They look forward to crashes and, yes, maybe even seeing people killed."

I used to believe that. Without arguing with Clark's memory, I don't believe it now.

Much of the 500 infield—so vast that a nine-hole golf course takes no more than a tiny swatch of it—is a babbling, drunken, filthy parody of humanity.

Some infielders look as though they were let out of a pigpen for the day. Out there you are overdressed in a T-shirt and cutoffs. It makes the infield of the Kentucky Derby look like Parliament in session.

Still, I can't convince myself that either these slobs or the 257,500 people on the seats want to see anybody die on a racetrack.

Hoosiers in general may be the kindest and friendliest of Americans. It is very hard to assign any innate viciousness to most of the crowd.

Still, for some among them the 500 is a motorized Sodom and Gomorrah. They come here to become semiconscious. They could not care less that the 500 is the only competition that starts at 80 miles an hour. Or that Ongais, after his wild early sprint, goes out after 145 laps of the 200-lap grind with a busted rotor on his turbo-charger.

Whatever that is.

I've seen people drink whisky straight at football and baseball games, and especially, at hockey games. They take it straight out of the bottle in parts of the Speedway infield with cars blazing by like groundbound UFOs.

They are so far gone by early afternoon that even the women are unaware that, with 35 laps to go, Janet Guthrie is tenth and ahead of four-time winner A.J. Foyt and two-time champion Johnny Rutherford and another Indy king named Mario Andretti.

Guthrie finishes eighth. She has come a long way, baby, and if she never climbs into another racecar, which she surely will, this lady of poise and courage has cut herself an immensely satisfying slice of history.

At last she has made her mark on the classic where more cars go faster in front of more folks who see less of what they paid for and more writers who don't know what they are doing than any place in the world.

Oh, a few writers do. Like maybe one from *Popular Mechanics*. Or the Massachusetts Institute of Technology. Bob Collins of *The Indianapolis Star* does. Collins once said Bobby Unser, Al's big brother who came in sixth Sunday, "could swagger standing still."

I tagged along with Collins to Rutherford's garage a couple of hours before Mary Hulman, old Indy owner Tony's widow, agonized through: "Lady and gentlemen, start your engines!"

Rutherford, one of the good guys, was standing there wearing his lopsided grin and polishing his helmet. Not daubing at it. He was bearing down on the helmet, searching for spots. Then he would twist a rag and grind them off like a man smashing fleas on a dog.

"Why?"

"It's an edge," Collins said. "Even a tiny speck on his helmet could mean that much more wind resistance. I know it sounds ridiculous. But they do that."

Didn't help. All that rubbing never erased the lousy luck from Rutherford's hat. He came in 13th.

Then, in the last grit-spraying howl of the five hundredth mile, here came Al Unser, 170 pounds of smile.

Al is the youngest of three racing brothers. The oldest, Jerry, was killed here in 1959. In practice.

WHEN NOT TO JOG

APRIL 14, 1977

Thirty-eight excuses—as opposed to reasons—for not jogging, most used by some of us, and all heard by Dr. Richard Elias of Miami Heart Institute since he began proving his run-for-your-life thesis more than two decades ago:

It's too hot.
It's too cold.
I haven't got time.
It's raining.
Dust makes me choke.
Dogs bite me in the morning.
Somebody might mug me at night.
Teen-aged drivers try to "shave" me.
I'll be late for my appointment at the beauty parlor.
I'm too stiff in the morning
I'm too tired at night.
The sand on the beach is too hard.
The sand on the beach is too soft.
The tide is up.
Dr. Paul Dudley White said riding a bike is just as good.
My shoes get wet jogging on morning grass.
Jogging on concrete hurts my knees.
I can't afford a jogging suit.
Bugs get after me.
My jogging suit is too heavy to carry on trips.
Too much homework.
Too much housework.
I have to get the kids dressed and fed and driven to school, and then I'm too bushed to jog.
I have ingrowing toenails.
My wife won't jog with me.
My husband won't jog with me.

I have to eat when I get up, and jogging makes my breakfast jiggle in my stomach.

I knew a guy who dropped dead jogging when he was 68.

I have to mow the lawn.

Ever since a University of Oregon study established that jogging increases sex drive, people holler "Sex maniacs!" at us.

I tried jogging a whole week and didn't lose any weight.

I know Billy Graham says jogging saved his health, but I'm not Billy Graham.

I'm too fat to jog.

I'm skinny enough already.

I'm too old.

I'm too young.

Jogging makes me sick after a martini.

I can't jog straight after two martinis.

CULTURE SHOCK FROM VEGAS TO AUGUSTA

APRIL 10, 1987

AUGUSTA, Georgia—Try 100,000 volts of culture shock. Fly straight from Las Vegas-Sugar Ray Leonard-Marvin Hagler to the Masters tournament.

Take the word of a Vegas-lagged tourist: No greater contrast exists in sports. It is catapulting from all-out assault on sense and senses into sweet serenity. It is ascending in splendor from Iron Maiden to the Vienna Boys Choir, from sledgehammers to xylophones.

This happened in Las Vegas:

Finally fighting my post-fight way through the dregs that mob every over-hyped match, I was confronted in my Caesars Palace hotel corridor by a glassy-eyed dandy who asked," Want to make $50?"

"What do you mean?"

"Tell me where the coke party is," he leered. This cat wasn't talking about soft drinks.

"Try the lobby," I said.

Dandy wasn't giving up so easily. "One hundred dollars for your press pass," he said, flashing a roll big enough to choke the casino.

"The fight's over, it won't get you into anything," I said.

Anything, I thought, but trouble for me. I beat it on into my room before Cocaine Charlie tried to find out how a shiv would fit between my ribs and simultaneously separate me from my credential.

Enough money will buy just about anything but class in Las Vegas. Five thousand bucks cash won't even get you past the gate at Augusta National Golf Club. Almost the only thing that will is having a granddaddy who was a Confederate general or helped found General Motors or Chase Manhattan.

Vegas bastardizes heaven's handiwork. The Masters is man's gentle adaptation of nature at its visual apex.

The Masters is not perfect. In certain doldrums, it can be substantially less exciting than a $2 blackjack hand. But the pink dogwoods do not make your head ring like the inside of a bell, nor do flowering peach buds pluck you clean.

Most of the numbers in Las Vegas hit with death-dealing impact. Here the numbers go gracefully onto huge boards without harming a soul. Well, maybe a golfer's bank account, but don't worry, those guys do all right.

Thursday, in the exquisite little cathedral that is the Masters' fourth hole, John Mahaffey wafted a majestic iron that hung in the breeze and then dropped 10 feet from the hole. He two-putted for a par three, to a pleasant smattering of applause.

Applause, and smiles.

Insensitivity is Las Vegas' chief staple. "Neither Leonard nor Hagler will be here this morning," a Top Rank Inc. flunky deigned to inform some 300 reporters staggering sleeplessly into an early Tuesday "press conference."

Upset winner Sugar Ray and Mumbling Marvin had taken their $23 million and run like thieves in the night.

Billy Kilmer, the old Redskin quarterback, strolled with former Dolphin Jake Scott across Augusta National's tranquil acres on opening day. Kilmer had just come from Vegas. "I'm convinced that fight was scripted, just to set up a rematch," Kilmer said.

Kilmer has company. Me, I'll be convinced these things are 100 percent on the square when one fighter takes the whole $23 million and the other gets nothing.

You couldn't buy a Masters for $23 *billion*.

Of course, too, the object of boxing is to maim. A golfer plays the course rather than the opponent. No golfer has ever destroyed a golf course. Even if he wins a classic, once is not enough. He doesn't give it one rematch and/or move up to a harder division. Golfers play the same tournaments and the same courses again and again.

Golf's beauty and consistency thus contrast the vicious here-today-gone-tomorrow of boxing. Not to mention your money in Las Vegas.

"One ought, every day at least, to hear a little song, read a good poem, see a fine picture," wrote Johann Wolfgang von Goethe.

In Vegas at big-fight time, the songs are all bloody. The only poetry is graffiti scrawled on men's-room walls by losers. The most memorable pictures are those show-offs swaggering across casinos with thousands of dollars' worth of rope-thick gold chains around their necks.

Bear with me for one last little story on the sadly stark contrast between Las Vegas and Augusta.

The Masters' par-five second hole was already jammed at 9 a.m. when 85-year-old Gene Sarazen, 75-year-old Byron Nelson and 74-year-old Sam Snead approached. They were playing as past-champion invitees, not actually participating, for obvious reasons. I won't embarrass them by reciting their scores, but they were hard up for low numbers.

Yet, as they walked together onto the green, a swelling roar went up from another of those Masters galleries that never forgets.

"My God," said Sarazen, "I had tears in my eyes! Where else could this happen?"

Just for openers, Gene, I wouldn't bet on Vegas.

Index